Chaucer and the English Tradition

D0082033

BY THE SAME AUTHOR

Chaucer's Prosody (1971)

Chaucer and the English Tradition

IAN ROBINSON

*Lecturer in English in the University
College of Swansea*

Mr Robinson's book re-establishes Chaucer as the 'father of English poetry', but not as the genial, tolerant figure of tradition, at his best in simple comedy. In a series of critical studies, beginning with Chaucer's earlier works, especially *The Parliament of Fowls*, and through to *The Canterbury Tales*, Mr Robinson writes of Chaucer as a serious and sometimes tragic author. Mr Robinson's first book, *Chaucer's Prosody* (CUP, 1971) situated Chaucer in the tradition of English rhythms; in this companion study he places Chaucer, in a more straightforwardly critical way, in the setting of English literature and some of its European neighbours. There are comparisons with Langland and *Sir Gawain and the Green Knight*, then with the parallel Scottish poetic tradition (especially Dunbar), and finally with the greatest of the contemporary traditions – the Italian.

Mr Robinson's book has things to say about all the great works of Middle English literature which students and readers generally may find thought-provoking. It compels us to re-read Chaucer and to listen to him as a fourteenth-century voice, but a voice which speaks to us now.

Chaucer
and the English Tradition

IAN ROBINSON

Lecturer in English in the
University College of Swansea

We are to adopt a real, not a
historic, estimate of poetry.

MATTHEW ARNOLD

CAMBRIDGE
AT THE UNIVERSITY PRESS
1972

Published by the Syndics of the Cambridge University Press
Bentley House, 200 Euston Road, London NW1 2DB
American Branch: 32 East 57th Street, New York, N.Y.10022

© Cambridge University Press 1972

Library of Congress Catalogue Card Number: 79–163179

ISBN: 0 521 08231 5

Printed in Great Britain
at the University Printing House, Cambridge
(Brooke Crutchley, University Printer)

164570

Contents

v

To

Frances Copsey

Preface
Dan Chaucer and/or Transformational Metrics

If ever there is a place for formal literary criticism, for discussing how a poet's work lives, how it matters and where it belongs, there is a place for criticism of Chaucer. Chaucer is marvellously accessible,[1] yet there are obvious difficulties in the way of reading and thinking about him. And if we are to read Chaucer well, that certainly involves thinking about his poetry as seriously as we can. But criticism, which should be the natural language of that thought, has here rarely been better than commonsense. There is plenty of room for improvement and even, perhaps, for serious attempts at improvement.

The old way of explaining the vitality of Chaucer's poetry, namely that he was a 'cheery dear old man, who so loved women, and the "glad light green" of spring'[2] or even that it proceeded from 'his large, free, simple, clear yet kindly view of human life'[3] says nothing worth saying; but remarks like these accurately represent the central stream of Chaucer criticism between Dryden and the beginning of this century. The general encomium, the insistence on the poet's genial tolerance (in which I do not believe at all) and the feeling that he is at his best in simple comedy, are the marks of this tradition, which reached its best in Kittredge's book and those parts of Chesterton's that are not simply propaganda for the past.

Chaucer has become one of our recognized classics (which he was not in the eighteenth century) by a kind of general acclaim, uneasily mixed with the institutionalization of English studies in the first quarter of this century. Other classical authors have achieved their classicality by the consensus of a reading public, but

---

[1] 'It is worth while here to observe, that the affecting parts of Chaucer are almost always expressed in language pure and universally intelligible even to this day' – Wordsworth, Preface to the second edition of *Lyrical Ballads*.

[2] F. J. Furnivall, Preface to *Handlyng Synne* (1862), p. iv. The quoted phrase is from the (spurious) *Flour and the Lefe*.

[3] Matthew Arnold, 'The Study of Poetry', *Essays in Criticism*, second series. Arnold's essay is, of course, elsewhere deservedly classical, and I shall recur to it gratefully.

elsewhere the process has usually been marked by very good literary criticism. Shakespeare's establishment as our great classic is hardly separable from the criticism of Dryden, Pope, Johnson and Coleridge; and in almost every generation since literary criticism began, Shakespeare has called forth the best work of the best critics. But all the best critics, even those of his native land, have always left Chaucer alone (I shall in due course mention some lesser exceptions to this remark) unless to misunderstand him like Arnold. For Samuel Johnson, English literature really begins with Shakespeare. Johnson had read Chaucer (and Gower and everything else) but the *Dictionary* does not delve back so far, and the *Lives of the Poets* begin with Cowley and Milton: which is to say that for Johnson Chaucer does not really belong to our literature. It is still true that the great critics usually ignore Chaucer. Dr Leavis has, I think, written about every other great English poet.

He who adds to the Work Done on Chaucer (that growing pyramid of solid assurance that the poet is safely dead) must know remorse, and look forward, as his reward, to his work's sinking unseen to the stacks of a few libraries. But I cannot accuse this book of making worse a superfluity of *criticism*. If it is seen to have added to the very small heap of Chaucer criticism I shall be more than satisfied.

In the absence of criticism, Chaucer has usually been handed over to The Language. A bad historic joke has made the study of English language in many of our universities quite separate from the study of English literature (as if the latter were written in something else or the former never rose into significance) and in this scheme Chaucer is classifiable as language as opposed to literature. For many years it has been the task of universities to make him grist to the mills of etymology and phonology, which have in common with those of God only that they grind slowly and that they grind exceeding small. More recently, a different kind of scholarship has been used to scare us into the belief that we have no right to read Chaucer before we have thoroughly understood all the books he may have read, from Augustine to Boccaccio. The future holds the prospect of scientific linguistic analysis that will prevent reading even more expeditiously. (I recently came upon an essay which, after proving that metre has *no* connection with reading poetry, worked up to a mathematical formula for Chaucer's pentameter whose triumph was its sheer abstraction, its freedom from the touch at any point of any 'subjective' sense of what the poetry is like to read.[1])

Yet Chaucer *is* a classic; his poetry's survival in individual experience is the proof of its continuing life, in a way that transformational grammar or St Augustine cannot hint at.

This book is the record of my effort to improve on the usual ways of thinking about Chaucer – and without good ways of thought reading is incomplete. The subject has forced me back all the time to the great problems of literary criticism, the questions of where poetry comes in our lives, of how poetry lives, of how we *know* it is alive, of the pastness and the presentness of old poetry, of how poetry can be a criticism of life, of what it is for the poet or the reader to see something 'as in itself it really is'. None of these questions can be quickly answered. They belong with the great questions that keep philosophy going not by being answered but by being asked differently, the continued vitality of the subject being the continued asking.

One of the inventions I have attributed to Chaucer is the common reader. Only the common reader, should he survive here and there, can keep Chaucer alive (and, in one way, be kept alive by Chaucer). It follows from my argument that only the common reader can judge what I have written; therefore to him I must leave it to decide between what I have said, what is said by the various historicists, and what is said by the multitude for whom the poet is still simply dear old dan Chaucer, petrifying in his well of English undefil'd.

I. R.

February 1971

[1] 'V → # P_1 P_2 P_3...Pn # (s (s))
where V = verse
P = position
s = syllable
# = verse boundary
( ) = elements enclosed thus are optional; that is, may or may not be present
n = the total number of positions in the line; in the pentameter line n = 10; in the tetrameter line n = 8, etc.' (There follow the substitution transformations.) Morris Halle and Samuel Jay Keyser, 'Chaucer and the Study of Prosody', *College English* XXVIII (1966), 219.

Acknowledgments

I have tried to trace to their sources and make due acknowledgment for the ideas in this book which I cannot claim to have originated and which are not merely common property but, particularly in the case of one source, I am sure I have not always succeeded. Much of the book derives in one way or another from the conversations I have had over a number of years with my friend and colleague Mr David Sims; and I am not always sure now what originated with him, what with me. If Mr Sims recognizes and wishes to claim any of this book I shall be flattered. I owe him a further substantial debt of gratitude for detailed comment on the penultimate draft. I am similarly indebted to Mr Michael Black for many helpful comments, and I am also grateful to Mr Black for the sight of some parts of an unpublished book which, I think, helped to refine some of my general notions.

Mr S. W. Dawson made useful objections to a version of Chapter 8, which has also benefited by the criticisms of the editors of *The Cambridge Quarterly*. From Mr M. B. Mencher I received encouragement at a time I needed it, as well as some sharp criticisms I have tried to meet. Chapters have been tried out on the Doughty Society of Downing College, Cambridge, and on the University of Exeter English Society, and modified in the light of subsequent discussion. A version of Chapter 9 appeared in *The Critical Review* (Melbourne, 1967) and I am grateful for the editors' permission to reprint.

Most of this book has been offered in one way or another to generations of undergraduates of the University College of Swansea and to them I am grateful for the critical attention (or inattention) which more than anything else gave me a sense of what was and what was not worth saying. The dedication records a special case of this gratitude.

Note on Texts

The words of Chaucer are quoted from F. N. Robinson's second edition of *The Works of Geoffrey Chaucer* (Boston, 1957) and I follow the older of the systems of line-numbers in that edition as well as its system of abbreviation. Shakespeare is quoted from the Nonesuch edition of his works, the First Folio text, edited by Herbert Farjeon (1953 reprint). Details of all other editions used are given after the first quotation from them: London is the place of publication, except of periodicals, unless otherwise indicated.

I have supplied a few glosses to the quotations of Middle English verse, and words which are glossed appear within asterisks and daggers in the quotations. Having earned a living for more than ten years by discussing Chaucer, I am not ashamed to admit that there are still words (not necessarily the ones glossed) I forget and am tripped by: the glosses are an encouragement to readers to read the quotations, in English. Those who do not need the glosses will, of course, simply ignore them.

In most of the quotations from the medieval poets I have removed editorial punctuation (except quotation marks) and printed the verse in phrases separated by spaces, as Anglo-Saxon verse is usually printed. The reasons for doing so are argued in my *Chaucer's Prosody*; but I hope that once the strangeness of this convention has worn off, it will explain itself in the increased naturalness with which it allows us to read Middle English.

Part One: Chaucer's Ways Out

I

Two Stanzas of
'The Parliament of Fowls'

I might be alive in a primitive way to the ideas of a work if I said, 'Putting *those* together in that way would never have occurred to me. And it is wonderful'...

I say it is wonderful – not that it is good or skilful or perfect. And it is this difference that makes the problem.[1]

The Parliament of Fowls is Chaucer's first wonderful poem, although both the earlier ones have wonderful moments.[2] And *The Parliament of Fowls* is not an obscure poem; you read it and see that it is wonderful. But it has created more confusion and contradiction amongst critics than perhaps any other English poem before *The Waste Land*. My belief that *The Parliament of Fowls* is wonderful (without which time devoted to it would be a kind of academic frivolity), and that its wonder is largely obscured by the ways people talk and write about it, makes me think the poem the right place to begin these chapters.

It begins:

> The lyf so short   the craft so long to lerne
> Thassay so hard   so sharp the conquerynge
> The *dredful* joye   alwey that †slit so yerne†
> Al this mene I by Love   that my felynge
> Astonyeth   with his wonderful werkynge
> So sore iwis   that whan I on hym thynke
> Nat wot I wel   wher that I flete or synke
>
> For al be   that I knowe nat Love in dede
> Ne wot how that   he ‡quiteth folk here hyre‡
>   * doubtful   † slips so quickly   ‡ pays people their wages

---

[1] Rush Rhees, 'Art and Philosophy', *Without Answers* (1969), p. 139.

[2] The chronology of Chaucer's poems is unlikely ever to be fixed. I write as if *The Book of the Duchess* is followed by *The House of Fame, The Parliament of Fowls, Troilus and Criseyde, The Legend of Good Women* and *The Canterbury Tales* in that order. This is thought likely by reputable scholars, but the main reason for the assumption is that it makes sense.

Yit happeth me ful ofte   in bokes reede
Of his myrakles   and his crewel yre
There rede I wel   he wol be lord and syre
I dar nat seyn   his strokes been so sore
But 'God save swich a lord'   I can na moore

At one extreme of the range of critical comment on these lines, Professor Lawlor writes, in an interesting essay, 'The opening stanza is miraculously poised. Here is that quiet exaltation, an open-handed acceptance of life as it unalterably is, which is the individual and unmatched mark of Chaucer's workmanship', and he also finds in the stanza 'a particular kind of delicate gravity'.[1] Chaucer, that is, is saying here, with appropriate seriousness, what he really thinks of love. Mr Brewer writes in the same volume (p. 30), 'It is possible even for those who think that poetry should speak sincerely from the heart to respond to such a beginning.' At the opposite extreme we find, from Professors Robertson and Huppé:

The poem opens with a mocking and humorous account of the 'wonderful werkynge' of Love...The poet humorously pretends to be afraid to take the name of this god in vain. He can say only 'God save swich a lord!' This is a god who, as Andreas Capellanus had put it, carries unequal weights when he 'quiteth folk her hyre.' The subject of the poem, then, is Love, an 'unkind' lord who seeks tyrannical rule over mankind. The tone is ironic.[2]

In literary criticism it is not unheard of to find disagreements even as flat as this one. Is Chaucer earnest or not? Lawlor thinks so; Huppé and Robertson are sure the tone is ironic. But how do they – or we – know? What Chaucer means depends on his tone, but how can we get his tone right?[3]

There are obvious difficulties about reading a poem 600 years old. Our knowledge of the tone of modern poetry follows from confidence in the movement of our own English; but whether we can achieve a comparable confidence in Middle English is at least an open question. In the books I have read, two main alternatives are offered. Either one believes like Lawlor that the poem is still capable of being read, and that if we read well enough it will communicate its tone (the difficulty then is how to read well

[1] John Lawlor, 'The Earlier Poems', in *Chaucer and Chaucerians*, ed. D. S. Brewer (1966), pp. 50–1.
[2] Bernard F. Huppé and D. W. Robertson, Jr, *Fruyt and Chaf* (Princeton, 1963), pp. 101–2.
[3] On Robertson's method of determining Chaucer's tone see below, pp. 271 ff.

enough), or one gives up as hopeless the attempt at reading and makes one of a variety of appeals to history which is to tell us what the poet must have meant.[1] I will quote – from a critic of some standing, to prove I am not tilting at windmills – one representative instance of the latter, a commentary by Mr F. W. Bateson on these opening stanzas which appeared in *Essays in Criticism* XI (1961). According to Mr Bateson, in the first stanza

The first problem to settle – it has not been raised hitherto as far as I am aware – is whether the abrupt reversal of style at l. 4 is deliberate. Instead of sticking to Vinsauf's *stylus grandiloquus* in which he has started, Chaucer apparently throws decorum to the winds and suddenly sinks into the *stylus humilis*. Did he know what he was doing?   (p. 257)

Having thus defined a problem Mr Bateson solves it to his own satisfaction by some history combined with a particular view of the stanza's tones:

We must assume in the first place a sophisticated minority who would welcome the rhetorical bag of tricks; it is likely that Richard II himself, an addict of contemporary French poetry, was something of a connoisseur in these things. But it is difficult to believe many of the ladies of the court shared his taste, and the King's uncles may well have preferred stronger meat. Hence, perhaps, the dualism of tone in our stanza. The King must be placated, and the highbrows must be shown that Chaucer's poetry was as capable of rhetorical refinement as that written in Latin or French. So we get the first three lines.

But the Wicked Uncles must not be forgotten either, and there are also the great ladies who, bewildered perhaps by the intricate enigmas of ll. 1–3, had to be reassured. And so Chaucer's voice changes. Instead of continuing to pile up the rhetoric to an appropriate climax ('O Love! O mystic mighty Love!') Chaucer steps outside his original part with an almost perceptible wink:

Al this mene I by Love...

'Cheer up! What I'm getting at after all these fine phrases is our old friend Sex!' Is that to read into the stanza's four last lines a good deal more than they will bear? Perhaps, but that there is a change to some sort of a new informality seems clear. Apart from the absence of rhetoric and metrical regularity, the writing becomes careless and even slovenly. Thus *myn felynge* must just mean 'me'; *sore* too is weak (Chaucer's astonishment at Love's wonder-working powers is not painful but enormous) and *iwis* is a mere 'filler', one of those empty phrases the oral poets used to pad out their lines.   (p. 259)

---

[1] The dilemma of criticism of *The Parliament of Fowls* is exemplified in Professor Wolfgang Clemen's *Chaucer's Early Poetry* (1963), pp. 130ff. Clemen's *forte* is the work of synthesis (cf. his useful *Development of Shakespeare's Imagery*) but his attempt to keep to the centre, using the best of all extremes, here leads only to a kind of flat disconnection from Chaucer's poetry.

Putting a passage in context can certainly be a way of understanding it. But I have to object to this attempt that Mr Bateson's
appeal to history is being used in support of a misreading of the
passage. The history, too, is indistinguishable from fantasy – and
this is typical enough of such criticism to be worth remarking,
though this is not the main objection. 'The original "publication",'
he says, 'must have been a court occasion. . .' Why 'must' it? We
know so little about the publication of this or any of Chaucer's
poems that (even after Mr D. S. Brewer's informative introduction
to his edition *The Parlement of Foulys* (1960)) we could not say we
know the poem was read in the fourteenth century at all. Nothing is
known of its original publication or reception: all we can do is
make informed guesses, based on knowledge of the Middle Ages
and the poem itself. By these criteria there is, however, nothing
unlikely about Mr Bateson's belief that the poem was read, by
Chaucer, to a courtly group; so let us grant it him. We will grant
also that the group was 'aristocratic, largely royal', though once
more we just don't know. (Apart from a critic's natural liking for
having to do with people he has heard of, we have here just the
feeling that the poem *ought* to have been read to a royal audience;
this feeling may be fair enough as literary criticism of the poem
but can add nothing independent to it.) Would these suppositions
about the poem's history explain a change of tone in the way Mr
Bateson wants to? There is fortunately no necessity for any
account of Richard II's accomplishments as compared with those
of John of Gaunt, Thomas of Woodstock etc., together with a
list of the dates when they were not feuding, for Mr Bateson's
notion of courtly ladies can be shown to be erroneous merely by
references to Chaucer's other works. When Chaucer or his
characters address ladies, so far from accommodating their style to
the weaker sex by refraining from embellishment, they usually
adopt the most refined, even effete, rhetorical flourishes. To quote
Troilus to Criseyde might be thought unfair (though *Troilus and
Criseyde* demonstrably provided the phrases in which generations
of courtiers addressed their ladies) but the style of proper address
to a lady extends as far down the social scale as the Host of *The
Canterbury Tales*. When he speaks to the Prioress, whose passion
is (A 132, 137–41) to counterfeit the manners of court though she is
not quite a real lady, the normally blunt and plain Harry Bailly
asks for a tale in one of the most delicately High passages in
Chaucer:

6

> B 1635   and with that word he sayde
> As curteisly   as it had been a mayde
> 'My lady Prioresse   by youre leve
> So that I wiste   I sholde yow nat greve
> I wolde demen   that ye tellen sholde
> A tale nexte   if so were that ye wolde
> Now wol ye vouche sauf   my lady deere?'

So Mr Bateson has produced no evidence for any of his historicaⱼ reconstruction and it is easy to produce conclusive evidence against an important part of it.[1]

The historical inaccuracy and misunderstanding is, however, only the outworking of a failure to be precise enough about the tones that are there to be read in Chaucer's lines. When Mr Bateson offers paraphrase it looks more like parody.

> Al this mene I by Love   that my felynge
> Astonyeth   with his wonderful werkynge

becomes, 'Cheer up! What I'm really getting at after all these fine phrases is our old friend Sex.' If one feels that that is not a satisfactory account of what Chaucer is doing, the feeling may challenge also Mr Bateson's account of the end of the stanza as bathos. Chaucer's stanza seems to me at once subtler and clearer than the critic allows. Mr Bateson is right to point to the change of tone in the fourth line and Huppé and Robertson are right to say that the tone is ironic, but Lawlor is right, too, to take the whole thing seriously.

For surely Chaucer's change is not the lapse into vulgarity Mr Bateson takes it to be. The solemnly rhetorical opening lines seem to be working out the old tag *ars longa vita brevis*; and the change in the fourth line expresses the surprise that they are, instead, about love. The device of a surprising or inappropriate application of a commonplace is not rare in the medieval poets (Thomas Hoccleve often does it, for instance at the beginning of the *Male Regle*), but this would not be obscure even if the device

---

[1] There are signs of tentativeness in Mr Bateson's original essay, but next year he had come to regard his thesis as securely established: '...the particular literary artifact in the context of its original audiences (e.g. Chaucer's *Parliament of Fowls* as addressed to people like Richard II's uncles, on the one hand, and people like "moral Gower" and "philosophical Strode" on the other)' (*Essays in Criticism* XII (1962), 107). Finally, by a process familiar to all students of literary criticism, behold Mr Bateson's original idea apotheosed in his *Guide to English Literature* (1965, p. 23) into mere fact: [Chaucer] 'was never able to maintain this artificial elegance for more than a few lines at a time... the lapse from decorum was perhaps unintentional.'

were unique. The surprise is there, right enough, and it is a comic surprise. But is it the devaluation of love into 'our old friend Sex'? Is the comedy of that reductive kind? It seems to me on the contrary that the shock here, though a comic one, is genuinely a shock of wonder. And I take the following lines as expressing a similar seriousness in the midst of their comicality. There is a genuine thrill, even of a romantic sort, at the same time as the comic astonishment of

> my felynge
> Astonyeth   with his wonderful werkynge
> So sore iwis

I do not agree that 'sore' is the wrong word or that Chaucer is referring to his 'felynge' only through carelessness. 'Sore', with its connotations of pain as well as intensity, goes well with the assertion in the next stanza.

> 12   There rede I wel   he wol be lord and syre
>   I dar nat seyn   his strokes been so sore
>   But 'God save swich a lord'   I can na moore

The outcome of Chaucer's serious comicality is a wry contemplation of love 'as in itself it really is', a detachment from the object viewed which is yet not an escape from it. The mixture of styles here is Chaucer's way of realizing love. I am even able to defend 'iwis'. This certainly is, as Mr Bateson says, a 'filler', but it has the typical rhetorical function of Chaucer's pads, from final -e upwards, of emphasizing the preceding word or phrase. 'Iwis' puts just the right comic-serious emphasis on 'sore'. The end of the stanza is to me as good as the beginning; the tone is that characteristic one of Chaucer's where a subject is treated with irresistible humour without being made coarse or cheap. The combination of this humour with continuing thrill is there in the last lines for anyone who can read English:

> So sore iwis   that whan I on hym thynke
> Nat wot I wel   wher that I flete or synke

Chaucer's comic uncertainty, and the terror of floating or sinking, are created simultaneously in this verse-movement. So when Chaucer writes of the 'wonderful werkynge' of Love, and of his 'myrakles and his crewel yre' he is not writing with his tongue in his cheek. At the same time the comedy is of a kind one is tempted to call frivolous; and here lies one of our problems.

Chaucer is writing in these opening stanzas of *The Parliament of*

8

Fowls with a wonder appropriate to his subject, love. He is therefore writing seriously. At the same time he is writing with a light
playfulness that we do not easily see as serious: the problem is not
just the one we face in all comedy; we may see that Aristophanes or
Dickens is a serious comic writer without being able to extend the
perception to include something as lightweight as the *Parliament*
seems.[1] Mr Bateson's remarks on line four are, after all, only his
falling into a trap set by our world and our language: this rhetorical
build-up would, now, be inevitably followed by a let-down.

To think about the opening of *The Parliament of Fowls* we seem
to need a category of the 'frivolously serious' which modern
English condemns as merely contradictory – and yet the phrase
points to something I find in an English poem. What Chaucer is
doing there is at any rate hard to discuss (and so perhaps worth
discussing) in modern English: but we can only know as much if
the style – the poetry – is accessible to the modern reader.

We can proceed from this first sight of the fascination and the
difficulty of *The Parliament of Fowls* in at least two ways. It is
possible to consider the poem more or less in isolation from all
other poems, to ask what this and other styles are doing, and by
seeing the place of the frivolous seriousness in the poem to point,
however feebly, to its wonder. Alternatively it is possible to take
the peculiar kind of comedy as a given, and to try to understand
it by comparing the *Parliament* with other works where similar
styles are found and so, by giving the poem its place in literature,
to make it easier to perceive.

Both these possible methods are historical as well as critical;
both, indeed, can only be one to the extent that they are the other.
I shall argue that if they are 'possible' *The Parliament of Fowls*, as
well as Chaucer's first wonderful poem, is the first of his works to
belong to English literature; and I shall also tackle the question
why that should matter.

[1] Mr J. M. Newton made a serious attempt to define this kind of comedy in
'One of the Great English Poems?', *The Cambridge Quarterly*, IV (1969).

2

'The Book of the Duchess' and Courtly Literature

I

If instead of *The Parliament of Fowls* we begin with *The Book of the Duchess*, the poem itself looks altogether baffling; but the second kind of commentary, the comparison with other works, makes the poem all too explicable. Merely reading *The Book of the Duchess* like any other poem, beginning at the beginning and going through it to the end, you are likely to be mystified. To show this one has only to compare some of the poem with what is said about it by all the scholars. F. N. Robinson's version of the usual history is:

According to a tradition recorded by John Stow and still accepted by nearly all critics, the poem was written in commemoration of the death of Blanche, duchess of Lancaster and first wife of John of Gaunt...
It is at once an eulogy of Blanche and a consolation addressed to her bereaved husband.[1]

This makes us feel at home and gives us a strong impression of what the poem is going to be like. The elegiac tone in English is established and well-known; perhaps we think of

> The curfew tolls the knell of parting day,
>   The lowing herd winds slowly o'er the lea,
> The plowman homeward plods his weary way,
>   And leaves the world to darkness and to me.

Then we look at the way *The Book of the Duchess* begins, and gasp.

> I have gret wonder be this lyght
> How that I lyve for day ne nyght
> I may nat slepe wel nygh noght
> I have so many an ydel thoght
> Purely for defaute of slep
> That by my trouthe I take no kep

---

[1] Chaucer's *Works*, p. 266.

Of nothing how hyt cometh or gooth
Ne me nys nothyng leef nor looth
Al is ylyche good to me
Joye or sorowe wherso hyt be
For I have felynge in nothyng
But as yt were a mased thyng
Always in poynt to falle a doun
For sorwful ymagynacioun
Ys alway hooly in my mynde
   And wel ye woot agaynes *kynde*   nature
Hit were to lyven in this wyse
For nature wolde nat suffyse
To noon erthly creature
Nat longe tyme to endure
Withoute slep and be in sorwe
And I ne may ne nyght ne morwe
Slepe

In elegy a poet concentrates on the dignified presentment of grief, keeping himself austerely out of the picture. Here the poet, in a light and affected manner (affected because a *persona*) retails his own troubles, in particular the rather undignified one of suffering from insomnia. It is not apparent whether his sufferings are as desperate as he says, for of the several ways of taking the passage the one we are likely to light on first is to be swept along by the tripping couplets at a quick pace and see the whole thing as gossip – the movement suggested by fitting 'sorwful ymagynacioun' to a trochaic tetrameter. Certainly English verse has never been further from the lapidary. 'And wel ye woot' is the poet, after the exclamations with which he seizes our attention, getting hold of the reader's buttonhole with the obvious intention of having his talk out. What on earth is he doing and how can this be elegy? We go on reading, perhaps, to find out. Chaucer continues to maunder entertainingly along about his insomnia. Perhaps those who know Curry's book[1] or other medieval poems realize that Chaucer, like Phil Squod, is 'limping round the gallery with his shoulder against the wall, and tacking off at objects he wants to lay hold of, instead of going straight to them',[2] the train of indirection here leading from insomnia by way of beds and sleep to a DREAM – perhaps we realize this, perhaps not. In either case we go on simultaneously being amused and wondering why the poet is going on like this. By line 30 Chaucer is ready to put the question himself:

[1] W. C. Curry, *Chaucer and the Medieval Sciences*, 2nd edn (1960).
[2] *Bleak House*, Chapter XXI.

> But men myght axe me why soo
> I may not sleepe and what me is

He seems to be playing with us: he must know that we're more
likely to ask, 'Why are you telling us all this?' But having asked his
question Chaucer answers it with a similar garrulity:

34   Myselven can not telle why
The sothe / but trewly as I gesse
I holde hit be a sicknesse
That I have suffred this eight yeer
And yet my boote is never the ner
For ther is phisicien but oon
That may me hele   but that is don

This has some hint of the frivolously serious tone I pointed to at
the beginning of *The Parliament of Fowls*: perhaps one can glimpse
in it the reticence of real disappointed passion. But, at the same time,
it certainly brings us no closer to the elegiac.

So, Chaucer tells us, unable to sleep, he was reading a book 'to
drive the night away (49)'. He obligingly tells us not only the subject (57 This bok ne spak but of such thinges / Of quenes lives
and of kinges / And many other thinges smale) but in particular
one tale that follows, the tale of 'Seys and Alcyone'. Here perhaps
we begin to think the elegy is coming closer, for the story is at least
about the death of a marriage-partner and his reappearance in a
dream. But where we expect it to be pathetic the tale seems to be
comical, and the rest is a very ungodly account of some very
commonplace activity by the gods, successfully and indubitably
funny, and as far from elegy as ever. Seys is polished off without the
slightest effort at feeling by the poet:

68   To tellen shortly whan that he
Was in the see thus in this wise
Such a tempest gan to rise
That brak her mast and made it falle
And clefte her ship and dreinte hem alle

Here the jog-trot of the verse and the repeated 'and' make the
drowning ridiculously sudden and unimportant, as far from a
realization of death as could well be. As for the fun and games
associated with the gods, one need only instance Juno's chatty
instructions to her messenger,

136 'Go bet' quod Juno 'to Morpheus
Thou knowest him wel the god of slep'

– which must surely take place in a back street of Olympus – or the famous passage where Morpheus receives the same messenger:

178   This messager com fleynge faste
        And cried 'O ho awake anoon'
        Hit was for noght there herde hym non
        'Awake' quod he 'whoo is lyth there?'
        And blew his horn ryght in here eere
        And cried 'Awaketh' wonder hye
        This god of slep with hys oon ye
        Cast up axed 'Who clepeth ther?'

and so on. After this we return to Seys, whose ghost comforts Alcyone with the remark that

204   certes swete I nam but ded
('It's all right, darling, I'm only dead.')

It now transpires that the whole episode is still connected rather with Chaucer's lack of sleep than with an elegy on the Lady Blanche; for the idea he gets from the tale is that sleep might be obtainable by the offer of a bribe to the god of sleep, whom he has never heard of. No sooner has Chaucer elaborated the idea with a description of the marvellous bedding he offers, than at line 274 he falls sound asleep and, pausing only for the hyperbolic puff that his dream will be more wonderful and difficult to interpret than the most famous ones in history, begins to relate the dream which (primed about the medieval dream poems) we know is to be the substance of the work. Chaucer is already a quarter of the way through his poem and has as yet given no sign of any elegiac intention, but with the dream we perhaps expect the poem proper to begin.

If so, Chaucer has fooled us, for no such thing happens. The dream turns out to be a real one. After some dream-like wanderings it develops into a hunt which Chaucer joins by mounting his horse and riding out of his bedroom:

354   Anoon ryght whan I herde that
        How that they wolde on huntynge goon
        I was ryght glad and up anoon
        Took my hors and forth I wente
        Out of my chambre

Having established whose hunt it is –

366   'Say felowe who shal hunte here?'
        Quod I and he answered ageyn
        'Syr themperour Octovyen'

– and when the hunt itself has occupied some lively and quite irrelevant lines, Chaucer, walking from his hitherto unmentioned tree, meets a whelp which leads him into a beautifully described courtly garden, the first sketch, perhaps, for scenes in *The Knight's Tale* and *The General Prologue* as well as *The Parliament of Fowls*. Finally, at line 445, Chaucer mentions the 'man in black' who turns out, much later, to be the mourner for whom the poem is written. (This is not to say that the digressions are now over or that the poem now changes tone into the elegiac. There is plenty of further expansiveness like the disquisition upon the physiology of the heart and blood, lines 490–9, or the other, on the origin of harping, around line 1160.)

Yet this account of the opening of *The Book of the Duchess* is very incomplete. Read quickly and lightly – one very natural way – the opening goes well as described above. But if one's mood is different and the pace slower it is quite possible to see in the same lines an ease and elegance which cover a real sadness:

23   and thus melancolye
      And drede I have for to dye
      Defaute of slep and hevynesse
      Hath sleyn my spirit of quyknesse
      That I have lost al *lustyhede*   liveliness

'Ceys and Alcyone' is also at times genuinely pathetic; and at lines 90–100 we get a taste of the manly–simple tone that is later seen as the heart of the poem, ending

96   I which made this book
      Had such pittee and such rowthe
      To rede hir sorwe that by my trowthe
      I ferde the worse al the morwe
      Aftir to thenken on hir sorwe

One critic goes so far as to say that lines 77ff. set forth 'the mental sufferings of Alcyone who, left without news from her husband, finds herself in a serious state of concern, which is described by the poet with no small degree of tender compassion'.[1] Yet the tale is certainly ridiculed, as I have shown. The more one gets to know the beginning of this poem, the more puzzling it becomes, because no one tone or range of tones is enjoined by the lines; there is no way of understanding the simultaneous presence of so many contradictory things.

We are puzzled because the poem is puzzling: perhaps it is

---

[1] Claes Schaar, *The Golden Mirror* (Lund, 1955), p. 20.

possible to go further and say that its intention is to be puzzling. In so far as it succeeds, the opening is poetry about the poet's puzzlement. 'Ceys and Alcyone' is a tale told by a man deliberately not seeing what there might be in love, a man escaping from his sympathy and puzzle into amusement. The gap caused by the absence of a subject is filled with the intention to please. And Chaucer evidently enjoys this and does it well; but the intention to please is not so much his own as one given to him by any effective use of that language and style. This, as I shall show, is the same as saying that before his inspiration became fully effective Chaucer wrote in a way that is *only* traditional. Without a tradition, of course, he couldn't have written at all, but here a tradition is speaking through him rather than *vice versa*.

So he begins entertainingly and pathetically puzzled, and the rest of the poem is his search for something real, the attempt to advance into knowledge of love or death. Chaucer's failure to understand the Black Knight's trouble until he is told in words of one syllable is the continuing expression of puzzlement, a figure for his wanting to be told. He plunges into a real dream because there a serious person may see something; and what Chaucer tries to see in his dream is the Black Knight's love and its loss. So the poem might be an attempt to work out of some difficulty we have yet to explain, towards a real elegy. But it doesn't work; Chaucer is still, in the main body of the poem, caught in ways of talking that prevent him from understanding love. What can the Black Knight say about the lady? Firstly a few lines that are simply an old-fashioned troubadour lyric (on which style see the next section):

475 I have of sorwe so gret *won*   custom
    That joye gete I never non
    Now that I see my lady bryght
    Which I have loved with al my myght
    Is fro me ded and ys agoon

This is formal, beautiful and so simple as to be almost unliterary; part of its contrast with what goes before is its lesser degree of sophistication. After that we get a kind of catalogue of the kind of rhetoric the courtly poets could use when in their earnest vein. But the lines (600ff.) on the 'my *a* is *b*' formula, where *a* is something happy and *b* something sad, seem stiff compared with the parts of the poem that puzzle us, and not as interesting as the true-to-life plainness of the retort of the Knight about Socrates, at line 720:

15

717 'Remembre you of Socrates
    For he ne counted nat three strees
    Of noght that Fortune koude doo'
    'No' quod he 'I kan not soo'

Later Chaucer again seems to be enjoying himself with the chess image – which is very traditional and very long – but his enjoyment need not be ours; this section of the poem is just dull, because it has turned serious. It is as if Chaucer can only succeed when creating his puzzlement or when writing with the utmost simplicity. So the section about the Black Knight's love for the lady is not a convincing picture of love.

Love, for the Black Knight, comes *before* the lady, though it isn't Platonic: first he finds Love then, years later, a lady to fall in love with. The ideal comes first, fully worked out: and so it is difficult to connect it with life. His description of the lady is the poem's last effort to be a love-poem: it applies the ideal to a real person. But the ideal is so triumphant and the sense of a real person so feeble that I get no sense of love from the passage. Notoriously the picture of the lady is from Machaut not from life. After a very good beginning (848–77) it settles down into a list of the points of appearance and manners a courtly lady was expected to have. Coming here it reminds me of the solution by Larry the Lamb, in one of the Toytown tales of S. G. Hulme-Beaman, of a similar artistic problem: Larry, unable to paint but commissioned to do a portrait of the Mayor, inserts into the frame provided a picture, done by another artist, of what a Mayor should look like. In the tale the Mayor is not pleased; John of Gaunt's opinion is not recorded. Chaucer's passage doesn't read like anybody's sincere feeling for a woman (which, I know, can only happen in a tradition) but is rather a specification, as if the poet were telling Nature how the lady should be made. (Fielding commits the same fault in his list of the properties which define Sophia Western.)

Chaucer in the end forces the Black Knight to state his grief with a plainness remarkably unlike any of the various literary artifice – the lightness and different comedies of the opening or the different rhetorical devices of the serious middle – which come before. And this plainness, the final puzzle, seems to me when it comes effective and moving – but baffling because of its context.

1298 'Sir' quod I 'where is she now?'
    'Now' quod he and *stynte* anoon   stopped
    Therwith he wax as ded as stoon

> And seyde 'Allas that I was bore
> That was the los that here before
> · I tolde the that I hadde lorn
> Bethenke how I seyde here beforn
> "Thow *wost* ful lytel what thow menest   knowest
> I have lost more than thow *wenest*"   thinkest
> God wot allas ryght that was she'

Even this is not enough for the Dreamer, who comes back in his usual lightsome way and provokes the final flatness of statement:

> 'Allas sir how? what may that be?'
>   'She ys ded' 'Nay' 'Yis be my *trouthe*'   faithfulness
> 'Is that youre los? Be god hyt ys routhe'

With this simple half-line of commiseration, as one blunt English gentleman to another, the poem is, after a few perfunctory lines of conclusion, at an end. This is as close to 'what he means' as Chaucer gets; this is his only way of showing the loss that is 'more than he knows'. Only by abandoning all the poetic styles – by abandoning what might be called the 'poetry' of the poem – and writing simple sense can Chaucer make his love-elegy. (And it won't do to wish the poem different, either: Spenser's *Daphnaida* seems to proceed from a view of the poem's waywardness and puzzlingness very like the above: Spenser straightens it out, makes it decorous and a real elegy – and the result is quite flat.)

The Book of the Duchess, in all its spontaneity and gay life, is a self-defeating poem about the impossibility of writing poetry about love and death; hence it is a poem about poetry and Chaucer's own plight. His dream reveals nothing better than he could have had without it: the ways of speaking of love and death offered by poetry are insufficient. The poem is about what Chaucer might want from poetry but cannot yet say. But Chaucer writes with such grace and ease that although baffled here he is taking on the problems of a poet. (The objection that there is something curious about writing solemnly on such an enjoyable poem is one of the critical data about the poem.)

Because Chaucer cannot yet write of love the poem is obscure: it is only not obscure in so far as it is deliberately expressing puzzlement, Chaucer's pleased puzzlement in the face of life and art. *The Book of the Duchess* is therefore not a fully self-sufficient work of art: it can't speak directly to us without, at any rate, provoking this kind of commentary. But if *The Book of the Duchess* doesn't carry its explanation within itself its curiousness can be explained (which is itself an adverse criticism) by the other sort of commentary, the appeal to history, in which I intend to show why I can call Chaucer's first poem, and the first of its kind in English, thoroughly traditional.

II

Modern European literature began when troubadour poetry moved into the great provincial courts of France and the royal courts of France and England.[1]

It is well-known that in the treatment of love lies the great difference between the first and second age of medieval poetry, especially to the north of the Alps. In France first, then in England and Germany – even in Wales and Scotland – an age of heroic poetry is succeeded by an age of love poetry. *Beowulf* and the *Chanson de Roland* are closer together in their ideals of heroism, comradeship in arms and submission to the chancy dictates of warlike fate than either is to *Le Roman de la Rose* or *Troilus and Criseyde*. When the troubadours began writing their always charming and sometimes forceful and beautiful love-poems, they were certainly taking Europe into a new age, though they were perhaps unaware of so doing and their importance was perhaps unrecognized until Dante met Arnaut Daniel in Canto XXVI of the *Purgatorio*, and later centuries produced their largely fictitious *Lives*.

The new thing with the troubadours is simply their celebration of heterosexual emotion. Troubadour poetry seems to me always simple, lyrical and amateur. It has, however, more real passion than one would expect to be made possible by its simplicity of language. Many of these lyrics are still immediately likeable, and the music to which they were sung also stands out from the professionally complex music of the courts of later centuries in its immediate appeal and often in its vitality – as well as in the comforting sense it gives a listener that he too might be able to compose melodies as pleasing if he gave his mind to it.

The statement of passion in language is never a mean achievement (think how hard it is to say anything simply passionate in modern English). Troubadour poetry provided the European aristocracies with a language of love, whose particular content and style (with its religiosity, the submission of the man to the woman,

[1] I consider the special case of Italian literature, which cannot in the same sense be said to have 'begun', in Chapter 15, below. What follows is not intended as a history of European literature. I am separating a few strands that bind Chaucer to France.

18

the belief in love's ennobling powers and so on) is well-known.[1] To talk in this way at all is to give the troubadours an importance that may seem extravagant. If we say they were new do we mean that nobody made love in the Dark Ages? Not quite, though for all we know that may have been the case. (We know, from the survival of the human race, that during the Dark Ages people had children; but whether procreation had then anything to do with making love is another question.) What we can say is that the language of the poetry of the Dark Ages is not a language of love.

There is no love without a language of love (the 'thing' that presumably there always is is called 'copulation'). This is not a denial of the unlinguistic intensity of the experience of love: I do not say that language causes love. Nevertheless love has to be learned, and varies with the language – the life of the society as well as of the individual – in which it is learned. The fact that there are phrases like 'making love' and 'being in love' – that there are languages of love, including verbal ones – means that however unique and itself any particular love is, it is not alone. Love depends also on the interconnections within the whole of life for which the existence of language is the prime evidence.

This in turn means that human sexuality can never be reduced to a biological or zoological matter, for a language of love (I use the phrase in its broadest sense, not restricting it to verbal expressions) gives a place to sexual relationships within human life. Love in this way varies with the language used of it. It is not my present concern to say how.

The connection between the language of literature and the language actually used in life is always problematic: but we can at least say that poetry is not disconnected from life and that the language of love in art will have some effect on, as well as being affected by, the language of love in experience.

Between the classical age and the troubadours love was not a subject of poetry: that is, there was no creation or criticism in poetry of the language of this very important area of life. The troubadours' interest in love recreated the subject as a proper one for poetry and, by creating a language and style of love, gave great importance to the subject. Their achievement was to make love, in general esteem, in the language, 'anything but trivial', for the first time in a millennium. That is why troubadour style is more than

[1] Cf., for instance, the opening pages of C. S. Lewis's *Allegory of Love* (Oxford, 1936).

what is usually meant by 'just a way of talking'; and this is a leading example of the great truth that (in ways we are not at present exploring) when styles of language change the world changes. The troubadours' poetry develops a language of love that altered, and alters, the world.

But it was a language *only* of love, and so, of limited impact on European civilization. The troubadours' love is a language disconnected from other important styles of language and the life they express. The troubadours never ask what will happen if their new way of singing becomes common form.[1] (Where will the church go? What about marriage? etc.) They did in the end impinge on sensibility at the profound level of common speech by changing the meaning of words like 'love' and 'lady'; but they could never rise into the conscious criticism of life that we think of as the typical poetic function. Their criticism of life – the connection between their new inspiration and the rest of life – was accidental. Yet by its mere existence troubadour poetry said, very powerfully, 'Love has been missing from our civilization: here it is, what are you going to do about it?'

But to make its criticism of life explicit troubadour poetry had to come indoors: from serenading from without, it had to enter the courts. To become connected with the mainstream of courtly imagination, the troubadours had to sing at the only places where their new feeling might, by connecting with the rest of life, criticize the whole, and so change it. But as soon as the troubadours came in out of the cold they necessarily became courtly entertainers. Immediately, the lords and ladies (like those of Yeats's Byzantium) became patrons, and in their patronage demanded that new ideas and heresies should at least be continuously amusing. Within a hundred years of its appearance, the wild new feeling of troubadour poetry was in acute danger of being civilized out of existence. If two great things – wild, god-given inspiration and disciplined criticism of oneself and life – are the ingredients of great poetry, the troubadours ran the risk of beginning by having the first without the second and then at once gaining the second at the expense of losing the first. The new feeling has its lonely, disconnected life in their poems, but when troubadours became domesticated, their attempt to civilize the passions, to make them live at court, ran the danger of emasculating them; and

---

[1] One of the reasons for calling *The Owl and the Nightingale* a 'criticism of life' is that it does raise questions like this. (Below, pp. 36 ff.)

the new style of love became the great game and pastime of the late medieval courts.

Now that the troubadours have won their war, now that our common languages are to some extent languages of *fyn amour* and that old-fashioned girls expect declarations of passionate love as part of proposals of marriage (or *vice versa*), it is hard for us to imagine the radical novelty of troubadour style: but we may at least be able to see how it became acceptably ordinary; for the same thing easily happens in every language, perhaps in every life, where a style like the troubadours' is used seriously. The ironical inflection, the joking use, is a step any age or any person makes very easily. It is so much more entertaining and so much less dangerous to play a game of love than to recognize, consciously, its dangerous power.

The peculiar history of the reception of the troubadours into the courts, and the peculiar style to which it gave rise, can be shown from a few details about two people. The later stages of this basic development in our European psyche depended on the whims of one lady; but we will first consider Andreas Capellanus, if only because his work is always discussed at length, and quite mistakenly, by the books on this subject.

III

Moses returned from his meeting with God bearing the tables of the Law. In just such a way, according to a whole tradition of scholarship, did Andrew the Chaplain emerge from his study with the law of courtly love, *de Arte Honeste Amandi*, which is supposed to have codified the new impulse of the troubadours into rules carefully henceforth obeyed by the poets and courtiers of the later Middle Ages. The most rightly influential statement of this view is by C. S. Lewis who, after considering the ideals of courtly love in the poems of Chrestien de Troyes says,

Having thus studied the new ideal...we naturally look next for a professedly theoretical work on the same subject, wherewith to finish off our sketch. Such a work is ready for us in the *De Arte Honeste Amandi* of Andreas Capellanus...

The *De Arte* takes the form of methodical instruction in the art of love-making.[1]

In the same passage Lewis invites us to find in this work 'the

---

[1] Lewis, *Allegory of Love*, pp. 32–3.

characteristics of the theory of love as it existed in the general mind of the period'.

If we come to the book with these expectations we are likely to be as surprised as when we try to read *The Book of the Duchess* as elegy. Andreas Capellanus is certainly not the schoolman he is taken for. You only have to read the contents or the first few pages to see that the book is, at one level anyway, a parody of a scholastic treatment of love. (Parody is quite foreign to the original troubadour spirit.) The schoolmen liked to get everything categorized into its neat subdivision. Add up all the classes and you get a *summa*. It is plain from the contents list that Andreas is applying this procedure to the subject love: 'Book One: Introduction to the Treatise on Love: I. What Love Is. II. Between what Persons Love may Exist. III. Where Love gets its Name'[1] etc. Medieval philosophers were very fond of definitions, too, and Andreas obliges with a definition of 'love' together with an etymology I find rather nice:

Love gets its name (*amor*) from the word for hook (*amus*), which means 'to capture' or 'to be captured', for he who is in love is captured in the chains of desire and wishes to capture someone else with his hook. Just as a skillful fisherman tries to attract fishes by his bait and to capture them on his crooked hook, so the man who is a captive of love tries to attract another person by his allurements.[2]

This is a joke and a tone reminiscent of the first stanzas of *The Parliament of Fowls* – 'Al this mene I by Love...'

But it is notoriously difficult to be sure that anyone is joking when he speaks of love. I would gladly believe that when the British Broadcasting Corporation announced programmes for schools on what it called 'sex education' from which all mention of such indecencies as love and marriage is excluded, it was hoaxing us. The reasons for knowing that in this case we are not dealing with an intentional joke are rather complicated, to do with context, and the absence of an established language of love in our age. But may it not be that if we learn enough to see Andreas Capellanus in context he will turn out after all to be a solemn schoolman?

My reason for being sure that he is at least not wholly serious is that our allowing his book to be funny is a way of making sense of it: it seems to be itself and in character when it is amusing. Further, the sense one can make of Andreas as a humorist fits well

[1] I quote John Jay Parry's translation of *De Arte, The Art of Courtly Love*, (New York, 1941).   [2] Parry's translation, p. 31.

the above sketch of the reception of troubadour ideas into the courts. Once one allows oneself to find humour in *de Arte Honeste Amandi*, in fact, the comicality of the work soon seems indisputable.

In true scholastic spirit Andreas gives a full conspectus of all the kinds of love and so comes at length in Chapter VIII to 'The Love of Nuns', which itself follows a chapter on 'The Love of the Clergy'. The love of nuns, it is very properly said, should be avoided because 'by such love body and soul are condemned to death'.[1] But having said so Andreas goes on to what seems the real objection: 'Be careful, therefore, Walter, about seeking lonely places with nuns or looking for opportunities to talk with them, for if one of them should think that the place was suitable for wanton dalliance, she would have no hesitation in granting you what you desire.'[2] Andreas offers the opinion (Chapter XI) that the *correct* way of courting a peasant is to find a convenient field and then knock her down. He rounds off the section with a chapter on the love of prostitutes: 'Therefore we have no desire to explain to you the way to gain their love, because whatever the feeling that makes them give themselves to a suitor they always do so without much urging, so you don't need to ask instructions on this point.'[3]

De Arte Honeste Amandi is really a compendium of various amusing ways of talking about love. As well as the chapters of advice and definition I have quoted there is – the main bulk of the book – a set of specimen dialogues between different classes of lovers, the interest of which is, I suppose, partly novelistic and partly exemplary; there are also two fables, two sets of the commandments of love, decisions of cases in courts of love, and a final renunciation of love.

The decisions of the courts of love have provided much grist to the scholarly mills. The courts have even been assumed to be real, and it has been solemnly debated what authority their case-law assumed.[4] Need one say more than that the court of love was essentially a group of courtly ladies playing at administering justice in affairs of the heart? – and giving another example of love as game and parody. It is not hard to see some of the decisions Andreas records as deliberately outrageous. After a lengthy argument[5] Countess Marie de Champagne delivers the considered

---

[1] Parry's translation, p. 143.   [2] *Ibid.*   [3] *Ibid.*, p. 150.
[4] J. Lafitte-Houssat's sensible little book *Troubadours et Cours d'Amour* (Paris, 1950), gives examples, pp. 33ff., and cites so acute an observer of human affairs as Stendhal as one who believed these courts to have had a real juridical function.   [5] Parry's translation, p. 107.

judgment that love cannot exist between a husband and wife; and this judgment is the foundation of the orthodox view of courtly love as necessarily adulterous.[1] Perhaps, in a way we have yet to define, the Countess Marie was talking seriously. But at the same time I imagine her judgment must have brought the house down. It leads to such refinements as this, which I confess to being amused by:

A certain knight was in love with a woman who had given her love to another man, but he got from her this much hope of her love – that if it should ever happen that she lost the love of her beloved, then without a doubt her love would go to this man. A little while after this the woman married her lover. The other knight then demanded that she give him the fruit of the hope she had granted him, but this she absolutely refused to do, saying that she had not lost the love of her lover. In this affair the Queen gave her decision as follows: 'We dare not oppose the opinion of the Countess of Champagne, who ruled that love can exert no power between husband and wife. Therefore we recommend that the lady should grant the love she has promised.'[2]

Most commentators take very earnestly the first parts of *de Arte Honeste Amandi* and treat the concluding rejection of love as somehow 'conventional', though it flagrantly contradicts the rest of the work. (Professor D. W. Robertson inverts the procedure and takes the last part as the only earnest bit of the book.) But this last chapter is just the Chaplain's parting joke. Having squeezed all the amusement out of courtly love itself he tries his hand at the different tradition of anti-feminist diatribe, with the same end in view – to entertain.

Furthermore, not only is every woman by nature a miser, but she is also envious and a slanderer of other women, greedy, a slave to her belly, inconstant, fickle in her speech, disobedient and impatient of restraint, spotted with the sin of pride and desirous of vainglory, a liar, a drunkard, a babbler, no keeper of secrets, too much given to wantonness, prone to every evil, and never loving any man in her heart.[3]

That this magnificent invective is meant to be comic is not provable: but, for instance, try to take the following with full solemnity and bearing in mind that the 'Queen' mentioned was probably one of the Chaplain's intended readers:

So great is the avarice by which women are dominated that they think nothing of running counter to the laws, divine and human... Indeed,

---

[1] Cf. Lewis, *Allegory of Love*, p. 2, and this note of Professor E. G. Stanley's in his edition of *The Owl and the Nightingale* (1960, p. 141): 'The Nightingale's view that there may be true love between husband and wife commends itself so readily to the modern reader that it is important to remember that it runs counter to the tenets of the stricter doctrine of courtly love.'

[2] Parry's translation, p. 175.   [3] *Ibid.*, p. 201.

women think that to give to no one and to cling with all their might to everything, whether rightly or wrongly acquired, is the height of virtue and that all men ought to commend it. To this rule there are no exceptions, not even in the case of the Queen.

Woman is also such a slave to her belly that there is nothing she would be ashamed to assent to if she were assured of a fine meal, and no matter how much she has she never has any hope that she can satisfy her appetite when she is hungry; she never invites anybody to eat with her, but when she eats she always seeks out hidden and retired places and she usually likes to eat more than normal. But although in all other respects those of the feminine sex are miserly and hold with might and main to what they have, they will greedily waste their substance to gobble up food, and no one ever saw a woman who would not, if tempted, succumb to the vice of gluttony.[1]

But despite my conviction of André's comedy, I do not wish to go to the other extreme from conventional scholars and say he is wholly frivolous. For all his levity he does seem sometimes to be really speaking of love. The dialogues are often eloquent and sometimes, perhaps, genuine in their feeling. And the commandments of love, though funny, are also sometimes convincing; and they do not prettify love. The second commandment, 'He who is not jealous cannot love',[2] survives at least as late as Wycherley,[3] possibly because it is true. Nevertheless, put as a commandment it is bound to be funny. Similarly numbers xv and xvi are made ridiculous by their form, but aren't simply nonsense:

xv. Every lover regularly turns pale in the presence of his beloved.
xvi. When a lover suddenly catches sight of his beloved his heart palpitates.[4]

It is certainly unsolemn to say, almost, 'Thou shalt palpitate' – nevertheless the commandment may have some real relation to experience. With Andreas Capellanus we find ourselves in the same no-man's-land between earnest and game that perplexed us with *The Book of the Duchess*. If these works puzzle us with their frivolous seriousness, we have at least found some consistency of literary tradition, and it would be at least plausible to suggest that these works are as they are because they were supplying a demand of patrons who wanted them so. But why should anybody demand frivolous seriousness? This question takes us back to thinking about how the troubadours entered the courts; and I think the matter may be sufficiently illuminated by some consideration of the courts that gathered round Queen Eleanor of Aquitaine.

---

[1] Parry's translation, p. 203.   [2] *Ibid.*, p. 184.
[3] 'He wants, you see, jealousy, the only infallible sign of [love]', *The Country Wife*, II, i.   [4] Parry's translation, p. 185.

IV

Queen Eleanor was *in propria persona* a force quite able to take on and captivate the whole troubadour movement.[1] At the age of fifteen she was Queen of France, and within eight weeks of being divorced from her first husband, at twenty-nine, she married the man who within a few years became King Henry II of England. Her life as queen successively of France and England was a long exploration of the most extreme and characteristic ways of life of her century, to which she herself added one. She was more than a match for the church in its wildest sanctity. St Bernard of Clairvaux, whose great monument was the Cistercian order – the last of the austere reforming orders, whose ideal can still be seen expressed in the stone of Tintern and Fountains – had an authority well-nigh incredible to the modern mind. He concentrated within himself all the mad spiritual authority of the early medieval church, and pope and emperor did his bidding. Early in Eleanor's first marriage Bernard was called in, as was the practice at the time, to restore peace between the King of France and the Pope. He dictated terms to which both sides obediently submitted, but in the course of his visit to the French court he visited the Queen and found her much less docile than her husband. Both Eleanor and Bernard were perhaps at a loss in this meeting of temperaments from different worlds: Bernard found a lady not in awe of him (she had perhaps as little idea of that kind of sanctity as most modern women) and Eleanor met a man wholly insensitive to feminine charm.

Eleanor did more than any other single person to discredit the crusading movement. It is true that the crusade with which she was associated resisted, unlike the fourth, the temptation to plunder Constantinople instead of attacking the infidel – though it had its own share of new disgraces, no mean feat even at that moment of crusading history.[2] But Eleanor's attack was more insidious: she insisted on going on crusade herself. This was a quite unheard-of thing. Even in recent times women have rarely been the warrior class – but the mind boggles at the idea of courtly ladies fighting a war. Fighting, however, was not what Queen Eleanor had

---

[1] Most of my sense of Queen Eleanor comes from Amy Kelly, *Eleanor of Aquitaine and the Four Kings* (1952), a work of real imagination as well as of scholarship.

[2] For instance, the Frankish army during the second crusade was for a time hopelessly lost in Asia Minor because it had no maps. In the end it found itself

in mind. She was perhaps more interested in getting a sight of Constantinople, the biggest and richest city known, and with an imperial court of unparalleled splendour. On *chevauchee* Eleanor amused herself by dressing up as an Amazon, and spent her time in her gorgeous tent in the usual courtly pastimes. The holy war – preached by St Bernard with such fervour that no prince and not even the Pope had been able to resist his command to support it[1] – became a great holiday excursion in which the French court, instead of touring the king's lands in the usual way, made a progress through the fabulous East. This was hardly the idea of the crusade held by St Bernard. If Queen Eleanor could turn *that* into a courtly game it is not surprising that she could do something similar to the love-poetry of the troubadours.

She patronized troubadour poets at Paris – they all seem to have been in love with her – but the French court was somewhat puritanical, and her great chances did not come until her second marriage. In her early years in London she took her first opportunity of patronizing poets to her heart's content. To this period belongs the famous pursuit of Eleanor by the most celebrated of the troubadours, Bernart de Ventadour; but she also commissioned Wace's *Brut* (a patriotic history of Britain) and Benoît de Ste Maure's *Troy Book* which, *inter alia*, added to the Troy story many of the details of the episode of Briseis which gave Chaucer, by way of its amplification and ordering in Boccaccio's *Filostrato*, the plot of *Troilus and Criseyde*. Eleanor was thus responsible, perhaps directly, for the introduction of courtly love into the Trojan War.

At fifty, after a life of enormous variety at all the centres of Europe and the Christian East, at an age when most of her contemporaries were dead and the female survivors were expected to

at the Byzantine city of Satalia, where it was refused admittance, and where money ran out. The nobles scrounged transport and made off, leaving 7,000 men between the inner and outer walls of Satalia, facing hostile Greeks in one direction and hostile Turks in the other. The 7,000 found a way out of this dilemma by declaring themselves unanimously Muslim. They were welcomed by the Turks and disappear from history less heroically than their companions whose bodies were left hundreds of miles both from France and the Holy Land.

[1] The Holy Roman Emperor, Conrad, said to be a cleverer ruler than Louis, tried to escape by not giving audience to St Bernard, but capitulated as soon as the saint gained access. Conrad did later retrieve something of his reputation for sagacity; he set off before the other crusaders and so got the best foraging; and after the destruction of his army he was sensible enough to take the chance of making the best of his way home.

devote themselves to ugliness and good works, Eleanor embarked on the new part of her career that most makes her the subject of our attention. Eleanor became estranged from Henry and with his permission retired once again with his heir Richard to her own capital of Poitiers, where she reigned from 1170–4. In those years at Poitiers we see something unique in the Middle Ages and not common since: a splendid court, the centre of a peaceful and rich state, reigned over by a woman and largely governed by other women. Eleanor's court became a sort of European finishing school. Not only the leading Angevin ladies of Henry's family, but the princesses of the enemy French camp were often to be found there, and the effective controller of the household arrangements was Eleanor's eldest daughter, none other than Marie de Champagne, who brought with her her chaplain André and probably her court poet Chrestien, from her capital of Troyes. Probably also present was a lady perhaps half-sister to the King of England and now known as Marie de France. This was the court for which Andreas wrote *de Arte Honeste Amandi*, perhaps where Chrestien recited *Lancelot, ou le Chevalier de la Charrete*, where Marie composed some of her lais and fables, and where a whole host of minor troubadours flattered the ladies with their beautiful, amateur love-songs.

Eleanor's court at Poitiers flourished until 1174 when her husband Henry (incensed, probably, more by Queen Eleanor's politics than her morals or style) appeared with an army and captured Eleanor as she fled towards Paris. The rest of her long life was as full of event as the first fifty years[1] but does not concern us here. (Marie de Champagne, providentially widowed, later had a lesser version of her mother's court, at Troyes.)

The successive courts Eleanor gathered round her were forcing-houses of a courtly way of life, a civilization that hinged on the superiority of women through the civilizing force of love. In one way courtly love was the serious business of Eleanor's courts. The talk, the games, and no doubt the affairs, made the style, and the style was the creation of a new way of life. The people who expressed the new mood (and without expression it could hardly have existed and could certainly not have been known to us) were of course the poets. They brought to it the new poetic joy and inspiration in love.

Yet at the same time love must always be a game, a game under

---

[1] Shakespeare, of course, puts her extreme old age into *King John*.

the control of the leading players, the great ladies.[1] As far as I know the more ordinary feudal business of Eleanor's court was effectively transacted: she and her officers administered justice and made appointments. Love, like other pastimes, was for leisure. And that her serious life was in her leisure hours is itself a continuation of her criticism of the church we have briefly noticed: her frivolity was a comment on the most effectively solemn institution the West has yet produced. Anything we can see as a serious development of culture at Eleanor's courts had to take a frivolous form. The poets, as soon as they come into the court – the only place for them – have to submit to the dictation of feeling and ethos by courtly patrons.

V

In this way I explain the case of Chrestien de Troyes, the most interesting (with Marie de France) of the French writers attached to Queen Eleanor or her entourage.

Chrestien's subject is the new courtly one, the 'matter of Britain'. The Arthurian cycle gave several opportunities to the narrative poet of courtly love: it went in for magic and mystery, appealing to a taste alien to the romanesque simplicities of the earlier Middle Ages; its central story and many of the others concern adultery, and allowed Chrestien to include many of the 'debates' and 'questions of love' which belong so obviously to the same world as Andreas Capellanus. Knights in Chrestien fight commonly not in defence of their lord or for treasure, but to win the approval of a lady. Damsels in distress make here their first appearance in European literature.

The central Arthurian story is a glorification of the love of the best knight in the world for the first lady – adulterous love, since the first lady is Guinevere and the best knight not Arthur but Lancelot:

> Et la reïne li estant
> ses bras ancontre, si l'anbrace,
> estroit pres de son piz le lace,
> si l'a lez li an son lit tret,
> et le plus bel sanblant li fet
> que ele onques feire li puet,
> que d'Amors et del cuer li muet.
> D'Amors vient qu'ele le conjot;
> et s'ele a lui grant amor ot
> et il c. mile tanz a li,

[1] This traditional relation of lady and poetry survives at least to Skelton's day in *Speke Parrot*.

car a toz autres cuers failli
Amors avers qu'au suen ne fist;
mes an son cuer tote reprist
Amors, et fu si anterine
qu'an toz autres cuers fu frarine.
Or a Lanceloz quan qu'il vialt
quant la reïne an gré requialt
sa conpaignie et son solaz,
quant il la tient antre ses braz
el ele lui antre les suens.[1]

Chrestien's treatment of the Lancelot story was, he says, directed by his patron Marie de Champagne,[2] but he himself did not approve of adultery. When left to his own devices he wrote firstly *Erec et Enide*, in which the hero and heroine settle the courtly problem of the reconciliation of arms and love (also treated in *The Knight's Tale*) by marrying and going off on adventures together, then *Yvain*, in which the hero marries at the end of the first part – the rest of the plot being his efforts to propitiate his wife after he has offended her by leaving her for martial pursuits – and finally *Perceval*, where Chrestien takes his revenge on the 'matter of Britain' by adding a Christianizing end, the story of the quest not for a beautiful lady but for the Holy Grail.

Chrestien's verse is full of verve and life: that confident, sunny, short couplet of his abounds with the *joie de vivre* which becomes in

---

[1] Chrétien de Troyes, *Le Chevalier de la Charrete*, ed. M. Roques (Paris, 1958), lines 4654–73. The Everyman translation runs: 'And the Queen extends her arms to him and, embracing him, presses him tightly against her bosom, drawing him into the bed beside her and showing him every possible satisfaction: her love and her heart go out to him. It is love that prompts her to treat him so; and if she feels great love for him, he feels a hundred thousand times as much for her. For there is no love at all in other hearts compared with what there is in his; in his heart love was so completely embodied that it was niggardly toward all other hearts. Now Lancelot possesses all he wants, when the Queen voluntarily seeks his company and love, and when he holds her in his arms, and she holds him in hers...' Chrétien de Troyes, *Arthurian Romances*, transl. W. W. Comfort (1914), p. 329.

[2] 21 Mes tant dirai ge que mialz oevre
ses comandemanz an ceste oevre
que sans ne painne que g'i mete.

('I will say, however, that her command has more to do with this work than any thought or pains that I may expend upon it.') and

26 matiere et san li done et livre
la contesse, et il s'antremet
de panser, que gueres n'i met
fors sa painne et s'antancïon.

('The Countess gives and furnishes him the material and the idea, and he concentrates on putting it in form, so that he puts hardly anything in without her care and concern.')

his century for the first time typically French. He is not frivolous in the same way as André le Chapelain; his stories exemplify the courtly styles of love, chivalry and intrigue without ridiculing them. But neither when directed by a patron nor when pleasing himself does Chrestien really explore or question or value the courtly ideals he creates. He is as far from setting them in a real world as the troubadour poets. (Some critics argue the contrary, and certainly Chrestien's mixture of poetic celebration with the trickery of love might sometimes suggest irony: my point is that we can't be sure whether it is there within *Lancelot* or not.) Chrestien, that is, never quite rises into a criticism of life.

Yet one can sense a real poetic talent in Chrestien. The most memorable parts of his tales are, in my experience, the semi-mystical symbols – the stone in *Yvain* that causes a storm when water is poured on it, or, above all, the Sword Bridge which Lancelot has to cross in his pursuit of love, the alternative to the Water Bridge crossed by Gawain:

El cil de trespasser le gort
au mialz que il set s'aparoille,
et fet molt estrange mervoille,
que ses piez desarme, et ses mains:
n'iert mie toz antiers ne sains,
quant de l'autre part iert venus;
Bien s'iert sor l'espee tenuz,
qui plus estoit tranchanz que fauz,
as mains nues et si deschauz
que il ne s'est lessiez an pié
souler, ne chauce, n'avanpié.
De ces gueres ne s'esmaioit,
s'es mains et es piez se plaioit;
mailz se voloit il mahaignier
que cheoir el pont et baignier
an l'eve don ja mes n'issist.
A la grant dolor c'on li fist
s'an passe outre et a grant destrece;
mains et genolz et piez se blece,
mes tot le rasoage et sainne
Amors qui le conduist et mainne,
si li estoit a sofrir dolz.[1]

---

[1] *Le Chevalier de la Charrete*, lines 3094–115. Comfort's translation (p. 309): 'Meanwhile he prepares, as best he may, to cross the stream, and he does a very marvellous thing in removing the armour from his feet and hands. He will be in a sorry state when he reaches the other side. He is going to support himself with his bare hands and feet upon the sword, which was sharper than a scythe, for he had not kept on his feet either sole or upper or hose. But he felt no fear of wounds upon his hands or feet; he preferred to maim himself

This is not allegory, nor is the image *explained* by talk of the pain of attaining love. The image has to work as art; the reader responds to the imagined situation (my nerves tingle) and takes whatever meaning the image carries in itself. Any meaning only comes *in* the image. But in places like this, where Chrestien is at his best, his poetry is a sort of refinement of the poetry of the troubadours. It does not go beyond them into criticism of life; it is not connecting this style with the other courtly style, the serious frivolity of Andreas Capellanus. In the end Chrestien remains a poet of isolated, beautiful, passionate moments.

What Chrestien does with his occasional beautiful images is the whole achievement of Marie de France[1] – again, an achievement which I have neither the wish nor the capacity to belittle, but which takes place so comfortably within the courtly milieu established by Eleanor and Marie de Champagne that I cannot see it as truly great art. The lais are the perfection of the poetry of Eleanor's courts – perfectly worked out, touching, short symbolic tales which work like Chrestien's image of the Sword Bridge by putting (as Dr John Stevens has recently argued very persuasively[2]) one situation simply before a reader and allowing whatever emotion or significance it has to speak without comment. The obvious example is *Laüstic*, where the Nightingale just *is*, at the end, the love of the knight and the lady. The bird is not symbolic: it is a bird; but the image of the bird itself expresses the love, killed, but treasured up by both lovers:

> Un vasselet ad fet forgeér;
> Unques n'i ot fer në acer:
> Tut fu de or fin od bones pieres,
> Mut precïuses e mut cheres;
> Covercle i ot tresbien asis.
> Le laüstic ad dedenz mis;
> Puis fist la chasse enseeler,
> Tuz jurs l'ad fet od lui porter.[3]

rather than to fall from the bridge and be plunged in the water from which he could never escape. In accordance with this determination, he passes over with great pain and agony, being wounded in the hands, knees, and feet. But even this suffering is sweet to him: for Love, who conducts and leads him on, assuages and relieves the pain.'

[1] It is worth making the obvious remark that Marie was a woman. Vernacular poetesses were unthinkable in the heroic age.

[2] 'Le Granz Bienz de Marie de France', *Patterns of Love and Courtesy*, ed. J. Lawlor (1966).

[3] *Laüstic*, lines 149–56; Marie de France, *Lais*, ed. Alfred Ewert (Oxford, 1944): translated by Eugene Mason in *Lays of Marie de France* (1911; p. 60): 'So he caused a certain coffret to be fashioned, made not of iron or steel, but of fine

Marie's *Lais* are so beautiful and so *small*. How can one imagine a literature growing out of them? Theirs is the smallness not of a seed but of something finished and final. This is what happened to troubadour poetry when it became domesticated in Eleanor's splendid courts.

So Eleanor's poets have always to sing of love, of its beauty rather than its destructive powers; and they are never allowed to evaluate love. Moreover, they have to write of love in an un-remittingly entertaining way: they cannot afford to be critical to a society for whom they are defining love and to whom love is a game. Seriousness can only take the form of the images of Chrestien or the perfectly finished small beauty of Marie, refined from the simplicity of the troubadours – and which risks refining the original troubadour passion completely out of poetry.

Naturally, to take the further step which is always the desire of poetry, the poets had to move out of the situation in which Eleanor confined them, though it is also true that without that situation there would have been no medieval French or English poetry. The dilemma of the courtly poets was that their prison was very com-fortable and in some ways necessary. Nevertheless they had to break out of it if love was to be more than a game, and if literature was to be a criticism of life.

VI

The break-out came in France within a few years of Queen Eleanor's death, in a uniquely accidental way, with the composition (if that is the word) of *Le Roman de la Rose*. When Chrestien criticizes life it is dependent criticism, criticism according to values given to the poet and not to be questioned by him. The great step towards freedom taken by the *Roman* is its criticism of love by way of the comparison of courtly love with other things. And this criticism and comparative evaluation is a way of making love itself more serious and passionate.

Guillaume de Lorris, as is well known, composed the first part of *Le Roman de la Rose*, and in it he achieves the consummation of everything Chrestien was trying for and Marie on her smaller scale achieved. Guillaume's part is often beautiful, occasionally moving, and not infrequently dull. The Amant, the young man who

gold and fair stones, most rich and precious, right strongly clasped and bound. In this little chest he set the body of the nightingale, and having sealed the shrine, carried it upon him whenever his business took him abroad.'

tells the first-person story, wanders in the first of the medieval
May-morning-green-mead scenes, by a river, and sees a walled
garden which he desires to enter. He is admitted to a beautiful but
enclosed garden in the middle of which is a bed of roses including
one special bud that it becomes the obsession of Amant's life to
pluck. He swears fealty to Love and is shot by Love's five arrows.

This is the first thousand lines or so. The remaining 21,000-odd
recount Amant's adventures and discoveries before he at last
plucks the rose (or, in the less decent later image, makes his way
into the narrow gate of the castle); but of these thousands of
verses Guillaume composed only the first 3,000, and at the end of
his part Amant seems on the point of attaining his desire. He has
already kissed the rose, in a passage both very beautiful and very
reminiscent of Marie de France, which the English version attributed to Chaucer translates like this:

3753   Whanne the flawme of the verry brond
      That Venus brought in hir right hond
      Hadde Bialacoil with hete smete
      Anoon he bad withouten lette
      Graunte to me the Rose kisse
      Thanne of my peyne I gan to lysse
      And to the Rose anoon wente I
      And kisside it full feithfully
      Thar no man aske if I was blithe
      Whanne the savour softe and lythe
      Strok to myn herte withoute more
      And me aleged of my sore
      So was I full of joye and blisse
      It is fair sich a flour to kisse
      It was so swoote and saverous

In Guillaume's part of *Le Roman de la Rose* I know of only one –
very mild – joke (at lines 2536–41).

Forty years after the death of Guillaume de Lorris his un-
finished poem was taken up by one Jean Clopinel or de Meung,
who added thousands and thousands of lines consisting largely of
anti-feminist, political and other diatribes, and good advice about
trickery in love which Chaucer later used in various poems.[1] The
usual account in histories of literature is that Jean's addition is
cynical, longwinded and unreadable, and that it doesn't belong at
all with Guillaume's part:

---

[1] In one striking passage, Jean gave Chaucer essential bits of characters as
diverse as the Wife of Bath and the Prioress: cf. *Roman* 13378–426 and *Canterbury Tales* A 130–41 and D 467–8.

Towards the end of the thirteenth century the *Roman de la Rose* was continued by **Jean de Meung**. This writer was a man of great learning with a strong satiric bent, and the eighteen thousand lines in which he continued the poem are a bitter attack on all forms of vice, on existing abuses, and, above all, on the Church. His work is too long and discursive to be readable, but it contains many telling passages.[1]

It does seem true that Jean's temperament was the opposite of Guillaume's. He certainly enjoys satire, the more startling the better, and never rests for long in the older enjoyment of ingenuous beauty without turning ironical. He also turns the allegory indecent. Much of the latter part of the *Roman* is the kind of courtly entertainment we have discussed, but more biting, wider ranging, and, in a way I must try to define, more serious.

So I must dispute Weekley's account. I can at least testify that the poem is not unreadable: I have read it. But I want to go further and suggest Jean de Meun is a better poet than is usually allowed. In the first place he takes the chance, given to him by the allegorical form, to be dramatic. He speaks not in his own person but through monologues and interchanges between a wide variety of lively characters not all of whom could possibly be taken as mouthpieces of the author. The Old Woman, for instance, seems to be the Wife of Bath's grandmother, and has some of her drive of dubious vitality. As Mr Geoffrey Strickland put it, 'The form of *Le Roman de la Rose* has something in common with *The Canterbury Tales*, in which different views of human relationships are dramatically contrasted and weighed.'[2] It is in this dramatic evaluation that one can see a decisive step out of the attitudes and feelings prescribed to earlier poets.

Secondly, *Le Roman de la Rose* was enormously popular (we know from the vast number of surviving manuscripts) not as two separate poems but as one work. The very different parts were somehow seen to be necessary to each other, and only together create the new step in courtly literature. The new thing is a courtly-love poem which can also be called a criticism of life.

Jean de Meun moves out into a criticism of life through the poem's fighting, contradictory range of attitudes to love. Guillaume's beautiful image of courtly pursuit is the foundation, but immediately afterwards, for example, comes Reason (hated by lovers for the rest of the poem) who tries to persuade Amant that

[1] Ernest Weekley, *A Primer of French Literature* (1901), p. 13.
[2] *The Cambridge Quarterly*, 1 (1966), 186.

2-2

his love is of a very inferior sort. In *Le Roman de la Rose* courtly love has to make a place for itself in a world that includes many of its enemies. And that is at once a way of taking courtly love seriously and allowing its inspirational force. A poet who tries to tell the truth about love by giving it its place in life is going further about love, and making it more itself, than Marie de France could.

I grant the *Roman*'s incoherence, that its success is fragmentary: but in its chaotic way it does scramble out of the courtly prison. Afterwards many things were possible to the courtly French writers which were not possible to Chrestien de Troyes or Marie de France.

VII

Meanwhile in England a comparable development had taken place but (because of historical accidents) without any great effect on the future of English poetry. In England there was a kind of second generation of the influence of Queen Eleanor of Aquitaine. In her earlier years all the leading courtly poets, writing in French, had serenaded her or dedicated works to her; but this second generation wrote in English. The first of the historically-minded English country parsons, Laȝamon, translated Wace into English, often with some force. There were some lyrics. But the work which makes me mention English poetry before Chaucer is the anonymous poem *The Owl and the Nightingale*, probably written during Eleanor's lifetime and making references to Henry II and to Marie de France. *The Owl and the Nightingale* makes in English, more briefly and surely, the step forward that was later to happen in France by accident.

The Owl and the Nightingale has the same frivolously serious base I have been defining as the mark of the tradition. It brings all the brightness and lightness of the French short couplet into English – an achievement in itself at a time when the English metrical romances were using a similar metre in a stiffly clod-hopping way, and when the romance vocabulary that seems to belong to the style in early Chaucer had hardly begun to penetrate the very Anglo-Saxon word-hoard of English. But *The Owl and the Nightingale*, in all its entertainingness (and it *is* a very amusing poem, though the history of the language has removed it for ever from those classes who enjoy what they read, and given it instead to medievalists) makes all the necessary steps away from mere entertainment and the courtly game of love, towards real poetic

36

seriousness. It achieves a more genuinely dramatic form than *Le Roman de la Rose* but in the same general way, testing courtly love by surrounding it with some of the other things to be met with in life. Although it begins with a charming smallness like that of Marie de France and an entertainingness like André le Chapelain's, *The Owl and the Nightingale* can even be solemn when it needs.

At its surface level *The Owl and the Nightingale* is an innocently trivial 'debate' between the two birds, which swell with extreme spleen, try to fight, and accuse one another of such misdemeanours as fouling nests and eating spiders and flies. It is an evening entertainment, taking about two hours to perform, of the kind beloved by Queen Eleanor. Yet at the same time it gradually emerges through the characters of the birds that the Owl is the stoical, Boethian, moral, Winter, Anglo-Saxon monastic bird, and the Nightingale the gay, carefree, Summer, French courtly lover.[1] In its amusing, light way the poem goes as far as raising some of the greatest questions, whether fullness of life is to be found in church or court, whether to worship God in revelation or creation, whether to love God or women or both.

The Owl and the Nightingale manages to extend the courtly mode without any overt rebellion (such as Jean de Meun was sometimes driven to) against its restrictions. Its tones range from lavatory jokes to troubadour-like beauty, private jokes to solemnly prophetic passages. The author adopts a *persona* comparable with those of Jean de Meun or Andreas Capellanus, an inversion in anticipation of Chaucer's favourite pose as what Mr Bateson calls 'comic nincompoop'. Nicholas of Guildford is represented as preternaturally sage and knowledgeable, a general dispenser of sweetness and light, though it is hinted at the same time that there may be a few skeletons in his cupboard:

> Maister nichole of guldeforde
> He is wis and war of worde.
> He is of dome suþe gleu.
> & him is loþ eurich unþeu.
> He wot insiȝt in eche songe.
> Wo singet wel wo singet wronge.
> & he can schede vrom the riȝte
> þat woȝe þat þuster from þe liȝte...

[1] J. W. H. Atkins makes this case in detail in his introduction to his edition (Cambridge, 1922), unfortunately out of print, which I think by far the best published essay on the poem.

Ich granti wel þat he us deme.
Vor þeӡ he were wile breme.
& lof him were niӡtingale.
& oþer wiӡte gente & smale.
Ich wot he is nu suþe acoled.
Nis he vor þe noӡt afoled.
þat he for þine olde luue.
Me adun legge and þe abuue.[1]

The other extreme of the poem's range of styles may be seen in the following passage, which seems to me astonishing in its power of making those light couplets solemn and stately – a grand style, moreover, very unlike the plainness of the climax of *The Book of the Duchess*:

1191 Ich wot of hunger of hergonge.
Ich wot ӡef men schule libbe longe.
Ich wat ӡif wif luste hire make.
Ich wat þar schal beo niþ & wrake.
Ich wot hwo schal beon & honge.
Oþer elles fulne deþ a fonge.
ӡef men habbeþ bataile inume.
Ich wat hwaþer schal beon ouer kume.
Ich wat ӡif cwalm scal comen on orfe.
And ӡif dor schul ligge & storue.[2]

---

[1] Ms. Cotton Caligula A. ix, lines 191–8, 201–8. I quote from the edition of J. H. G. Grattan and G. F. H. Sykes (EETS, 1935), and have substituted 'w' for 'p'. I translate the passage as follows:

> The Reverend Nichol, of Guildford city,
> Is wise and careful, as well as witty.
> His judgment is centrality
> And he is very strong on morality.
> He knows all about singing technique,
> Whose style is strong and whose is weak;
> He can discriminate wrong from right
> And part dark sayings from the light...
> Yes, I agree that he should judge.
> His past is not without a smudge:
> Nightingales once were dear to him,
> And other creatures neat and slim.
> But now, I think, he has matured,
> And is of all such rashness cured,
> So that he will no more be fooled
> By you, not that his fires are cooled.
> He will not – for his former love –
> Place me below and you above...

[2]
> I know of famine caused by strife.
> I know the length of each man's life.
> I know if wife shall lose her mate.
> I know of vengeance and of hate.
> I know who, hanging, life shall leave

Professor P. F. Baum refutes the general drift of these remarks like this:

> Others, however, have gone farther and seen deeper. The Nightingale is the troubadour bringing the gaiety of the sunny South as far north as wet England;[1] it teaches love, yet warns against love's errors; it stands for the French, courtly element in the British [*sic*] character. The Owl belongs to the folk and represents the lower clergy and speaks English – did not the poet elect to write in English rather than French? There are other contrasts: two types of mind; the joyful and the serious view of life; youth and age; the erotic and the ascetic; or, as has recently been suggested, the astrological opposition of Venus and Saturn; or heavenly and earthly love; or (as usual) the active and the contemplative life; or, what you will . . . For we seem to have a whole anthology of themes; and this could hint that the poet was sprawling in uncertainty and disorder over too much ground; or else, and better, since he shows no little skill in other ways, that he had his eye sharply on the subject and the subject was just an exhibit of two talkative 'birds' hopping from branch to branch, enjoying themselves because they liked to argue.[2]

But a whole anthology of themes need only hint that a poet is sprawling in disorder if he is a feeble poet or if all poems have a simple design. If this man is a good poet he might be able to bring in more themes than the troubadours. And it doesn't follow in that case that he need take his eye off the squabbling birds: the surprising thing is that there is *no* tension between the amusement and the seriousness.

What appears incoherence to Professor Baum seems subtlety to me – and, I am thankful to say, to W. P. Ker, who makes the point that at the end of the poem both birds are trying to steal part of the case of the other.[3] As the poem progresses, in fact, it becomes more like an election than a trial. Now that the birds have defined their characters and attitudes, each tries to catch the other bathing and make off with her clothes. The Nightingale, who is

Or other viler death receive.
When men to a pitched battle come
I know who shall be overcome.
I know when stock shall die of pest
And when shall sink to death each beast...

[1] There is a passage complaining bitterly about the climate of Scotland but I don't recall anything is said in the poem about English wet.
[2] P. F. Baum, Foreword to *The Owl and the Nightingale*, translated by Graydon Eggers (Durham, N.C., 1955), pp. xiii–xiv.
[3] *English Literature Medieval* (n.d.), pp. 180–3. There is never likely to be a better introduction to the subject than this old Home University Library primer, which is good enough to make succeeding critics feel both crude and unnecessary.

really interested in love and bored by morality, yet bids for support by denouncing adultery (though it is true that this turns out to be a way of sympathizing with girls who are led astray: having said that the proper place for love is marriage the Nightingale can then indulge her sympathy without inviting a moral attack – which nonetheless the Owl makes). Then the stern, ecclesiastical Owl does an even more surprising thing: she bids for the floating votes of the centre by condoning adultery (if the wife is driven to it by the husband's locking and beating her up). This rings a little hollow: the Owl is as suddenly (and perhaps as unsuccessfully) compassionate as the Labour Party in election year.

The semi-dramatic form saves the poet from the simplicity of having to take sides, just as the Parlement saves Chaucer in *The Parliament of Fowls*. Each bird's attitude is tested and made clear by the other's – which makes the poem rather a criticism of life than statements about life. When *The Owl and the Nightingale* uses *Laüstic* it uses it *critically*. The tender feelings are both created and criticized in the later poem (lines 1043–108).

But to continue this argument would be futile: *The Owl and the Nightingale* is not available to us in the same way as Chaucer or even as Marie de France: its language is too archaic, and, as I write, the poem is not even in print – except in the Early English Text Society facsimile of the two extant manuscripts. It seems to me that to go further with criticism of the poem one would have to translate it into modern English: translation would be the line-by-line engagement with what the poetry is saying to us which we get from poets fully of our own language merely by reading them. I am at least confident that the translation by Mr Eggers won't do: its style (it has only one) is untrue to the poem's life. 'I reck not of your threats, I ween' and 'Forsooth, you are an evil wight', etc.[1] make me say that the poem is at least more like English than the translation: the poem dates from before the invention of Prithee English. But this is not the place for me to attempt my own translation – which is the only way I can think of to make criticism of the poem valid.

So I have to leave it as what the Nightingale calls a 'bare word' – an unsupported assertion, to which the Owl takes proper exception, that *The Owl and the Nightingale* begins like *Le Roman de la Rose* in a courtly prison and like it develops into a criticism of life. Its being in English was itself a sign of escape but also, perhaps, that

[1] Pp. 4 and 5.

the escape was premature. There was no real equivalent of Queen Eleanor's courts in England for over a hundred years, and without the courtly audience the poem could not have made its more than courtly statement. We are rather lucky that *The Owl and the Nightingale* survives at all: there are only two manuscripts and only the sketchiest indications that the poem was read after its own generation.[1] It has all the quality of a new development of the creative imagination, but historical accident made the development ineffective – a good example of the truth of the axiom that without a coherent public and its criticism there can be no literature.

VIII

The next courts in England capable of harbouring a literature were those of the sons, grandsons and great-grandsons of Edward III – John of Gaunt, Thomas of Woodstock, the Black Prince, Richard II, Humphrey of Gloucester. Their ethos is still basically what I have pointed to in the courts of Eleanor of Aquitaine: the demand is for entertainment and the great subject is love. Froissart is a good example of a writer whose work was naturally pleasing to this taste.

Chaucer meets in his early poems the demand for courtly entertainment, and does so with such brilliant spirits that it would be absurd to argue that he was in rebellion against the tradition. But yet one can see a certain tension between Chaucer's genius for making the best of things just as he found them, and his ambition to be a real poet and explore and express whatever significance he could find in life – including, it may be, speaking of love in ways that would have been displeasing to the ladies of Queen Eleanor's day.

The Book of the Duchess is just an unassimilated mixture of the different things the courtly tradition made available. It is amusing, rhetorical or simple because that is what courtly poems could be, and because Chaucer enjoyed writing such poetry. But it is not really an elegy, and not really a love-poem, because there was no place for elegy or for the real expression of passion in the courtly prison from which Chaucer had not yet escaped – though perhaps, like Alice at one moment, he was already bigger than the house and had one leg sticking out of the chimney.

[1] The editors have found some evidence of fifteenth-century manuscript revision.

41

3

Chaucer Lost in the
House of Fame

The solemnity of critics atones for the frivolity of poets, and *The House of Fame*, which takes the manner of *The Book of the Duchess* to an extreme of brightness and lightness, is kept firmly to the ground by the weight of the criticism attached to it. Professor Bennett's case, that *The House of Fame* really is about fame, and in particular the fame a poet might expect from writing of love,[1] is argued with the wealth of learning one expects from the author, and assumes the poem's great seriousness. Mr Koonce[2] goes even further and (in the tradition of Professor D. W. Robertson, below, p. 271) takes the lightness of the poem as a transparent disguise for its true intention, namely, to preach the moral doctrines of the church.

I would not wish, even were I equipped to do so, to challenge Professsor Bennett on his own ground. But there is a certain absurdity in writing such large and weighty tomes on a poem that, whatever else it is, begins by being sheer entertainment. Both these scholars make the poem relate to their own special areas of academic devotion, but only by not raising the questions about its tone which if they were asked would make academic devotion seem inappropriate.

For *The House of Fame* is even more amusingly frivolous than *The Book of the Duchess* – and perhaps I join in the critical absurdity by *arguing* the point. Isn't it just obvious? The poem begins with sixty-five lines of 'comic-nincompoop' chatter about dreams, jumbling together all the words ('dream', 'avisioun', 'fantome', 'oracles', etc.) the narrator has ever heard used of them,

---

[1] ...the plight of Dido, which Chaucer makes the high point of Virgil's story, will serve obliquely to introduce the twin themes of the rest of the poem: the nature of 'Fame' and the search for tidings of 'Loves folke', J. A. W. Bennett, *Chaucer's Book of Fame* (Oxford, 1968), p. 26.
[2] B. G. Koonce, *Chaucer and the Tradition of Fame* (Princeton, 1966).

asserting that he doesn't know which is which, and culminating in this magnificent puff:

59   For never sith that I was born
       Ne no man elles me beforn
       Mette/I trowe stedfastly   dreamed
       So wonderful a dream as I
       The tenthe day now of Decembre
       The which as I kan now remembre
       I wol yow tellen everydel

Before carrying out his threat Chaucer announces his intention of making an Invocation, the 'trusteth wel' being more or less equivalent to 'don't you worry!':

66   But at my gynnynge trusteth wel
       I wol make invocacion
       With special devocion

the invocation being (the first appearance in English of the joke about sending a reader to sleep?)

       Unto the god of slep anoon

The story begins at line 111 with a brief description of a temple of Venus (the curious reader will find a whole chapter on this temple in Professor Bennett's book and a longer discussion of the goddess in Mr Koonce's), leading to what I must call a send-up of the *Aeneid*. The manner is perhaps sufficiently apparent in the couplet by which Chaucer renders Virgil's famous opening phrase, '*Arma virumque cano*':

143   I wol now singen yif I kan
       The armes and also the man

In reducing the *Aeneid* to a couple of hundred lines, Chaucer concentrates on the Dido episode, and it may indeed be that this indicates his wish to comment on love. But one cannot know from the lines themselves whether this is so, because Chaucer's tone throughout is so amusingly but aimlessly frivolous that the frivolity is the only thing one can be sure of. What can one make of Aeneas bearing the old Anchises on his back *like this?* –

166   he
       Escaped was from al the pres
       And took his fader Anchises
       And bar hym on hys bak away
       Cryinge Allas and welaway

> The whiche Anchises in hys hond
> Bar the goddes of the lond
> Thilke that unbrende were

These combustible gods remind me of the information (*BD* 167) that 'Eclympasteyr' is 'the god of slepes *heyr*'. Chaucer goes on making the immortals ridiculously mortal by addressing

198   cruel Juno
> That are *daun* Jupiteres wif   master
> That hast yhated *al thy lyf*
> Al the Troianysshe blood.   [my italics]

Chaucer is not above *double-entendre*, either:

242   she
> Becam hys love and let him doo
> Al that weddynge longeth too
> What shulde I speke more queynte?

From the whole story Chaucer derives this useful lesson:

267   For he to hit a traytour was
> Wherfore she slow hirself allas[1]
> Loo how a woman doth amys
> To love him that unknowen ys!
> For be Cryste lo thus yt fareth
> Hyt is not al gold that glareth

But most of the Virgil summary is straightforward and even a little dull. It doesn't follow, though, that – because the first book is less brilliant than the rest – it is the centre of the poem. Chaucer's telling of the Dido story, like the story of Ceys and Alcyone, shows him puzzled by love, not knowing what to make of it – yet having to write about it because that is what poets do.

So he tries to make his escape; and it is a real escape from the claustrophobic temple of love. In a much admired passage the poem comes back to life at the end of the first book: Chaucer expresses his puzzlement pretty directly:

470   'A! Lord' thoughte I 'that madest us
> Yet sawgh I never such noblesse
> Of ymages ne such richesse
> As I saugh graven in this chirche
> But not wot I whoo did hem wirche
> Ne where I am ne in what contree
> But now wol I goo out and see
> Ryght at the wiket yf y kan
> See owhere any stiryng man
> That may me telle where I am'

---

[1] This is as nonchalant a death as that of Ceys in *BD*.

44

So he leaves the 'church' and finds himself in a desert which is the immediate alternative to the temple of love. But then appears the Golden Eagle which is to rescue Chaucer.

Book II, the journey in the Eagle's grasp, is an attempt to escape from love altogether. The Eagle is frivolously serious. He is a real, terrifying eagle – more so, perhaps, than Dante's – but his talk is a way of *not* providing Chaucer with a subject. The discourse is about various branches of knowledge and the humour comes from the masterfulness of the Eagle contrasted with Chaucer's timorousness: but if the book is *about* anything it can only be, like *The Book of the Duchess*, the problems that assail a poet.

Dante's sublime certainty that *he* is one of the chosen few is easy to see (*Inferno* IV, for instance). And that goes with the joy, the positive joy in the ordering of the world, that allows him to see (*Inferno* XX) Hell as evidence of divine love. It was not at all like that for Chaucer; for him Jove's eagle is, however comically, terrible; Chaucer is appalled, if comically appalled, at the idea of being 'stellified'. Instead of walking in respectful friendship with Virgil, Chaucer is dazed by being rapt up to heaven much against his will. (I shall follow some of the implications of this contrast below, Chapter 15.) Chaucer is sincere and modest when he answers the question later in the poem about what he is hoping to find:

1884   That wyl y tellen the
         The cause why y stonde here
         Somme newe tydynges for to lere
         Somme newe thynges y not what
         Tydynges other this or that
         Of love or suche thynges glade
         For certeynly he that me made
         To comen hyder seyde me
         Y shulde bothe here and se
         In this place wonder thynges

This certainly is a poet waiting for his inspiration: but instead of 'tidings', what he most strongly hears are rumours of the bewildering and terrifying complexity of things. The Eagle says,

1031 'Herestow not the grete swogh?'
         'Yis parde' quod y 'wel ynogh'
         'And what soun is it lyk?' quod hee
         'Peter lyk betynge of the see'
         Quod y 'ayen the roches holowe
         Whan tempest doth the shippes swalowe...'

45

This is one of the places where the lightness is *obviously* serious – and where the seriousness is the poetic creation of the poet's bewilderment which, as much as in *The Book of the Duchess*, is the heart of the poem.

The House of Fame itself is a rather mechanical and not very profound comment on Dante – well done at its own level, but not very much of an idea, as Chaucer recognizes by making it quite short. The real hint of genius and the real criticism of Dantesque certainty is the 'Domus Dedaly' passage (1916ff.): this sudden glimpse of the wild variousness of the world, the other extreme from the temple of the first book, is the pointer to the way out of the court and into *The Canterbury Tales*. But it remains a hint, and the surprising thing is that Chaucer can only get to a firm grasp of such an unliterary version of life by going back to books and to courtly love. Book III points back to Book I. Many critics have, of course, seen the end of the poem as prophetic of things to come.

2121	And Lord this hous in alle tymes	
	Was ful of shipmen and pilgrimes	
	With scrippes bret ful of *lesinges*	lying tales
	Entremedled with tydynges	
	And eek allone be hemselve	
	O many a thousand tymes twelve	
	Saugh I eke of these pardoners	
	Currours and eke messagers	
	With boystes crammed full of lyes	
	As ever vessel was with *lyes*	lees
	And as I altherfastest wente	
	About and dide al myn entente	
	Me for to pleyen and for to lere	
	And eke a tydynge for to here	
	That I had harde of som contree...	

Do we not seem here on the brink of *The General Prologue*? And may not the famous 'man of great authority' promised at the end of the poem be, in a final fancy, Chaucer himself on love?

But I doubt whether this could have been got from *The House of Fame* without hindsight. The poem remains an amusing exploration of the poet's difficulties; and his way out of them was not easy. Jove's eagle appears to rescue Chaucer from the imprisonment within the temple of love – but only that he shall hear tidings of love's folk. Chaucer had to try again in the temple. He again confronts the subject of love in a temple in *The Parliament of Fowls*, and there finds his way through – with the help of Macrobius, *Le*

Roman de la Rose and Alain of Lille's *de Planctu Naturae*, all mentioned in the poem. Only through books could he begin to find England.

II

Chaucer's career after *The House of Fame* is the break-out of the courtly prison – though having made what use I can of this image I must now discard it, for Chaucer was obviously delighted in the early poems to be a courtly entertainer, and throughout his life the courtly tradition remained his centre. But we might say that he was henceforth not restricted to the palace of courtly art but was able (on parole) to make expeditions into the English countryside.

The difficulty of developing within a cramping tradition is shown by the variety of directions Chaucer's growth took. One of the dangers for those with literary ambitions is to try to be a GREAT POET, and Chaucer sometimes showed symptoms. After *The House of Fame* he seems to fluctuate between the extremes of court entertainer and incipient epic poet. But he goes further with the former; he taught himself more easily than most poets that the high style epic was not his salvation. *Anelida and Arcite*, Chaucer's only thoroughly dull and heavyweight poem, is left scarcely begun; and though parts of *Troilus and Criseyde* have GREAT POEM written all over them – and that is one of the things wrong with *Troilus and Criseyde* – Pandarus alone is enough to ensure that the poem shall not be merely epically dull. The other extreme, pure entertainment, is found here and there throughout Chaucer's career (its place in *The Canterbury Tales*, a proper evaluation of it, is the tiny *Manciple's Tale*), but especially in as late a work as *The Legend of Good Women*.

And in the *Legend* we can still see how cramping the palace of art could be. *The Legend of Good Women* transcends the merely entertaining in its best passages, notably the wonderful Prologue (which I would classify with the 'pure Chaucer' I discuss below, Chapters 6 and 7) just as *Troilus and Criseyde* often transcends its pomposity; but generally the need in the *Legend* to be lightly entertaining gets in the way of the fineness of the poetry. We still find here the same mixture of simple pathos with frivolously ironical comment that I remarked in Chaucer's first poem, and the result is that both are made frivolous. As with Dido and Aeneas in *The House of Fame* Chaucer is still fond of amusing the reader with inappropriate morals. From the pathetic legend of Thisbe he learns this:

> LGW 917
> Of trewe men I fynde   but fewe mo
> In alle my bokes   save this Piramus
> And therefore   have I spoken of hym thus
> For it is deynte   to us men to fynde
> A man that can in love   been trewe and kynde
> Here may ye se   what lovere so he be
> A woman dar and can   as wel as he

The ambiguity of the last line ('A woman dares and knows how to do anything as well as a man') is a Wife-of-Bath-like sentiment. So from the legend of Lucrece Chaucer sagely concludes,

> 1883 And as of men   loke ye which tirannye
> They doon alday   assay hem whoso lyste
> The trewest ys ful brotel   for to triste

From the legend of Philomel he gets the moral, later elaborated,

> 2387 Ye may be war of men   if that yow liste

And the whole work ends with a repetition of the trick of the end of *The House of Fame* which breaks off just when Chaucer can no longer stave off a subject. The last line of *The Legend of Good Women* is

> 2723 This tale is seyd   for this conclusioun

– that is, for *no* conclusion whatever.

The frivolity here does prevent full poetic realization: or, love which is so much the subject for elegant and civilized amusement isn't love. Really to write about life was for Chaucer to develop other styles than this very attractive light courtly one, without dropping into epic solemnity. But the development had to be of the language of this frivolous seriousness.

Down the middle, between the extremes of pomp and frivolity (and able to include both) Chaucer found himself – and by so doing, I shall argue, became the father of English poetry. Like *The Owl and the Nightingale*'s (and unlike *Le Roman de la Rose*'s) his way out is by transmuting the frivolity and simple pathos of the courtly style without contradicting it: by making courtly poetry serious without making it leave its amusingness behind. The work in which he achieves this metamorphosis is, as I began by asserting, *The Parliament of Fowls*, where he simultaneously creates what I have been calling passion and also what I have been calling criticism of life – within a consideration of 'courtly love'.

48

4

'The Parliament of Fowls'

Part of the seriousness of *The Parliament of Fowls* is the tight construction that underlies its apparent aimlessness. The wandering of the narrative, so like that of the earlier poems at first reading, is only apparent, a kind of bait laid by the poet, an assurance to the readers that they are not to be bored by epic solemnity. Really the poem is as much a whole as anything in English.[1] *The Parliament of Fowls* has three main parts, the first about Macrobius, the second about the garden of love, and the third the Parliament itself; the early steps towards understanding the poem's comic seriousness are concerned with seeing how the parts belong to one whole.

I

The book Chaucer is reading at the beginning of *The Parliament of Fowls* is very unlike the love-poems with which he is passing the time at the beginning of the two earlier works. What he calls *Tullius of the Dream of Scipio* was one of the most influential books throughout the Middle Ages because this work of Cicero and especially the commentary by Macrobius attached to it expressed in an accessible way one of the streams of thought and feeling that the age most admired, a descendant of the stoic tradition, which attached importance to public and private decency, sobriety and particularly 'commune profit', that is, the interest of the community. Macrobius stands for reason and is interested in love, if at all, only when it appears as *amicitia* or *caritas* – asexual forms of friendship. These remarks, however, are not so directly relevant as Chaucer's own, since he himself gives a summary of what interested him in Macrobius.

43 Than telleth it that from a sterry place
    How Affrycan hath hym Cartage shewed

[1] This is demonstrated at length in J. A. W. Bennett's book *The Parlement of Foules* (Oxford, 1957).

49

And warnede hym beforn   of al his grace
And seyde hym what man   *lered other lewed*
That lovede commune profyt   †wel ithewed†
He shulde   into a blysful place   wende
There as joye is   that last withouten ende

Thanne axede he   if folk that here been dede
Han lyf and dwellynge   in another place
And Affrican seyde   'Ye withouten ‡drede‡'
And that oure present   worldes lyves space
Nis but a maner deth   what wey we trace
And rightful folk shul gon   after they dye
To hevene   and shewed hym the Galaxye

　　　* literate or uneducated   † with good habits   ‡ doubt

The service of 'commune profit' on earth will ensure salvation
from this wretched life; and 'the weye to come into that hevene
blisse' is also given:

73　　　　　Know thyself first immortal
　　And loke ay besyly   thow werche and *wysse*　　set an example
　　To commune profit   and thow shalt not mysse
　　To comen swiftly   to that place deere
　　That ful of blysse is   and of soules cleere

'Affrycan' is offering here the great alternative to the Love of the
opening stanzas: 'comune profit' is put forward as something
that the 'likerous folk' of the next stanza should repent and live by:

78　　　But brekers of the lawe   soth to seyne
　　And *likerous* folk   after that they ben dede　　sensual
　　Shul whirle aboute therthe   alwey in peyne

Here tone is of vital importance, because on the tone of this
passage depends whether we can agree with Professors Huppé and
Robertson[1] that Chaucer is giving us here the framework of real
belief on which the rest of the poem hangs. Is he simply telling us
that courtly love is insufficient and that we ought to take more
thought of 'comune profit'? Some of these lines certainly have a
solemnity Chaucer could not command in his earlier poems;
Cicero and Macrobius are not just being ridiculed like Virgil in
The House of Fame.

85   The day gan faylen   and the derke nyght...

This movement is one of the signs that Chaucer was learning to do
more than make game of Dante: the line translates, 'Lo giorno se
n'andava, e l'aer bruno...' (*Inferno*, II, 1.) Moreover, the three
stanzas from line 50ff. have a sort of philosophic clarity and
detachment quite beyond the poet of *The House of Fame*. But it

───────
[1] *Fruyt and Chaf*, pp. 107ff.

50

doesn't follow that Chaucer is speaking simply from the heart. He is sometimes playful about Macrobius:

32   Chapitres sevene it hadde   of hevene and helle

– isn't the naivety reminiscent of the description of the book Chaucer is reading at the beginning of *The Book of the Duchess*?

> *BD* 57
> This bok ne spak but of such thinges
> Of quenes lives and of kinges
> And many other thinges smale

Similarly the 'likerous folk' of line 79 seems to be spoken with such relish that it would be a mistake to make the stanza *only* sermon-like. He seems to be saying 'lecherous folk like *you*, dear reader'.

The way Chaucer immediately puts courtly love and 'comune profit' together saves him from committing himself to formal judgments of either. It is insensitive to take him as siding firmly with 'Affrycan' (or, perhaps, with anyone else): the procedure that comes plain right at the beginning is the placing of certain alternatives side by side which, in allowing them to *be* alternatives, shows both as in themselves they really are. Any judgment is of both terms: perhaps 'comune profit' makes clear the frivolity of love – but only to the extent that love makes clear the solemnity and self-seeking of 'comune profit'. Moreover *Tullius of the Dream of Scipio* is not Chaucer's main concern. It is here not as a judgment on what is to come, but a foil for it. So when Professor Baum comments that 'African offers six stanzas of admirable wisdom (the one wholly serious passage)'[1] he is taking 'serious' in a sense that does not do justice to Chaucer's poem – and reinforcing my sense that we are right to go on asking in what sense the poem *is* serious. It is not, at any rate, a poem that offers an extractable moral by which we judge the action. Similarly Professors Huppé and Robertson can make the poem an attack on courtly love from a Christian standpoint only by considering what amounts to a prose paraphrase, with the varying tones flattened. About the 'breakers of the law' stanza they say:

The punishment is like that which afflicts the carnal lovers in Dante's *Inferno*. [This is not so: cf. *Inferno* v, where the carnal sinners are whirled, but not about the earth.] Since Chaucer's poem is light in tone, he speaks only of the lecherous who have repented in time so that after 'many a

[1] P. F. Baum, *Chaucer's Verse* (Durham, N.C., 1961), p. 107.

world be passed' in Purgatory, 'than shul they come into this blysful place'.[1]

Their dependence on an interpretation of Chaucer's tone is more important even than they allow, since their gloss about purgatory is without any foundation in Chaucer's poem; he doesn't mention purgatory and he doesn't make the restriction to those who have repented in time which is certainly necessary to save his orthodoxy. The argument is that Chaucer's tone is light so he *must* have meant what they say. But the connection between style and content in poetry may be – let us hope – more subtle. So the conclusion that follows what I quoted, 'The theme of the *Parliament of Fowls*...is thus the futility of earthly love' is reached by adding contentious material not found in the poem, on the grounds that the poem's tone demands it – but at the same time by ignoring the poem's tone.

II

Any reader who persists through the first part of the *Parliament* in the belief that Chaucer has gone earnest is likely to be taken aback at the beginning of the Dream, where the poet gets up to his old tricks again by showing that the use of a solemn tone is still not the only way of proclaiming a debt to Dante. Dante was, of course, the great Christian and stoical poet for the later Middle Ages, and it is fitting that the first thing Chaucer should dream after being instructed about 'comune profit' is Dante's Hell gates – but with a difference. Perhaps the inscription above the gate of Hell is the only tag of Dante we all know:

> Per me si va nella città dolente;
>   per me si va nell'eterno dolore;
>   per me si va tra la perduta gente.

> Giustizia mosse il mio alto Fattore;
>   fecemi la divina Potestate,
>   la somma Sapienza e il primo Amore.

> Dinanzi a me non fur cose create,
>   se non eterne, ed io eterno duro:
>   lasciate ogni speranza, voi ch'entrate.[2]

---

[1] *Fruyt and Chaf*, pp. 107–8.

[2] *Inferno* III, 1–9. I quote the Temple Classics text (1900), whose translation is: 'Through me is the way into the doleful city; through me the way into the eternal pain; through me the way among the people lost.

Justice moved my High Maker; Divine Power made me, Wisdom Supreme, and Primal Love.

Before me were no things created, but eternal; and eternal I endure: leave all hope, ye that enter.'

Chaucer goes one better than Dante and has two gates. They have different inscriptions but both lead not into Hell but the eternal medieval garden of love. Or, to put it in a more literary fashion, Chaucer's gates lead not into *La Divina Commedia* but Guillaume de Lorris' section of *Le Roman de la Rose*:

> 127 Thorgh me men gon   into that blysful place
> Of hertes hele   and dedly woundes cure
> Thorgh me men gon   unto the welle of grace
> There grene and lusty May   shal evere endure
> This is the way   to al good aventure
> Be glad thow redere   and thy sorwe of caste
> Al open am I   passe in and sped thee faste
>
> Thorgh me men gon   than spak that other side
> Unto the mortal strokes   of the spere
> Of which Disdayn and *Daunger*   is the gyde
> Ther nevere tre   shal fruyt ne leves bere
> This strem yow ledeth   to the sorweful were
> There as the fish   in prysoun is al drye
> Theschewing   is only the remedye

*the power to make a man keep his distance

The rewards and penalties are, of course, those of courtly love: the alternatives are 'good aventure' or 'disdain and danger'. Chaucer is kicked through one gate (we are not told which) by Scipio Africanus, who thereupon disappears from the poem. Chaucer finds himself in the garden of love, that is, the rose-garden, which he describes delightedly. Those with no French who would like to know something of the feeling of the most beautiful passages of Guillaume de Lorris or Marie de France would do well to dwell on this part of the *Parliament*. It is a distillation of that French tradition just as the opening section is a concentrated sample of what the Boethian tradition offered. Chaucer's garden is as beautiful and as restricted as Guillaume's – truly beautiful, but excluding so much. It admits from the animal kingdom only

> 195 The dredful ro   the buk   the hert and hynde
> Squyrels   and bestes smale of gentil kynde

– 'little animals of civilized nature'. What has this garden to do with 'comune profit'? – or, for that matter, with the Love of the opening stanzas whose 'strokes been so sore'? The effect of placing this beautiful garden next to the preaching of 'Affrycan' is to bring out the insufficiency of both.

But Chaucer goes on to rescue his rose-garden from the littleness of its beauty; for the love which is enthroned in the centre turns out to be not Guillaume's simply innocent rose, but a creature of some complexity and of dubious propriety, such as we are perhaps more likely to have met with in life, as well as in Jean de Meun. Here, I believe, is where Chaucer's poem begins to show its final seriousness, its superiority over all commentaries, past, present or future. Here the critics usually betray their own limitations and illustrate Chaucer's poetic truthfulness: they demand that Chaucer shall take sides and either denounce love or make it simply noble and beautiful. The creative power with which he does neither is one of the things that allows me to call the poem wonderful.

Chaucer finds 'Cupid our lord' and accompanying him

218   Tho was I war of Plesaunce   anon ryght
      And of Aray and *Lust*   and Curteysie   liveliness, liking
      And of the Craft that can   and hath the myght
      To don by force   a wyght to don folye
      Disfigurat was she   I nyl nat lye
      And by hymself   under an ok I gesse
      Saw I Delyt   that stod with Gentilesse

      I saw Beute   withouten any atyr
      And Youthe   ful of game and jolyte
      Foolhardynesse   Flaterye and Desyr
      Messagerye and †Meede†   exchange of *billets*   reward

'Delyt that stod with Gentilesse' would make a good first definition of courtly love; but not all the things that belong to it are delightful. Chaucer can be aware of the 'delit' only at the same time as the 'craft' that is 'disfigured'. This passage leads naturally enough to Priapus (255 'In swich aray as whan the asse hym shente') and Venus.

260   And in a prive corner   in disport
      Fond I Venus   and hire porter Richesse
      That was ful noble   and hautayn of hyre port
      Derk was that place   but afterward lightnesse
      I saw a lyte   *unnethe* it myghte be lesse   hardly
      And on a bed of gold   she lay to reste
      Til that the hote sonne   gan to weste

      Hyre gilte heres   with a golden thred
      Ibounden were   untressed as she lay
      And naked from the brest   unto the hed
      Men myghte hire sen   and sothly for to say
      The remenaunt was wel kevered   to my pay
      Ryght with a subtyl coverchef   of Valence
      Ther nas no thikkere cloth   of no defense

This sultry Venus broods over the garden of love. She is the goddess of this section of the poem as surely as Nature is of the next. And I

have no defence to offer of her morality: she is certainly voluptuous, and Chaucer's tone about the 'coverchef' is an example of
the uncertain humour, on the edge of being lewd, that this style of
voluptuousness invites. But I cannot agree with all the commentators that because Venus is sultry and Nature admirable Chaucer
is arguing a case in favour of nature and against Venus. The comments I have just made seem built in to Chaucer's passage: but he
may yet think Venus is more wonderful than Nature. So I must
argue against Professor Bennett, who says, with a flatness remarkable in so subtle a stylist, and which may mean that he feels himself
safe here if nowhere else, 'In making the appearance of Nature the
climax of his poem, in displaying her superiority over Venus *in
beauty and power* [my italics], he follows the pattern that Jean de
Hanville adumbrated.'[1]

But this voluptuous Venus is here to complete Chaucer's initial
exploration of the different kinds of Love. The question of approval
or disapproval of Venus need not yet arise; what is necessary is to
see her as the goddess of love. This Venus is a surprising deity to
find in the rose-garden: but Chaucer is showing a necessary connection. Without *this* side of love, the picture of love would be so
incomplete as to destroy the other sides. Without this Venus the
rose-garden remains beautiful but small and disconnected: with
her it is the garden of love. This seems to me so important, and so
generally misunderstood by the critics, that I must try to explain.
(If what follows is the elaboration of the obvious I have at least a
heap of printed evidence that it is not obvious to the authorities.)

Medieval exegetes were always trying to rescue the idea of love
from the faults of passion, heat or even any kind of sexuality.
Astrologically, or theologically, this meant the division of Venus
into two goddesses: one, to be approved of, the patron of what we
might call respectable love – rational friendship, concord, amity –
the other, to be frowned upon, the inspirer of sexual desire and the
mother of Concupiscence in the shape of Cupid. This division more
or less follows the old Christian distinction of a good and a bad
love, *caritas* and *cupiditas*.

All the commentators I have ever seen want to say that the
goddess of *The Parliament of Fowls* is the bad Venus and is there-

---

[1] *The Parlement of Foules*, p. 112. Cf. 'For Gower, as for Chaucer, Kind
['Nature']...ranks above Venus', *Selections from John Gower*, ed. J. A. W.
Bennett (Oxford, 1968), p. ix; cf. also *Chaucer's Book of Fame*, pp. 16ff. and
p. 67.

fore to be condemned, especially in comparison with Nature. I quote an extreme version, from Mr Koonce:

> The first Venus, as Boccaccio indicates, is associated with the love expressed in marriage, which God ordained in Paradise for the purpose of increasing and multiplying...In Christian theology this bond of love is defined as the motion causing all of God's creatures to act according to their natures, such as to reproduce their species. In man this love is fulfilled by means of reason...As such, Venus signifies the natural and virtuous behavior of man when he exercises his rational nature...
>
> The disruption of the divine bond of love through sin is symbolized by the second Venus, who, as Boccaccio explains, is commonly called 'the goddess of love'. Her carnal rather than spiritual nature is suggested by the various names ascribed to her, such as 'lechery', 'lasciviousness', 'voluptuousness', 'carnal delight', 'concupiscence of the flesh', and 'mother of all fornication'.[1]

But Mr Koonce also says (of the Venus of *The House of Fame*) that 'Chaucer makes no attempt to distinguish between the two Venuses.'[2] That is putting it very mildly. Chaucer is not merely not attempting to distinguish two Venuses; his achievement is to show the links between all the kinds of love – that they are rightly all called by the same name – and the feat the poem performs of seeing love whole is much more interesting than the scholarly pastime of analysing her into parts. Chaucer is upholding the truth there may be in the classical idea of Love as deceitful as well as divine[3] against the simple-minded moralizings whether of his Christianizing contemporaries or our academicizing ones. The English word 'love' is arguably a more useful tool than the three New Testament Greek words it can translate[4] *because* of the great range of different things it can be used of. This is perhaps most striking with the verb.

I love my grandmother. I love Mozart. I love Miss So-and-so. I just love crispy noodles. I love God. So with the adverb: it's a lovely day. We had a lovely time on the beach. Miss So-and-so is a lovely woman. The force of these words comes from their use in *very* different situations. I know that loving God, Miss So-and-so and crispy noodles are all different. There is no one unchanging

---

[1] Koonce, *Chaucer and the Tradition of Fame*, pp. 90–1.

[2] *Ibid.*, p. 92.

[3] Peacock gives a handy list of examples of the deceitfulness of Venus in Chapter XXIX of *Gryll Grange*, 'The Bald Venus'.

[4] ἀγάπη, love towards God, ἔρως, passionate erotic love, and φιλότης, friendship or affection, all translated 'love' by the Revised Version. The use of a special word for the love of God – that is, the urge to make it understandable without reference to other loves – was apparently developed by Plato.

thing, love, that we think of in connection with each, and it may be that one could produce two examples of love with nothing in common above the level of vapid generality (for example, that both are predicated of human beings). Nevertheless the words are important in our organizing of life *because* of their variousness. Can even specifically erotic love be the same for men as for women? – or for different men? – or for the same men at different moments? No, what can be the same is the language, and the offer it makes of a shared seriousness: the capacity of living and thinking these same words.

The word 'love' points out likenesses as well as differences – and at the same time, for the steps of likeness are also the steps of difference. 'Love' is (as Wittgenstein argues of 'game') a great family. There are family likenesses between different 'loves' – some strong, some weak, some a family joke – and the family has a black sheep or two. Loving God can be, in some of the ways that give a language the power to be meaningful, like loving a girl; part of the comicality of life is that both have occasional aspects of resemblance to loving crispy noodles. (The sudden impulse of delight when the noodles appear, or the feeling of gratitude that there should be noodles in the world, or the compulsion to eat more of them than is good for one...) This is not to say that the resemblances are definable (though they may be) any more than we can always (though we can sometimes) point to any single feature or expression as characteristic of a family face. The resemblance comes out, if at all, in the language. Wittgenstein says of two very different instances of admiration,

To compare them seems almost disgusting. (But you can connect them by intermediate cases.) Suppose someone said, 'But this is a quite different kind of delight.' But did you learn two meanings of 'delight'? You use the same word on both occasions. There is some connection between these delights.[1]

But if 'resemblance' is found misleading, if it suggests that two loves must be like each other (as if two members recognizably of the same family must be alike!) I will suggest another, also possibly misleading, analogy. The different uses of 'love' are *like* metaphor. One love is *as if* another. The force of metaphor depends not on observable likeness (that is simile) but on the convincing use of one

[1] L. Wittgenstein, *Lectures and Conversations*, ed. C. Barrett (Oxford, 1966), p. 12. Note his final omission of inverted commas around 'delights'.

style of language of a subject which usually has another. A language that uses different words for loving God and women is impoverished not because the two are really the same and not because there is necessarily a close resemblance between them, but because the word links both, and the sense of the link is made within the language. I like Miss So-and-so or am attracted by her or fancy her or want to tear her clothes off; but if I say I *love* her, that word can draw across into this situation (where it has its new particular force, also now made available elsewhere) the sense it has had in other situations in my life and other lives. If I use it well I create my own seriousness, but one permitted by the whole range of the word in our language – love, that is to say, comes from the gods, but only within an effective language of love. And 'love' is the word to use whether the love in question is sultry or moral or both. It belongs to this family, one of whose most famous members is represented by 'God is love', another being sexual passion.[1]

The parallel to the range of our word 'love' in Chaucer's mythology is his whole dream of the garden and its inhabitants. He is showing us in brief the great variety of things to which we properly give this name. And the perception expressed in the walk through the rose-garden (or in the temple of Venus in *The Knight's Tale* or the prayer to the goddess in Book III of *Troilus and Criseyde*) is of the wholly unpredictable variousness of this divine force. Chaucer gives us a glimpse of two young lovers praying to Venus in her sultry mood:

277   amyddes lay Cypride
      To whom on knees   two yonge folk ther cryde
      To ben here helpe

This poor couple are obviously in for it. But is it not true that *this* Venus must be one of the possibilities wherever there is sexual passion? This is one of the ways it might go; and without this possibility the other possibility, of something less immorally wonderful, would not be there either. Venus is destructive but also civilizing: in either case, the same goddess. She may be in the mood we see in the *Parliament*, or she might be as she is when Troilus praises her so triumphantly:

[1] Although the range of English 'love' is so wide we have what is very odd in European terms, the distinction between 'love' and 'like', as well as the more common one between 'loving' and 'being in love'. If I say the strength of 'love' is in its range that doesn't deny that the word can be usefully exclusive. (Cf. below, pp. 97, 176–80, 252.)

III 1254
Than seyde he thus   'O Love O Charite
Thi moder ek   Citherea the swete
Aftir thiself   next *heried* be she   praised
Venus mene I   the wel willy planete
And next that   *Imeneus* I the grete   Hymen
For nevere man   was to yow goddes holde
As I which ye han brought   fro cares colde

Benigne Love   thow holy bond of thynges...'

Troilus is not distinguishing two Venuses: one will not suspect him of opposing this benign goddess to the sexy one when one remembers that as he speaks these words he is in bed with Criseyde for the first time.

No, there is only one Venus, a planet of very various aspects: and to try to separate two Venuses is to destroy both, for the nice one lives only as a mood of a personality who knows how to be the opposite. Blake, I think, is in agreement when in 'The Clod and the Pebble' (*Songs of Experience*) he makes the second speaker say

> Love seeketh only Self to please,
> To bind another to Its delight,
> Joys in another's loss of ease,
> And builds a Hell in Heaven's despite

and when he is able in 'The Sick Rose' to use the phrase 'dark, secret love'. 'There are many wonderful mixtures in the world which are all alike called love', says George Eliot.[1] But they are all 'wonderful'. That Chaucer shows Venus at her worst is one of the signs that he is taking her seriously and recognizing her wonder.

The medieval scholars who tried to redeem Venus from sex were not in general admirers of imaginative literature, and their attempt is understandable: it is more difficult to see how Messrs Koonce, Bennett, Huppé and Robertson and the rest can labour so diligently to untie the knot of Chaucer's meaning – for they have, presumably, read and thought about Shakespeare and Milton, amongst others, who both show that whatever is splendid in love is not easily separated from quite another side. There is obviously a great deal wrong with Cleopatra's passion – it is only not a gypsy's lust because it is so full of trickery and acting – but that is the love in which she rises into splendour. Milton shows himself something similar – perhaps against his will – in the course of *Paradise Lost*. When Adam so righteously and properly eats the

---

[1] *Middlemarch*, Chapter XXXI.

apple (what sort of a man would he have been if he hadn't, in those circumstances?) he does so out of love of Eve:

> IX 911
> Should God create another *Eve*, and I
> Another Rib afford, yet loss of thee
> Would never from my heart; no no, I feel
> The Link of Nature draw me...

That is a man speaking a language of love. But the immediate result is the introduction into Eden of just those sultry aspects of Venus Chaucer has put before us so clearly. Milton will hardly be thought of as encouraging concupiscence; indeed, the classically masterful statement of the need for morality in the relations of the sexes occurs also in *Paradise Lost*, in the hymn to 'wedded Love' (IV, 750ff.). But there is something missing in the bliss of the married life of Adam and Eve before the fall. The thing missing is not sexual passion, but the possiblity that it should be under the guidance of Chaucer's Venus. Adam and Eve are better at the end of the poem: their love is better,[1] because with the entry of concupiscence their language of love is complete. They have become human beings and their fall has given them the possibility of human love in compensation; just as in the *Parliament* this possibility follows from the recognition of the sultry Venus.

The extreme case here is Macbeth, whose love for his wife (what else could it be called?) is the inspiration of his blood-lust. It is when Macbeth has recovered his spirits by thinking of the murder of Banquo that he naturally calls his wife 'dearest Chuck' (III, ii). So too Conrad of Martin Ricardo: 'His passions being thoroughly aroused, a thirst for blood was allied in him with a thirst for tenderness – yes, tenderness.'[2]

The fear of Venus is the beginning of any wisdom attainable by the poets of love. Anything good in love, as well as everything bad, follows from it. We are not, after all, in a strong position to lecture Chaucer like marriage-guidance counsellors; it is not as if we have got Venus all taped in our own world. Making something human of passion is a worthy end (not that anything *else* can be made of it).

---

[1] As Adam says,
> XII 473   full of doubt I stand,
> Whether I should repent me now of sin
> By mee done and occasiond, or rejoyce
> Much more, that much more good thereof shall spring,
> To God more glory...

[2] *Victory*, Part IV, Chapter VI.

Poets including Chaucer certainly do ask and show what is good and what makes for health in human life, in love and sex as elsewhere. But the first poetic function is 'to see things steadily and see them whole'. Chaucer can and does go on later to other things, but he begins in *The Parliament of Fowls* by seeing love 'as in itself it really is' – moral, immoral, pleasant and nasty; anything but trivial, and one of the forces in relation to which we are human. Without some such understanding the continued interest of writers in love would be hard to understand.

In these pages the phrase 'the language of love' has occasionally appeared. Chaucer's achievement in the *Parliament* is to develop a poetry in which love can be spoken of. This verbal recognition, this bringing into consciousness of something passional, seems to me *the* poetic achievement, the intersection of a man unusually alive and adventurous with the agreed sense of a tradition represented in a language. It is a failure to recognize the depth of Chaucer's achievement to ask that his love should be more proper. He is giving English a style in which love can be both proper and improper but without which there would be no love at all.

In this way Professor Bennett spoils his book's groping towards a recognition of the diversity of love in Chaucer's poem by adding an 'envoy' in which he lists six points of belief which, however tentatively, he attributes to Chaucer.[1] The principal thread running through these is the superiority of Nature to Venus, which I believe is mistaken; but the more important error is the attempt to extract any such creed. To ask an artist who has seen something steadily and whole what he believes about it is to miss the point of art.

And if Chaucer is not simply against his sexy Venus it is equally true that he is not simply *pro* Nature. He allows himself to be amusing about that goddess in the same stanza as the noble description of her as the 'vicar of the almighty Lord' –

379 Nature   the vicaire of the almyghty Lord
That hot   cold   hevy   lyght   moyst and dreye
Hath knyt   by even noumbres of acord
In esy voys   began to speke and seye
'Foules   tak hed of my sentence   I preye...'

We shall see that his admiration is often at least tinged with irreverence.[2] Nature appears as the other great alternative, with

[1] *The Parlement of Foules*, pp. 186ff.
[2] Jean de Meun, though more of a Nature worshipper than Chaucer, is also capable of amusing himself at her expense: *Roman de la Rose*, 19687ff.

'comune profit', to the different kinds of passionate love. Love is despised by Affrycan; Nature doesn't despise it (courtly love in the shape of the female Eagle sits on her glove and is kissed by her) but she is only interested in how it can be used. For Nature love is justified in so far as it is functional and promotes the continuance of the species – in which, as we have seen, Mr Koonce agrees with her. The effect of the plea by the male Eagles at the beginning of the Parliament is to hold up these proceedings: hence, according to that line of argument, Chaucer is siding against the courtly birds and with Nature (and presumably with the Goose).

The royal eagle in fact desires the formel; but because he is a follower of the wrongful Venus, he cannot act upon Nature's intention with a correct and natural offer. Obedient to the commands of Venus, he will have his lady 'soverayn', not his 'fere' as God created her. Instead of the wife and companion which Nature ordained as proper, he wants a sovereign lady... He asks of the formel 'merci' and 'grace' with death as an only alternative. She has the power to make him 'lyve' or 'sterve'. Thus he places her in the supreme position which should be reserved for God...The speech in all its exaggeration is, moreover, a profession of idolatry. The first speaker, the one who should be an example to the rest, sees the formel eagle, in which all virtues are at rest, merely as an object of physical desire. In abasing himself before her, he reveals himself as one prepared, as it were, to bedeck Priapus with garlands.[1]

Yes, perhaps bedecking Priapus with garlands has always been one of the activities of the love-poet (cf. *Lady Chatterley's Lover*, Chapter 15) – the trouble is that the alternative seems to get rid of the idea of love altogether. Baum has a different but connected confusion when he calls 'love' simply 'the biological urge'.[2] Hence our love is *the same* as the coupling of animals (without any offence to the latter)? Decking Priapus with garlands might be a sign that love is more than a 'biological urge' – or that Venus is more than Nature. This may come clearer in some consideration of the Parliament itself.

III

The courtly birds are the highest creation of Nature:

372   Nature held on hire hond
   A *formel* egle   of shap the gentilleste   mateable
   That evere she among hire werkes fond
   The moste benygne   and the goodlieste

[1] Huppé and Robertson, *Fruyt and Chaf*, p. 129.
[2] *Chaucer's Verse*, p. 106.

and she calls the first Tercel

394 The foul royal   above yow in degre
     The wyse and worthi   secre   trewe as stel
     Which I have formed   as ye may wel se
     In every part   as it best liketh me

The love of the first Tercel, which begins the debate, is shown
standing forth in Nature's world but somehow separate from it as
well. The difference between the three Tercels which are all
suitors for the Formel is not one of natural capacity and therefore
not, for Messrs Huppé and Robertson, a very important one.[1]
Each could fulfil the female's 'need' and thereby satisfy Nature's
purpose. Their differences lie in the different poetry they speak; it
is a difference in the quality of their feeling. This has no correla-
tion with reproductive efficiency, but has much to do with the
value and importance of love. And if Nature is reproduction,
courtly love, the humanizing of the 'biological urge', may be
argued to be an advance on Nature – or her metamorphosis into
human nature, which is not to be condemned simply because it
places, on the broad road that leads to reproduction, obstacles
unknown to the animal creation. The real difference between the
birds, the difference of quality in the poetry they speak, is of no
concern to either Nature or Huppé and Robertson; but it may
interest a mere reader of poetry and even allow him to see something of what the poem says of love.

The first Eagle is far and away the best. His proposal is beautiful
and effectively solemn. It has the power – and the simplicity – of
the best troubadour lyrics; and in his speech Chaucer shows
himself for the first time able to express passion directly. These
lines could have been spoken by Troilus:

421 Besekynge hire   of merci and of grace
     As she that is   my lady sovereyne
     Or let me deye   present in this place
     For certes   longe may I nat lyve in payne
     For in myn herte   is korven every veyne
     Havynge *reward*   only to my trouthe   regard
     My deere herte   have on my wo som routhe

This carries full conviction in its halting rhythmic phrases. If this

[1] I am not a biologist, but I would have thought the 'Nature' of these scholars
biologically indefensible. Is it not notorious that human sexuality is unlike
that of other mammals in not being so straightforwardly functional? For
instance, in human females orgasm and conception are equally natural but
not necessarily connected.

is not the authentic language of love, nothing in Chaucer is recognizable. Which is not to say that there is no amusement to be got from the courtly lovers, in their context in the poem. This Eagle's declaration is a type of what I have been trying to show as the essential history of love-poetry. The Eagle makes his bold statement of love with no thought of consequences. But he has to make it in the world of Nature, with the result that the Parliament is thrown into some confusion and a whole range of comments on love results, including cries from the 'lewedness behind'.

The first Eagle seems to me to be fulfilling the desire of all love-poets (but not of Nature) in making of sexual attraction something serious and human, something not allowed for simply by talk of reproduction. No disdain for Nature is implied;[1] without Nature there would be no love, but it does not follow that love is included in Nature.

The second Eagle is comparatively vulgar ('of lower kynde' (450)). He begins by boasting ,'I love her bet than ye' – and so, having gone too far, has to qualify the boast at once,

452   Or at the leste   I love hire as wel as ye.

He swears ('by seint John' (451)). He makes the strong point that he has served longer, but wrecks it by appealing mathematically: he ought just to have hinted his length of service before throwing

[1] There is such a disdain in *The Owl and the Nightingale* in these words of the Owl, rebuking the Nightingale for being like peasants whose love (the Owl thinks) is just the 'biological urge':

509   A sumere chorles awedeþ.
     & uorcrempeþ & uorbredeþ.
     Hit nis for luue noþeles.
     Ac is þe chorles wode res.
     For wane he haueþ ido his dede.
     Ifallen is al his boldhede.
     Habbe he istunge under gore.
     Ne last his luue no leng more.
     Al so hit is on þine mode.

I freely translate:

     In Summer peasants are the same.
     The lustful peasants, all agape,
     Contort themselves, and tend towards rape,
     Which has *nothing* to do with *love* –
     It's just a low, mad, rushing shove.
     For once a peasant's done his deed
     His boldness all has run to seed;
     And once he's stung under the gown
     His 'love' goes quickly sinking down.
     Just like that is *your* change of mood.

himself on her mercy (which he has not yet done). He is committing the obvious breach of good manners of arguing about the
Formel in the third person as if she weren't there. By contrast the
first has managed to address her with direct sincerity and delicacy
without affronting the chairmanship of Nature. But the real let-
down in the second bird's speech comes in his second stanza:

456	I dar ek seyn if she me fynde fals	
	Unkynde janglere or rebel any wyse	perverted
	Or jelous do me hangen by the *hals*	neck

The first bird, in the certainty of his 'trouthe', has mentioned the
possibility of being untrue, and has proposed a fitting punishment:

432 That with these foules   I be al torent
That ilke day   that evere she me fynde
To hir untrewe   or in my gilt unkynde

This is a way of asserting love: love breathes through the image of
the lover's being torn, almost as if he were, in the image, faithful –
a 'love lies bleeding' air. The difference in the second bird's verse
is wholly of tone. The 'I dar ek seyn' is vulgarly contentious; and
although he uses the same words in 'if she me fynde' their different context and different stress pattern quite change their sense.
In the first bird's speech the word is surrounded by stresses on
'evere' then on 'untrewe' in the next line. But this one seems to be
saying 'if she me *fynde* false' – if she *catches* me. The hint of a
bedroom-farce world is perhaps taken up with 'jelous'. He is
suggesting that he won't object to the goings-on that are only to be
expected from her (and, of course, transgressing one of André le
Chapelain's great commandments). 'Janglere' is more obviously
vulgar: he ought not to mention the word even as a possibility.
(The Miller, we recall, is a 'janglere and a goliardeys'.) The last
straw is the punishment he imagines for himself, also fittingly
vulgar. Execution for treason was a death common enough to the
more adventurous members of the medieval aristocracy, but
hanging – execution by the common hangman – was the punishment of a churl, a fate worse than death to the noble because it
deprived him of honour. The honourable mode of execution was
decapitation. This bird perhaps is saying, 'Degrade me...' –
itself a lapse of taste – but sounds as if he doesn't know that hanging is not for a gentil bird. He talks in his forthright way like the
churl he is.

But the third Tercel is even worse. The second has at least been doing his best to achieve courtly love; the third abandons the effort and lapses into the natural. He gives himself away in his first two lines,

464 Now sires ye seen the lytel leyser heere
   For every foul cryeth out to ben ago
   Forth with his *make* or with his lady deere   mate

For him 'make' is the ordinary word, which he paraphrases, with a gesture towards an incomprehensible fashion of speech, as 'lady' – the two being really the same, he thinks. Moreover, he is using an argument familiar to anyone who has ever sat on a committee: Time is passing, let us cut short mere talk and get down to business. (The extreme of the position is when 'wretches hang that jurymen may dine'.) That is to say, this character is not speaking remotely like a man in love. So when he tries to come up to scratch with the required language all he can produce is

479 But I dar seyn I am hire treweste man
   As *to my dom* and faynest wolde hire ese   in my judgment

The feebleness of 'to my dom' is the sign that he is trying to talk a foreign language, with the result that he naturally relapses into what he can understand: he offers to fulfil a need by satisfying a natural appetite, which is more or less what Nature (and of course modern Nature-lovers like Huppé and Robertson) think he should offer. But what he says is feebly uninteresting and uncivilized compared with the poem of the first Eagle.

Love here is, of course, *fyn amour*; the first Eagle's concern is how to make it civilized (and that is another thing at which the twentieth century can hardly afford to sneer). Love has to be beautiful, and if the style goes wrong the quality of love suffers. But our stress should not be on the *courtly* of 'courtly love'. This fine form is the only one love can take in the poem; but it is none the less love for being politer than we think natural. The first Eagle is creating love; and Chaucer, by letting him speak and by putting his speech in a context, is showing that love is important. It so happens that it is also charming and beautiful; but what matters for us is its significance, the fact that the poet is taking it seriously – by giving an example of how it *can* be taken seriously, however ridiculous it is at the same time. Showing that love can be taken seriously (which is not the same as approving or disapproving of it) is what I meant by saying that the medieval poets are developing a language of love. Chaucer isn't discussing it, he is creating it; and any evaluation is not a question of comparing it with external standards, but of the style of the creation.

By siding with Nature against Venus the scholars show that they cannot understand Chaucer's language of love – or, it may be, human love of any kind. Love in so far as it is human has to be different from 'the biological urge' (whatever quite that is); there has to be something that from Nature's point of view is superfluous. It is in the superfluity that we are human and in which human society, by developing a language of love, is a civilization. This is, after all, one of the great human problems: how to make something human of a life that is in some ways shared with the animals. And these are some of the reasons why it is possible to see the poets of courtly love as the initiators of our own literature, for they are the writers who for the first time propose the great theme of the place of sexual passion in the human world. *The Parliament of Fowls* belongs rather with D. H. Lawrence than with the modern critics. Shaw's Don Juan says, 'Sexually, Woman is Nature's contrivance for perpetuating its highest achievement. Sexually, Man is Woman's contrivance for fulfilling Nature's behest in the most economical way.'[1] Clifford Chatterley's view at one moment is similar: 'I suppose it's natural, and it's no use me trying to go against nature. The war should have taught us that. – All right, my dear, breed! It is nature's law.'[2] But:

What then of this excess that accompanies reproduction? The excess is the thing itself at its maximum of being. If it had stopped short of this excess, it would not have been at all. If this excess were missing, darkness would cover the face of the earth. In this excess, the plant is transfigured into flower...

Yet we call the poppy 'vanity' and we write it down a weed. It is humiliating to think that, when we are taking ourselves seriously, we are considering our own self-preservation, or the greater scheme for the preservation of mankind. What is it that really matters? For the poppy, that the poppy disclose its red...Seed and fruit and produce, these are only a minor aim: children and good works are a minor aim. Work, in its ordinary meaning, and all effort for the public good, these are the labour of self-preservation, they are only means to the end. The final aim is the flower.[3]

After the speeches of the Tercels comes the debate in which the Parlement subjects courtly love to criticism and definition by a

---

[1] *Man and Superman*, some pages from the end of the most interminable scene in Act III.

[2] *The First Lady Chatterley*, Chapter VIII.

[3] D. H. Lawrence, 'Study of Thomas Hardy', *Phoenix* (1936), pp. 402–3.

3-2

number of points of view. It is still marvellously serious and funny, and here it is plainer than ever that Chaucer is not simply endorsing or condemning anything. The advice of the noble birds is delivered by the 'gentil Tercelet' of the Falcon. He sees how difficult it would be to prove which male deserves the female and concludes with the kind of bluff solution of a delicate problem that one might expect from the military classes:

538   I can not see   that argumentes avayle
          Thanne semeth it   there moste be batayle

which reminds me that Chaucer was by birth burgess not 'gentil'. Then there is the Goose, a first sketch for Pandarus, whose remedy is very simple:

566   I seye I *rede* hym   though he were my brother   advise
          But she wol love hym   lat hym love another   unless

This speaks for the 'lewednesse behind' (520) to which (519) Nature always had an ear. The ordinary birds, like the third Tercel, cannot understand the delay, and just want to get on with it. The *Parliament* ends, of course, without a decision, when their demands can no longer be postponed.

But the Sparrowhawk rebukes the Goose, very sharply. (It is noticeable throughout the debate that the 'gentil' birds are much ruder than the rest, possibly an early observation about our Barbarians.) Nature has to keep the peace not because of a popular tumult but because the courtly Merlin has completely lost his temper and in very unparliamentary language accused the Cuckoo of (among other things) murder (610ff.). The Cuckoo causes this explosion by pleading (605–6) to be left in peace with his mate – so reasonable a point of view, especially in Nature's eyes, but one that puts the courtly bird into a blind fury because it denies the existence of his courtliness. So ends the Parlement, with the decision postponed because the Formel does not as yet wish (652 – so much for the critics' impression that she is eager to go to it) to serve Venus and Cupid, and with the lesser birds getting their mates and singing the February 14th rondeau whose beauty is not at all spoiled by Chaucer's very funny introduction of it.

IV

By the *Parliament*'s exploration (one can use the word) of love, Chaucer moves beyond his early poems into a seriousness that is not the less genuine because it is still consistently amusing. In the speech of the first Tercel and the response of the Formel we see courtly love briefly but finely not as amusement but as the civilized adventure in consciousness, the launching off into the unknown. Chaucer's valuation of love is in this serious treatment of it – serious but not uncritical, for courtly love is seen in the real world, not in the court. Its value has to do with its surviving the sneers of those for whom love is an amusement and the incomprehension of those who wish it to be suppressed so that the ordinary world of procreation may go round.

The first Tercel too wants procreation, but he wants it as the significance there may be in love. The possibility that love may be significant is what makes love of interest to poets; and the great achievement of the medieval poets is to express such a significance by developing their language of love. They make the passions a human adventure without insisting that the passions be other than themselves.

The Parliament of Fowls ends with this ordinary-looking stanza:

693   And with the shoutyng   whan the song was do
     That foules maden   at here flyght awey
     I wok   and othere bokes toke me to
     To reede upon   and yit I rede alwey
     I hope ywis   to rede so som day
     That I shal *mete*   som thyng for to fare   dream
     The bet   and thus to rede nyl I nat spare

– ordinary but more prophetic than anything in *The House of Fame*. Having worked his way out of the palace of courtly art in *The Parliament of Fowls*, Chaucer felt himself free to do virtually anything.

His means continue to be, as he says so plainly here, reading. He has found his poetic voice within the tradition of French courtly poetry: he goes on to use it by doing in English many of the things possible to the other literary traditions of the age. And that is how Chaucer sees life whole and creates a literature.

Part Two:
Some of Chaucer's Stories

5

Chaucer's Great Failure,
'Troilus and Criseyde'

Having worked his way out of the palace of courtly art, Chaucer seems to have celebrated his freedom by determining to treat the subject of love without any indirection or frivolity. *Troilus and Criseyde* looks like his monumentally serious attempt to settle love once and for all.

In so far as the poem succeeds it is through the direct present-ment of the different states of love – the sudden fall, the hopeless-ness with the stratagems, the 'time of such quality',[1] the parting, the betrayal or hopeless faith. *Troilus and Criseyde* is a kind of amatory *Everyman* or *Pilgrim's Progress* or, if one may say so with no blasphemous intent, the stations of the lover's cross. I shall show that the depth of the creation of the characterizing *moments* of love is what makes it right to call the poem a 'great' failure, the emphasis here being on the 'great'.

But a failure nonetheless. There are many great parts but they don't cohere into a great whole. *Troilus and Criseyde* simply doesn't hold the attention like *The Parliament of Fowls* or half a dozen of the Canterbury Tales. To begin with the most obvious example: there is no way of making the end of the poem (I mean the so-called Palinode, not the whole of Book v) follow from its

---

[1]   What we did as we climbed, and what we talked of
        Matters not much, nor to what it led, –
    Something that life will not be balked of
        Without rude reason till hope is dead,
            And feeling fled.

    It filled but a minute. But was there ever
        A time of such quality, since or before,
    In that hill's story?

                                        Hardy, 'At Castle Boterel'

beginning or middle. Many explanations have been offered, of varying degrees of ingenuity. Mr Speirs writes:

> When Troilus' soul rising above the earth finally condemns
> > The blinde lust, the which that may not laste
>
> and profane love is described as 'worldly vanitee', the voice may not sound distinctively Chaucerian. Yet there is no ground whatever for supposing that these stanzas are a *moralitas* added perhaps by a Chaucer fallen into age, sickness and proximity to death...If the voice is not distinctively Chaucerian, it is distinctively mediaeval, and makes explicit what has without doubt been implicit throughout the poem – a portion of Chaucer's mediaeval gravity – that above the human love is to be set the love of God.[1]

Certainly this is a medieval voice – one might almost call it a medieval cliché – the trouble is that the love of God is seen in contradiction with human love, and is made to assert the valuelessness of the subject of the poem. Chaucer's passage is a very insensitive criticism of his own poem:

> v 1847
> And syn he [Christ] best to love is   and most meke
> What nedeth feynede loves   for to seke?

– but how is Troilus's love for Criseyde in Book III 'feyned'? And

> v 1852
> Lo here   the fyn and guerdoun for travaille
> Of Jove   Appollo   of Mars   of swich rascaille

But one might as well retort, 'Lo here', the guerdon is quite different earlier in the poem. On

> v 1840
> > thynketh al nys but a faire
> This world   that passeth soone as floures faire

Professor Muscatine comments, 'Were the world not fair, it would not have its deep and tragic attractiveness; were it not mutable and passing, it would not be the world.'[2] But this attempt to show that the end of *Troilus and Criseyde* belongs to the rest of the poem cannot survive a quoting of the rest of the same passage. As well as what we have already cited, there are the last thoughts of Troilus, who is not able to see the world as a fair:

[1] John Speirs, *Chaucer the Maker* (1951), p. 81.
[2] Charles Muscatine, *Chaucer and the French Tradition* (Berkeley, 1957), p. 165.

74

v 1814
And down from thennes   faste he gan avyse
This litel spot of erthe   that with the se
Embraced is   and fully gan despise
This wrecched world   and held al vanite
To respect   of the pleyn felicite
That is in hevene above

Having written most of the poem as a dutiful worshipper of the
God of Love, Chaucer has suddenly gone over to Scipio Africanus –
or rather, Dante.[1]

Once, under the potent spell of Professor Muscatine's views of
Gothic Form, I tried to persuade myself that although the end of
Troilus and Criseyde violently contradicts the rest of the poem it
might yet belong to it. Gothic art is not linear and has no necessary
logical unity: you enter a cathedral and perceive it not all at once or
from an ideal point of view but by walking through it or worshipping in it in different ways and at different times, so that the unity
of the building is a series of disconnected experiences or vistas;
nevertheless, there is point in calling Ely Cathedral one building. So
may it not be that Chaucer's story leads from love to the rejection of
love; may it not be that though Book III contradicts the Palinode if
they are put side by side, taken with the bulk of the poem between
them, as Chaucer intended, what we have is not a contradiction but
a journey between opposites? This now seems to me mere condescension to Chaucer, of which all critics should beware. When
he seems to go wrong we shall not rescue him by that kind of
intellectual ingenuity.

The lack of fit between the poem and its end is only the extreme
case of a general fault, that *Troilus and Criseyde* is at once a novel
and not a novel, with the result that much of it is plain dull. (As if
Chaucer, no longer feeling the need to be continuously amusing, is
taking his chance of boring us.[2]) *Troilus and Criseyde* has been
called (by Kittredge and all his followers) 'the first English novel',
and it certainly has to be understood as a story: it only works if we
understand Troilus and Criseyde as characters and take the events
of their tale as significantly related. We imagine, often very strongly,

[1] Cf. *Paradiso* XI, 1–12, XXII, 133–54.
[2] I don't mean that attempts to shorten *Troilus and Criseyde* could be other
than barbarous. (Cf. the abridgment by D. S. Brewer and L. Elisabeth Brewer
(1969), in which the most difficult parts have been omitted – 'Book IV...
almost entirely' – in a paradoxical effort to induce students to read the whole.
The students I know need little persuasion and often think more highly of
the poem than I do.)

the actions and the emotions of the people concerned, and that is how we go with them through their lovers' progress. But the more naturalistically we take the story, the more like a novel, the more strongly are we forced to make objections or to ask questions that damage the story.

Why don't Troilus and Criseyde get married as the obvious solution of their difficulties? Because, retort the scholars, marriage is not permitted by the code of courtly love. But if the story is like a novel and the characters are like real people, as they are for much of the time, this defence would not do even if we admitted the existence of any such code. Again, part of the triumphant love of Book III is that when Troilus and Criseyde get to bed,

1685 Agon was every sorwe   and every feere

– *every* fear? Including the fear that Criseyde might become pregnant? Are they then using contraceptives, or is one of them infertile, or is Troilus after all, as he feared, impotent? These realistic and squalid questions are quite against the mood of the poem (even as it concerns Pandarus) but they arise just to the extent that we take it as a novel.

We have to take as a *donnée* that there is no marriage and that babies aren't born, just as in *The Clerk's Tale* (below, p. 165) we take as something given that Walter and Griselda have made that incredible contract. But in *The Clerk's Tale* Chaucer carefully controls the mood so that at the difficult moment we accept the *donnée* as we could in a fairy tale; whereas in *Troilus and Criseyde* he just seems to ignore these difficulties.

The first long conversation between Pandarus and Troilus is as natural-looking as many of the conversations in Dickens – so natural-looking, indeed, as to be more than a little tedious. It is Troilus's gradual confession of his plight, leading to the naming of Criseyde, and Pandarus's offer of help.

1 876
And whan that Pandare   herde hire name *nevene*   named
Lord he was glad   and seyde 'Frend so deere
Now far aright   for Joves name in hevene
Love hath byset the wel   be of good cheere
For of good name   and wisdom and manere
She hath ynough   and ek of gentilesse
If she be fayr   thow woost thyself I gesse'

But Chaucer has not yet told us that Pandarus is Criseyde's uncle. The information actually alters the meaning of this stanza, and the lack makes it less naturalistic. It is as if Chaucer is having it both ways, committed to some of the things only a novel can do, but at the same time working through a quite different lyric procedure.

What does Criseyde mean by 'honour'? She uses the word a good deal, but it is basically and necessarily obscure. It goes with her concern for her 'name', her reputation: but she seems to mean more by 'honour' than just wanting not to be caught. To show what Criseyde means by honour the poem would have to be much more like a novel set in a recognizable real world. For 'honour' must depend on the existence of a world including marriage, which the poem excludes.

If as I asserted Chaucer's aim was to concentrate on love by considering it separately from the rest of life, we may explain these failings. He seems to want to detach courtly love in order to see it more clearly. But that cannot be done in a story that is like a novel: the novel has to give us a 'world' in which we can become familiar with and then take for granted a whole web of relationships and assumptions. In particular, the comparison with Tolstoy that Mr Speirs's essay begins with cannot stand: *Anna Karenina* is so much more complete a picture; Anna and Vronsky have so much more the difficulties of real life than Troilus and Criseyde.

By disconnecting courtly love from, in society, marriage, and, in biology, reproduction, Chaucer has condemned himself *not* to give the novel-like treatment of it he seems to want. The way to show the full reality of courtly love is to put it in the world – as Chaucer does at times, notably in Book IV – just because it can't be separate. (The language of love exists in its connections with the rest of our language.)

These objections could not be made to lyric poetry, and much of the time Chaucer knows full well that his story is nearer to lyric than naturalistic narrative. He deliberately omits details necessary to the story *as* a story which are plain enough in his source. Criseyde is a widow: what was her husband like, and has she any children? Chaucer deliberately doesn't tell us. To ask about Criseyde's children is not like worrying about Lady Macbeth's, because in a naturalistic tale of love the woman's other relationships will have some importance, like Anna Karenina's love for her son. But if we take the poem as a sequence of lyric moments we needn't ask anything about Criseyde's children. So, too, Chaucer casually throws in a description of his characters – towards the end of

77

Book v, when the story is nearly over. This isn't postponement of essential information but one of the signs that we don't need to ask how to picture Troilus and Criseyde – that the poetry does not work in that way.

But yet a lot of the poem is given to narrative – narrative cut off from the sources of a novel's convincingness. Chaucer is committed to a lot of social scenes but can never allow himself to be lively or realistic for fear the poem might turn into a novel. We have therefore all those descriptions – not creations – of social festivities, when we are told, but not made to believe, that the characters 'pleye'. For instance the scene at King Sarpedoun's in Book v is too particular to be pure lyric but not particular enough to be novelistically interesting.

Even when the conversations are lively and well done (II, 155ff., for instance) they seem against the form both of the rhyme-royal stanza and the poem itself. What is that lively conversation doing? It seems long for this poem.

The places where the story succeeds are where it is most lyrical. I don't mean by that the absence of narrative detail, but those passages where all is concentrated into some particular scene with its appropriate feeling, some particular moment of the pilgrimage of love. (The nightingale's song in Criseyde's garden, Troilus and Pandarus waiting for Criseyde's return, or the feeling of the night of the 'smoky rain'.) These are examples of the eternal moments of love, and the true narrative of the poem is just their succession.

II

Yet there is a narrative progression in *Troilus and Criseyde*, though not like a novel's; and by exploring it I hope to come at the great critical problem, how to say what (for all the poem's shortcomings) is fatal and splendid in Troilus's love. To try to say directly what this quality is would be a mistaken endeavour; it would be setting up in competition with the poem. But unless one sees something deep, something fatal in the love, talking about the poem will be a waste of time. We might get there by asking what sense there might be in calling the love fatal: by showing that Troilus is not, as he thinks, predetermined, but a man meeting his fate, co-operating with Venus (and, of course, with Criseyde) to attain a depth of splendour of life, and also a sadness of life, beyond what he could arrange or control, but which couldn't happen

without his reverencing the gods. I neglect this line of advance into
the poem's astrology because, firstly, I don't know enough to
undertake it and, secondly, Mr David Sims is writing a book in
which he does it. But if I illustrate the poem's 'narrative progression' not from its main centre in the relationship of Troilus with
Criseyde but in the increasing divergence of Troilus and Pandarus,
we may see that what Troilus finds in love is suggested by what
Pandarus fails to find.

Pandarus begins very like everyman's idea of Chaucer himself,
a calm, amused, sympathetic but dispassionate observer. In the
first two books the friendly reader might find Pandarus very
likeable and, if any suspicions of his shallowness arise, they can all
be explained away by his high spirits and friendly wish to help.
Pandarus is himself a lover (II, 57–63) and that makes us feel assured
of his earnestness as well as his niceness – just as 'himself a poet'
on a publisher's blurb used to incline us kindly towards the
critical vapourings of some don or other. Pandarus's advice to
make the most of our time seems a little better than sensible:

II 281

For to every wight   som goodly aventure
Som tyme is shape   if he it kan receyven
But if that he wol take of it no cure
Whan that it commeth   but wilfully it weyven
Lo neyther cas nor fortune   hym deceyven
But ryght his verray slouthe   and wrecchednesse
And swich a wight   is for to blame   I gesse

He even for just one stanza seems to make something profound out
of a commonplace:

II 393

Thenk ek how elde   wasteth every houre
In ech of yow   a partie of beautee
And therfore   er that age the devoure
Go love   for old *ther wol no wight* of the
Lat this proverbe   a loore unto yow be
To late ywar quod beaute   whan it paste
And †elde daunteth daunger†   at the laste

      * nobody wants   † age cows stand-offishness

That is certainly, at least, putting the case as its strongest, with a
distinction of verse-movement that is a guarantee of the feeling.

But if for any reason our suspicions about Pandarus were
thoroughly roused we could go back to these early passages and see
that there is more than one way of taking them, that what looks

79

like friendliness might be a rather unattractive frivolity, and what looks like sympathy an indecent curiosity.

> I 617
> 'How hastow thus   unkyndely and longe
> Hid this fro me thow fol?'   quod Pandarus

– the intervention of a friend or the curiosity of an insatiable gossip?

> I 862
> 'Look up I seye   and telle me what she is
> Anon   that I may gon   about thy nede
> Know ich hire aught?   For my love telle me this
> Than wolde I hopen   rather for to spede'
> Tho gan the veyne   of Troilus to blede
> For he was hit   and wax al reed for shame
> 'A ha' quod Pandare   'here bygynneth game'

– sympathetic wish to help or sex-hound scenting the great game of love? The second alternative may seem wildly unjust: but if it be for a moment conceded even the passages which look at first so attractive become quite different. The stanza about 'good aventure' becomes an opportunist's urging to snatch whatever comes; in particular the 'gather ye rosebuds' theme is seen to get its urgency from a very unbeautiful prodding to 'go love', so that when Pandarus comes to restate the theme his urgency to get on with it is frenetic:

> II 1737
> 'Fy on the devel   thynk which oon he is
> And in what plit he lith   com of anon
> Thynk al swich taried tyde   but lost it nys...'

(Troilus shows his love in the opposite extreme of hardly knowing what to do when he gets into Criseyde's bed.)

But why should I suddenly start looking at Pandarus in this severe way? Isn't he then the great 'protagonist of life, the natural joy of the natural heart in the spring'[1] for which so excellent a critic as Mr Speirs takes him?

Why is Pandarus so anxious to give his niece to Troilus?

> I 860
> Were it for my suster   al thy sorwe
> By my wil   she sholde al be thyn to morwe

Isn't that at least taking friendship to a point which in this sub-lunary world it is not unreasonably cynical to be suspicious of? To

---

[1] *Chaucer the Maker*, p. 58.

put it with the kind of crudity such suspicions demand, What's in it for Pandarus? *Why* is all this so delightful to him?

Pandarus is sexually interested in *both* Troilus *and* Criseyde. In a poem which as I have insisted is not much like a novel, one of the things Chaucer rarely omits is the physical movements of Pandarus when either Troilus or Criseyde is near. It is of course true that manners have changed and that a medieval uncle who embraces, kisses, nudges and strokes his niece would not necessarily be making any sort of love to her; but in Chaucer's poem the cumulative effect of many passages seems to me to put it beyond doubt that Pandarus is more than strictly avuncular. So, too, men who were friends might take quite innocently physical liberties which for us would indicate homosexual inclinations: but Pandarus is, whatever else he may be, not an innocent. Pandarus's tactic is to manoeuvre Troilus or Criseyde into getting hold of him.

> I 1044
> Tho Troilus gan   doun on knees to falle
> And Pandare in his armes   *hente* faste   seized

after which in the course of the poem Pandarus seems to spend almost as many nights with Troilus as Criseyde does. (For Troilus and Pandarus see II, 935ff., III, 229ff., III, 694–700.) But, to economize and consider only his 'play' with Criseyde,

> II 87
> 'Ey uncle myn   welcome iwys' quod she
> And up she roos   and by the hond in hye
> She took hym faste...

> II 1154
> 'Refuse it naught' quod he   and hente hire faste
> And in hire bosom   the lettre down he *thraste*
>   (my italics)
> III 115
> And Pandare wep   as he to water wolde
> And *poked* evere his nece   new and newe
>   (my italics)

Mr David Sims has recently suggested that Pandarus 'hath fully his entente' by himself enjoying Criseyde the morning after her first night with Troilus:[1]

> III 1574
> With that his arm   al sodeynly he thriste
> Under hire nekke   and at the laste hire kyste

[1] David Sims, 'An Essay at the Logic of *Troilus and Criseyde*', *The Cambridge Quarterly* IV, 142.

I passe al that which   chargeth nought to seye
What! God foryaf his deth   and she al so
Foryaf   and with here uncle gan to pleye
For other cause   was ther noon than so
But of this thing   right to theffect to go
Whan tyme was   hom to here hous she wente
And Pandarus   hath fully his entente

But whatever happens under Criseyde's bedclothes, and however interested Pandarus (who, like the Wife of Bath, 'wel koude ech a deel / The olde daunce')[1] is in Troilus and Criseyde separately, he is more interested in them together. His real joy in the 'game' is half as pandar, half as voyeur. The great climax of the poem consists, in one way of putting it, in the very detailed bedroom farce which Pandarus brings to a satisfactory conclusion by throwing Troilus into Criseyde's bed, then stripping him, then joining with Criseyde in some more physical action,

III 1114
Therwith his pous   and paumes of his hondes
They gan to frote...

then retiring – but only, says Chaucer (III, 1141) as far as the 'chimney', from whence he no doubt enjoyed subsequent events. (Where else does Pandarus spend that night, and how else is he so ready to turn up at the right moment in the morning?)

But let us say, being liberal and enlightened, that there's nothing wrong in voyeurism; if that's where Pandarus's impulses lead he can but follow them, and perhaps his charm and good humour can survive our understanding of his motives. Certainly the Pandarus scenes go on through the book being among the more amusing; a lot of this comedy is plain enough to see. Grant all this: what can't survive is the opinion that Pandarus is *serious*, in any sense, about love. ' "A ha" quod Pandare "here bygynneth game" ' – a game which he plays with an energy derived from sex but which has to remain a game. This kind of sexuality could never be 'anything but trivial', it could never show a man what there might be that is wonderful even in 'the olde daunce'.

Pandarus and Troilus are *inter alia* another allegory of love; Troilus is the old, solemn, dejected troubadour, Pandarus is love as the great amusing courtly game. Pandarus's frivolity is essentially that of Chaucer in *The Book of the Duchess*, or Marie de Champagne as reported by Andreas Capellanus. Yet Pandarus is

---

[1] III, 694–5.

necessary to Troilus who – because of his style of seriousness – is absurdly unable to act for himself. Chaucer is here repeating in a different way the creation of love from solemnity plus amusement that we saw in *The Parliament of Fowls*: by that I mean the odd way in which Troilus and Pandarus seem to add up to a whole greater than either of the parts. *Both* are necessary for the splendid moments of Book III: Troilus cannot ascend Criseyde's bed until he is thrown there – emblematically as well as literally – by Pandarus. If the poem is as I asserted a journey through the characterizing moments of love, Everylover is not Troilus alone or Pandarus alone, but Troilus-with-Pandarus. Troilus supplies the solemnity – and the depth, I feel, for all his well-observed absurdity; but Pandarus supplies the trickery and calculation and horse-sense that are equally necessary to a successful affair. Troilus is *so* decent and good that he cannot ever admit that what he wants is to have her: Pandarus has to think that for him. But for Pandarus the fascinating physical game is everything.

So if I say that Pandarus and Troilus are necessary to each other that need not deny that Troilus shows up Pandarus's shallowness, or that Pandarus can suggest a real depth in Troilus. This is especially the case with the later books. When Criseyde departs Pandarus takes a commonsense line which proves he knows nothing of love. He offers Troilus the comfort that he has had Criseyde – which, in a different form, might have been right, for all Troilus can hold on to in Book v is that he has known love and cannot pretend he hasn't. But Pandarus talks of it as a simple question of appetite and repletion:

IV 393
'But telle me this   whi thow art now so mad
To sorwen thus?   Whi listow in this wise
Syn thi desir   al holly hastow had
So that by right   it oughte ynough suffise?'

and he falls into the final stupidity of supposing Troilus just wants a woman – the appetite having come on again – and of offering him others. So, when Pandarus asks his rhetorical questions, Troilus, one feels, could answer them 'YES':

IV 1095
Artow for hire   and for noon other born?
Hath Kynde the wrought   al only hire to plese?

'Kynde' – Nature – has no more to do with this than with the first Tercel's love. Pandarus and Troilus end the poem with a characteristic difference: Troilus thinks that divine vengeance ought to fall – on Diomed (v, 1706–8), but Pandarus hates Criseyde (v, 1732).

Troilus stands out as wonderfully and as ridiculously for love as the first Tercel, equally in Book v with Book III. This is what he has known and cannot help being true to – but in the context of Pandarus and Criseyde. She knows Troilus's fatal magic, so to speak, in reverse. For Troilus, physical desire naturally takes the form of the love he feels for Criseyde, but after she has left him Criseyde's frail love turns into the lusts of the flesh:

v 715
Ful ofte a day   she sighte ek for destresse
And in hireself   she wente ay purtrayinge
Of Troilus   the grete worthynesse
And al his goodly wordes   recordynge
Syn first that day   hire love bigan to springe
And thus   she sette hire woful herte afire
Thorugh remembraunce   of that she gan desire.

So she succumbs to Diomed. Her failure and Pandarus's unseriousness suggest Troilus's tragic splendour.

III

Finally, and briefly, I can say that Shakespeare's treatment of the theme also helps me to see something unique and great in Chaucer's *Troilus*. *Troilus and Cressida*, it would only be a little unfair to say, is *Troilus and Criseyde* from the point of view of Pandarus. (Shakespeare's Pandarus, too, is *only* a friendly fool: though he is more of a pandar in Shakespeare's story than Chaucer's, he isn't given that drive of dubious sexuality.) Shakespeare's play vividly suggests some of the adverse comments on Chaucer I myself have tried to make: Shakespeare must have felt the dullness of much of the poem, and the undue solemnity of Troilus, who weeps more than all the Metaphysicals drowning in their tears and who is at death's door so often that one can be forgiven, sometimes, for wishing him to cross the threshold. Shakespeare sees this feeble side, but he sees nothing else, and so the play is only an onslaught on love.

Of course the onslaught is written with a variety of rich device beyond the powers of Chaucer. Shakespeare incidentally demolishes the Troy myth (the *cheek* of Shakespeare – annoyed by this foundation of the Renascence he just blew it up) and such old-fashioned notions as that there can be honour in politics or that there is any sense in the world. The attack seems to me far richer than anything in Swift – the debunking of the grand style of the Troy story follows an authentic example of a non-Miltonic English grand style in the Prologue; those who think Chaucer's Pandarus lively should look at Shakespeare's (or those who think that Pinter can write convincing conversation); and the attack on honour and decency can only be so shocking, in the murder of Hector, because Shakespeare has prepared the mine by making us respect Hector. And yet. . . Chaucer's failure is the greater achievement, because the splendour of its great moments is as far beyond Shakespeare's play as Shakespeare's dramatic vividness is beyond Chaucer's poem. Shakespeare's Troilus is *only* a youth suffering from the disease of desire; his Cressida *only* a very clever but light-minded woman. A criticism of *Troilus and Criseyde* which doesn't notice that it is a splendid love-poem is comparatively stupid and, if these were Shakspeare's only words on love, one would say that of him. Shakespeare is far closer to Chaucer when Chaucer is not at the top of his mind – in *Antony and Cleopatra*, whose equivocal wonder, such a great advance over the boyish gush of *Romeo and Juliet* or the sourness of *Troilus and Cressida*, depends on a combination of the trivial, the indefensible, and the splendid very comparable with love in *The Parliament of Fowls* or the combined Troilus-with-Pandarus of *Troilus and Criseyde* – that great failure.

6

Chaucer's Pure Poetry:
1, 'The General Prologue'

The Prologue to *The Canterbury Tales* has, ever since Dryden's day, been recognized as one of Chaucer's sure masterpieces, but critics never seem to have got very far towards saying why. My own purpose is not to fill this gap with one sudden revelation, but to raise some of the questions that commentary on some of the tales may make clear.

The abundant life which every reader senses in *The General Prologue* used often to be taken as chunks of gratuitous liveliness. On the other hand one influential modern school writes learned commentaries to show how didactic, solemn and exegetical a work the Prologue is, and in this endeavour the life of the poetry somehow seems to slip away and be forgotten. I want of course to have it both ways, to show that the seriousness and the liveliness, properly understood, are the recto and verso of the same leaf, and that Chaucer is here on the same road – though much further along it – that he began to take in *The Parliament of Fowls*.

This may seem obvious enough; but for the modern reader it is not easy to understand how Chaucer manages to contemplate the shocking and the evil not merely without being shocked but in a way that is very positively comic. 'Genial tolerance' is the traditional explanation, and it won't do at all. The asking why it won't do may take us into the questions of how Chaucer is involved with and untouched by his poetry, how it may speak to us, and how it belongs with the rest of our literature, which will be the themes of the rest of this work.

Chaucer is not tolerant. He sees the grim things as straight as Dante; he shows their grimness (which is to be intolerant of them) and finds them funny nevertheless. The Friar is a depraved and mean villain, and we see his depravity and meanness if we see the man at all. There is no attempt by the author to make him nice or genial.

86

A 240
He knew the tavernes wel   in every toun
And everich hostiler   and tappestere
Bet than a lazar   or a beggestere
For unto swich a worthy man as he
Acorded nat   as by his *facultee*   profession
To have with sike lazars   aqueyntaunce
It is nat honest   it may nat avaunce
For to deelen   with no swich poraille...

A 253
For thogh a wydwe   hadde noght a sho
So plesaunt   was his *In Principio*
Yet wolde he have a ferthyng   er he wente

Nothing is hidden here and nothing is made cosy; yet the effect of the whole portrait is a comic one.

A 221
Ful swetely   herde he confessioun
And plesaunt   was his absolucioun

This is the opposite of condoning the Friar's notion of penance, yet the man's wickedness is created with such joy in the language that we positively like the contemplation of his evil.

Take that horrifying pair the Summoner and the Pardoner. 'Horrifying' is by no means too strong a word, but horror is not – at least not alone – the reader's response, because there is something desperately funny at the same time. It is said of the Summoner that

A 628
Of his visage   children were aferd

– and quite right too; this is the child's instinctive fear of the deformity of character expressed in his body and face. He bears in his face the unmistakable signs of his gross and manic life. It is the face of a man suffering – with 'natural justice' – from a horrifying disease which is itself an essential part of the character as presented.

Now, in spite of all the Elizabethan jokes about pox, pox was no joke to them...They didn't think it funny, for by God it *wasn't* funny...And no man can look without a sort of horror on the effects of a sexual disease in another person. We are so constituted that we are all at once horrified and terrified. The fear and dread has been so great that the pox joke was invented as an evasion.[1]

[1] D. H. Lawrence, 'Introduction to these Paintings', *Phoenix*, p. 554.

What Lawrence says would fit this very well:

2nd Man. I am a knight, Sir Pockhole is my name,
    And by my birth I am a Londoner,
    Free by my copy, but my ancestors
    Were Frenchmen all; and riding hard this way
    Upon a trotting horse, my bones did ache;
    And I, faint knight, to ease my weary limbs,
    Light at this cave; when straight this furious fiend,
    With sharpest instrument of purest steel,
    Did cut the gristle of my nose away,
    And in the place this velvet plaster stands:
    Relieve me, gentle knight, out of his hands!
Wife. Good Ralph, relieve Sir Pockhole, and send him away; for in truth his breath stinks.[1]

This is funny only in so far as it isn't realized – after the manner of all those horns-and-cuckolds jokes which a man might laugh at so long as they could never remind him of his wife's infidelity. It is literary humour, depending on the mock-heroic. Chaucer's Summoner is fully realized and, as I said, desperately funny. These lines follow the description of his face:

A 634
Wel loved he garleek   oynons and eek lekes
And for to drynken strong wyn   reed as blood
Thanne wolde he speke   and crie as he were wood
And whan that he wel dronken hadde the wyn
Thanne wolde he speke   no word but Latyn
A fewe termes hadde he   two or thre
That he hadde lerned   out of som decree
No wonder is   he herde it al the day
And eek ye knowen wel   how that a jay
Kan clepen Watte   as wel as kan the pope
But whoso koude   in oother thyng hym grope
Thanne had he spent   al his philosophie
Ay 'Questio quid iuris'   wolde he crie

This is the opposite of a disguise of the Summoner's nastiness: all the same, the imagery of his drunken shouting (and the Pope's) is comic. How and why it is our task to explore.

So too the Pardoner, that sinister madman. Although the Pardoner is a eunuch, and pathetically touchy about it (cf. his claim to have a jolly wench in every town and his insane fury when the

---

[1] Beaumont and Fletcher, *The Knight of the Burning Pestle*, III, iv.

88

Host requites his tale with just the right insult (c 952)) he is not without sexual gratifications:

A 669
With hym [the Summoner] ther rood   a gentil Pardoner
Of Rouncivale   his freend and his compeer
That streight was comen   fro the court of Rome
Ful loude he soong   Com hider love tome
This Somonour bar to hym   a stif burdoun

I have elsewhere[1] argued that the spelling 'tome' records a form in which the *e* is soft, giving an effeminate, falsetto effect suitable to the Pardoner. The character of the duet, which expresses also the character of the pretty plainly insinuated relations between the 'freends', is not pleasant. Yet the Pardoner too is wildly funny – to the same extent, one might say, that he is disgusting. This is especially true of his ecclesiastical racket.

A 705
And thus with feyned flaterye   and japes
He made the person   and the peple   his apes

That is a truth put as flatly as possible: and it is not humorous to degrade people. But the next two lines, which are even worse, are much funnier:

A 707
But trewely to tellen   atte laste
He was in chirche   a noble ecclesiaste

– *this* creature a noble ecclesiastic! Then we realize that such a man *could* look the part – such is the chaos of human life.

Spenser and Dryden were quite right; Chaucer is the well of English undefiled and here in truth is God's plenty. Coming back to the Prologue after having earned my daily bread by talking about Chaucer for ten years, I am still always refreshed by the sense of abundance. (I wouldn't intend to be at all blasphemous if I said Chaucer was come that we might have life and that we might have it more abundantly. . .) And the poem reads like the work of a man utterly sure in his genius; it reads as if it were written with ease and certainty. Like *Hamlet* (*pace* T. S. Eliot) it seems to have come out effortlessly, extruded by sheer force of genius. All the same, 'sheer genius' is misleading, for *The General Prologue* is the observation, the disciplined observation, of what mattered in life

[1] *Chaucer's Prosody*, Chapter 5.

89

to the poet, of the styles of life he must live and die with. The comedy is not the easy amusement of detached observation: this poetry is lived through by the poet; and what that might mean is one of the themes of later chapters. But though there are horrors the Prologue is still a *comic* masterpiece, confident and sane.

Now I want to say that the observation of life, the comedy, and the seriousness are all necessary – without all, none. Chaucer's liveliness isn't separate from his observation of the realities, including the horrors, of life. What we have in the Prologue is a keenness and depth of observation of life – not trivial and not detached, but a comic depth of observation. The comic depth is the poet's serious evaluation and balancing of what matters in the world. The exhilaration of reading Chaucer is the joy of seeing things – including the horrible and the mean – as they really are. It is the pure poetic joy of recognizing the truth as the poet creates it.

The comedy is the seriousness – the seriousness of a poet, not of a moralist or exegete. *The Parson's Tale* is in comparison feebly frivolous because Chaucer has abandoned in it the central vision which he achieves as comic poet. One modern critic says, 'Both symbolically, that is (in the medieval sense), truly, and architectonically the Parson's Tale is the pinnacle, reaching heavenward, upon which the diverse earthly tales converge.'[1] But he has already said the page before that 'The longest of the Canterbury Tales is not a tale, is not literature, is not art.' That is why it cannot be the pinnacle of a work that can only express the truth possible to art. *Melibee* too is unserious: in these solemn prose works Chaucer loses the poetic vision of the world that is the same as his wonderful vigour of language.

The General Prologue is the culmination of the achievement that begins in the first stanza of *The Parliament of Fowls*. This is Chaucer's pure poetry; this is the centre where all his other achievements interconnect. I do not mean that the centre is necessarily his greatest achievement though I think in a sense it makes the rest possible. This central comic ground is only a small proportion of the whole; the only tales belonging it are the Nun's Priest's, perhaps the Miller's, and *The Wife of Bath's Prologue*.

But I call this Chaucer's pure poetry because this is as near as he comes to doing everything at once. Elsewhere he can be solemn or

---

[1] Robert M. Jordan, *Chaucer and the Shape of Creation* (Cambridge, Mass., 1967), p. 228.

tragic or funny but not all at once ('Of his visage children were aferde' is a tragic line; so is A 400, By water he sente hem hoom to every lond). Elsewhere Chaucer can't do anything like Lear on the heath, where the fool's contributions are as much part of the scene as Lear's. But there is this centre, and the other works, straining a little towards each other, meet in it.

7

Chaucer's Pure Poetry: 2, The Miller and the Wife of Bath

Chaucer is most comic when not *merely* comic. Fabliaux are supposed to be short, fast-moving tales, made amusing by their bawdry or irreverence; Chaucer's fabliaux are at their most taking when this definition is at its least adequate. This is why *The Shipman's Tale*, the purest fabliau of all, with nothing extraneous to its quick-moving plot of the wife who deceives the husband and the monk who enjoys the wife and deceives both wife and husband, is Chaucer's only fabliau that could be called unmemorable. *The Summoner's Tale* is enlivened by the merciless sketch of the canting friar; *The Reeve's Tale* by the undergraduate's northern uncouthness, the miller's snobbery and the narrator's mean passion to be one up – all these things being superfluous to the fabliau proper. It is the fabliau elements in conjunction with other things that make the tales go.

I

I said that in *The Parliament of Fowls* we see courtly love standing forth in the real world. We can see the same thing in *The Miller's Tale*, though in a somewhat different way. Absolon, rigged out as a lover and provided with the correct musical equipment, comes singing in a *castrato* voice beneath Alison's window:

A 3355
And forth he gooth   jolif and amorous
Til he cam   to the carpenteres hous
A litel after   cokkes hadde ycrowe
And dressed hym up   by a *shot* wyndowe   openable
That was upon   the carpenteris wal
He syngeth   in his voys gentil and smal

'Now deere lady   if thy wille be
I praye yow   that ye wol rewe on me'

The husband awakes and – addressing the lady more familiarly –
makes a fair comment whose reduction of Absolon comes out in the
scorn of 'chaunteth':

A 3364
This carpenter awook   and herde him synge
And spak unto his wyf   and seyde anon
'What Alisoun   herestow nat Absolon
That chaunteth thus   under oure boures wal?'

So, too, when Absolon tries again he makes a very tender speech
which is demolished in one line of retort. He says,

A 3698
'What do ye hony comb   sweete Alisoun?
My faire bryd   my sweete cynamome
Awaketh lemman myn   and speketh tome[1]
Wel litel thynken ye   upon my wo
That for youre love   I swete there I go
No wonder is   thogh that I *swelte* and swete   swoon
I moorne as dooth a lamb   after the tete
Ywis lemman   I have swich love longynge
That lik a turtel trewe   is my moornynge
I may nat ete   na moore than a mayde'

The Miller's creation of courtly love in this falsetto dandy is
unlike the ones Chaucer has offered before, but is as finely done.
Absolon is betrayed by alliteration into 'sweat', but the main
characteristic is the effeminacy of the verse-movement. The Miller
despises this style enough to create it delicately, with the close
observation of contempt. The tale is full of debunking rhymes, and
the one with which the Miller makes Alison judge Absolon is the
best of all

A 3707
'...I may nat ete   na moore than a mayde'
'Go fro the wyndow   Jakke fool' she sayde[2]

The pleasure one gets from these passages certainly has to do
with the tale's bawdiness; but it comes from bawdiness adulter-

---

[1] On this rhyme cf. above, p. 89.
[2] Cf. the other rhyme, the one that records Absolon's realization that his kiss
has not been quite what he intended:
A 3739   [He] seyde 'Fy allas   what have I do?'
      'Tehee' quod she   and clapte the wyndow to

93

ated, as it were, by poetry. The power is not in the indecency itself but its context, its attack on things that are far from indecent. Here the delight is in the sudden demolition of Absolon: but that depends on the delicacy with which he has been created.

The verse of *The Miller's Tale* is often delicate – delicate the antonym not of robust or of indelicate, but of crude. That is enough to make us pause before thinking that the tale's power, its effect as indubitably one of Chaucer's greatest creations, could be explained in terms of simple comedy or narrative pace. The most impressive thing in the whole tale isn't particularly comic at all – the description of Alison, the longest description of a person in Chaucer.

A 3233
Fair was this yonge wyf   and therwithal
As any wezele   hir body gent and smal
A *ceynt* she werede   *barred* al of silk
A *barmclooth* eek   as whit as morne milk
Upon hir *lendes*   ful of many a *goore*.
Whit was hir smok   and broyden al bifoore
And eek bihynde   on hir coler aboute
Of col blak silk   withinne and eek withoute.
The tapes   of hir white *voluper*
Were of the same suyte   of hir coler
Hir filet brood of silk   and set ful hye
And sikerly she hadde   a likerous ye
Ful smale ypulled   were hire browes two
And tho were bent   and blake as any sloo
She was ful moore blisful   on to see
Than is the newe   perejonette tree
And softer than the wolle is   of a wether
And by hir girdel   heeng a purs of lether
Tasseled with silk   and perled with *latoun*
In al this world   to seken up and doun
Ther nys no man so wys   that koude thenche
So gay a popelote   or swich a wenche.
Ful brighter   was the shynyng of hir hewe
Than in the *Tour*   the noble yforged newe
But of hir song   it was as loude and *yerne*
As any swalwe   sittynge on a berne
Therto she koude skippe   and make game
As any kyde or calf   folwynge his dame
Hir mouth was sweete as *bragot*   or the *meeth*
Or hoord of apples   leyd in hey or heeth

ceynt, girdle; *barred*, decorated; *barmclooth*, apron (lit. bosom-cloth); *lendes*, loins; *goore*, pleat; *voluper*, house-cap; *latoun*, brass; *Tour*, the Mint; *yerne*, ready; *bragot*, mulled ale; *meeth*, mead.

94

Wynsynge she was   as is a joly colt
Long as a mast   and *upright* as a bolt.   straight
A brooch she baar   upon hir lowe coler
As brood as is   the boos of a bokeler
Hir shoes were laced   on hir legges hye
She was a prymerole   a piggesnye
For any lord   to leggen in his bedde
Or yet for any good yeman   to wedde

In its immediacy and depth that passage is one of the great things in our literature. We are given not only the details about the young wife, but also the remarkable depth of life she embodies. The Miller will typically present some snippet of information about Alison's clothes or movements, then immediately (whether or not by formal simile) will flash an image from nature, so that the two are apprehended as one, and the natural image and the detail about Alison are compounded. It is right that at the end simile is abandoned and she is simply called a primrose. But the other comparisons aren't really similes either: reading

A barmclooth eek   as whit as morne milk

we don't extract the idea of whiteness from the picture of milk and then apply it to the picture of an apron; Chaucer is not wasting words and if that were what happens it might as well be the evening milking. But 'morne milk' is wholly right: the reader takes the force, all the associations, of morning milk, together with the 'barmclooth' – and of course with a hint of the 'barm' it clothes. This is a passage where the poet's apparent inconsequentiality is no such thing. Even when the abruptness is not merely an elliptical omission of connections,[1] it is a necessary part of the onward movement, the pace that makes the verse paragraph quoted a real unit. This unity made out of a quick succession of perceptions is somewhat obscured by the usual heavy editorial punctuation of a passage in which I see only three pauses, which I have marked. But I do not suggest by 'onward movement' that the passage has a bullying rush or one that distracts from the subject; its speed is unlike the rhetoric of Marlowe, or of Swinburne. It is necessary for the poetry to bewilder the reader with all these impressions at this pace, because it is saying in one piece – almost in one breath –

---

[1] As it often is in Chaucer. For instance
A 99   Curteis he was   lowely and servysable
          And carf biforn his fader   at the table
– here the transition from general to particular disguised by 'And' may take the reader a little by surprise.

95

something of great complexity and force which has to be taken as near whole as possible. The whole effect is that the narrator seems to be seeing the girl delightedly for the first time; but this spontaneity is, as usual in Chaucer, the art that conceals art.

The impression Alison makes is in one sense neutral: we see her natural attractiveness, and it is certainly the attractiveness of the female of our own species; but the emphasis on her natural life is a way of leaving obscure what sort of a person she is. We don't know anything about her character or style of life beyond what is implied by her fashions of dress and eyebrows. She may be, to the reader coming newly to the tale, like Pansy Osmond, 'really a blank page, a pure white surface, successfully kept so'[1] – on which therefore anything could be written; and the Miller mentions two of the possibilities when he says she could marry a yeoman or be laid in the bed of a lord. He doesn't hint, though, at her actual fate.

The passage is very striking, and its impressiveness is confirmed by the variety of attitudes to Alison in the tale. As well as the different loves of Nicholas and Absalon there is the feeling of her husband, which despite the Miller's evident contempt for and severe punishment of the old man, I confess to being touched by:

A 3519
   'This world' he [Nicholas] seyde 'in lasse than an hour
Shal al be *dreynt* so hidous is the shour   drowned
Thus shal mankynde drenche and lese hir lyf'
   This carpenter answerde 'Allas my wyf
And shal she drenche? allas myn Alisoun'
For sorwe of this he fil almoost adoun[2]

The Miller sees this as dotage; why should we?

But the predominant attitude to Alison has yet to be mentioned – predominant because obviously the Miller's own. If his description of her is striking, so is, in another way, the next passage, in which we see her in action, or rather in passion, for it is the passage in which Nicholas makes what is best described as his grab.

A 3271
   Now sire and eft sire so bifel the cas
That on a day this hende Nicholas
Fil with this yonge wyf to rage and pleye
Whil that hir housbonde was at Oseneye
As clerkes ben ful subtile and ful queynte
And prively he caughte hire by the queynte

[1] Henry James, *The Portrait of a Lady*, Chapter xxx.
[2] Cf. the very unexpected couple of lines of feeling in *The Reeve's Tale*, A 4247–8.

And syede 'Ywis   but if ich have my wille
For *deerne* love of thee   lemman I †spille†'   secret   die
And heeld hire harde   by the haunchebones
And seyde 'Lemman   love me al atones'

It is its putting these passages together that gives the tale its
comic malignity. Within the lines just quoted the indecency comes
not so much from the action itself as from its mixture with the
language of courtly love. The grab by the queynte, like the thak-
king her about the lendes weel with which he concludes the day's
action, could just be Nicholas's animal high jinks: but the Miller
will insist that he also talks about what he's doing as if it were love.
The fascination then isn't in the action but in the action *as* an
onslaught on love.

This is the first sign of the procedure of the whole tale. The tale
is the Miller's manic proof that *that* gorgeous creature is really
made to be reduced to farting and hairiness. The 'grace and oore'
(A 3726) that Absolon asks for turn out to be her arse. The Miller
is insisting that life is like *that*. It is a tale full of poetic justice –
Nicholas, Absolon, gullible John, all get their deserts, according to
the Miller's view of the world; and Alison's desert is to have *that*
story attached to her. And we are again faced with the old problem
of the ways in which Chaucer's comedy can be serious – as well as,
here, how it can be comic. But I postpone discussion of the latter
until we get to the extreme case, *The Merchant's Tale* (Chapter 10).
Is Chaucer here hiding behind the Miller's persona in order to
indulge himself after the strain of keeping up seriousness in *The
Knight's Tale?*[1] *The Miller's Tale* certainly fulfils its threat of
'quiting' (A 3127) *The Knight's Tale*. But the question of how the
tales commit Chaucer is more interesting and more difficult than
such an offhand account would suggest. I reserve until the discussion of *The Clerk's Tale* (Chapter 9) my own consideration of it.

At any rate the Miller's tale is wholly consistent with his character
as we see it in the Prologue: there too he has just the same mixture
of roaring destructiveness and delicacy – he *wants* to break doors
by running at them with his head, but he is also a musician, even if
his instrument is the bagpipes. And the above remarks are coldly
written in the study: in reading we experience a sweeping away by

---

[1] This looks like an excuse:

A 3182   The Millere is a cherl   ye knowe wel this
So was the Reve eek   and othere mo
And harlotrie they tolden   bothe two
Avyseth yow   and put me out of blame

the pace and life of the tale, a fusion of everything in it, which leaves no time for question about whether we ought to be fascinated.

Chaucer's 'pure poetry', as well as being a compound of various kinds of poetry, is also always pointing beyond itself. *The Miller's Tale* pays out *The Knight's Tale* by debunking its notions of love; hence its full effect depends on the existence elsewhere in the *oeuvre* of some quite uncomic uses of the same words. The fabliaux are the most succinct realizations of the full power of Chaucer's genius: but their uses of language depend on relations with Chaucer's other uses. I would say – backed by a love of *The Canterbury Tales* even more than a taste for linguistic speculation – that the fabliaux can only be properly enjoyed by those who can also enjoy both *The Knight's Tale* and *The Clerk's Tale*. If they work by demolishing various solemnities their strength will depend on what they demolish being, elsewhere, *really* solemn. The Miller after the Knight is like a satyr play after the tragic trilogy, without which it would not have much point. But it is true that on this analogy the central concentration of Chaucer's poetry goes into his satyr play.

II

Perhaps I am using phrase 'pure poetry' as Descartes used the idea of God, something to stand for the part of the system that can't be explained or understood. I would certainly not claim to give any very complete account of *why The Wife of Bath's Prologue* is so good – or even of *how*. But the critic ought to grit his teeth and go on asking the questions as long as he goes on finding the work, without quite knowing why, wonderful. What follows is such an attempt, without even the degree of finality the rest of the work may attain to. I don't imply that I would like to be able to fathom the Wife of Bath. Heaven help any man who thinks he's got to the bottom of her: he would certainly be in danger of some condign punishment from Venus or Mars. Moreover the final understanding of any work of art would be a reason not for writing a book about it but for knowing it wasn't worth further attention. I know I haven't fathomed *The Knight's Tale*, either: but I am more confident that I know how to talk about it.

Some, but not all of the reasons for calling *The General Prologue* 'pure poetry' will also apply to *The Wife of Bath's Prologue*. The latter, too, is pure Chaucer because of the marvellous creativity, the abundant and delightful life that is the same as seeing the thing in itself (if one dare so call the Wife) as she really is, with any criticism implied by the creation, and not stated separately. But that – even if we can show it – will raise more questions than it answers.

The stress on the personal pronoun in her second line is the first sign of the Wife's dauntlessness:

D 1
>Experience   though noon auctoritee
>Were in this world   is right ynogh for me

and from then on her self-assertion is not in doubt. Sometimes it is boldness naked and unashamed:

D 460
>Metellius the foule cherl   the swyn
>That with a staf   birafte his wyf hir lyf
>For she drank wyn   thogh I hadde been his wyf
>He sholde nat han daunted   me fro drynke

Sometimes the force of personality is expressed as powerfully in a calmer assertion:

D 113
>I wol bistowe   the flour of al myn age
>In thactes   and in fruyt of mariage

'Will' expresses intention much more strongly in Middle English than modern English: if we did not know, that couplet would make us suspect as much. (It is very characteristic that even in the case of her fifth husband, the one she is in love with, the Wife *orders* him to marry her (D 567).) Her dauntless will is seen equally in the persuasiveness of her calm opening discourse and in the terrible life she boasts she has led her old husbands. This has the great takingness that is one of the marks of a great poet at the height of his powers: but does our enjoyment commit us to admiration of the Wife? 'Admiration' in the old sense is perhaps closer: we certainly wonder at her. But is there any question of approval or disapproval? – and if not, in what sense are we taking the poem seriously? The alternatives for many critics seem to be either that we approve or disapprove (in the sense of taking the Wife as a model whether it be of admirable independence or of depravity) or that, in asserting the question to be irrelevant, we treat the poem as merely entertaining and come no closer to explaining how it is 'pure poetry'. Must its connection with life be either exemplary or frivolous?

Then again the presence of so many contradictory elements in the poem might be seen as a reason for the success. It is well known that the Wife is created out of a great many earlier works of literature and in particular anti-feminist literature. This gives Chaucer the chance to put the words of her opponents into her mouth for her to pour scorn on, and gives us both sides at once.

So, too, it is tempting especially at the beginning of the Prologue to say it is so good just because of the way – at once so sane, funny and individual – in which the Wife talks about sex.

D 115
> Telle me also   to what conclusioun
> Were membres maad   of generacion
> And of so parfit wys   a wight ywroght?
> Trusteth right wel   they were nat maad for noght
> Glose whoso wole   and seye both up and doun
> That they were maked   for purgacioun
> Of uryne   and oure bothe thynges smale
> Were eek to knowe   a female from a male
> And for noon other cause   say ye no?
> Thexperience woot well   it is noght so

Here the Wife's constant appeal to experience falls together with her insinuations about the rest of us, and her circumlocutions that have quite the opposite effect from modest concealment. She is always implicating us (D 89 For peril is bothe fyr and tow tassemble / Ye knowe what this ensample may resemble; D 200 Ye woot wel what I meene of this pardee, etc.) or making very transparent suggestions – not that she can't be plain and blunt too (for example, D 332) – and at times we may feel that we simply agree with what she's saying so forcefully. The attraction of her first 150 lines is partly that she seems to have a strong case. But that takes us to the very edge of the principal pitfall the poem digs for us.

How is *The Wife of Bath's Prologue* a serious or significant work? 'By showing us *this* woman's way of talking about love' is only part of the answer. What is it that makes the Wife's view important? She is using real words about the real subject; she isn't trivializing it, and so she is contributing to the language of love. But her view isn't important as a view, for all the compliments we can pay some bits of it; and by talking of her Prologue as pure poetry I at least hope to sidestep the trap into which several of the other pilgrims, most modern critics, and perhaps even Chaucer himself[1] have fallen, the trap of taking the Wife as a serious thinker with a doctrine.

---

[1] In *The Envoy to Bukton* – but that poem is made of such depths of irony upon irony that I am never quite sure what is its purpose in using the Wife as a cautionary example.

She does certainly set going the discussion that Kittredge called the Marriage Group; but that can't be the debate it is sometimes taken for, if only because the Wife gives no case to answer.

She believes that marriage is a good thing and that in marriage happiness is assured by the dictatorship of the wife. She uses both her own marriages and the example in her tale to enforce this doctrine, but considered apart from the Wife herself it will obviously never convince any man. The doctrine falls neatly into two, and it is the second half, concerning 'maistrye', that the Wife makes no attempt to argue – perhaps because it couldn't possibly be argued.

She begins by arguing, hard and straight, the first part of her idea, the value of marriage. The second half bursts in in this disconnected way:

D 149
In wyfhod   I wol use myn instrument
As frely as my Makere   hath it sent
If I be *daungerous*   God yeve me sorwe   difficult
Myn housbonde shal it have   bothe eve and morwe
Whan that hym list   come forth and paye his dette
An housbonde I wol have   I wol nat lette
Which shal be   bothe my dettour and my thral
And have his tribulacion withal
Upon his flessh   whil that I am his wyf
I have the power   durynge al my lyf
Upon his *propre* body   and noght he   own
Right thus   thApostel tolde it unto me
And bad oure housbondes   for to love us weel
Al this *sentence*   me liketh every deel   saying, meaning

At this moment of perverse half-quotation she is interrupted by the Pardoner. The interruption is lively and in character and the Wife handles it almost as well as she later does the Friar's[1] – but the real use she makes of the interruption is to go over from argument to reminiscence. The Pardoner has saved her in the nick of time from the impossible task of showing some connection between the two prongs of her attack.

The connection is not between two parts of an argument but between two parts of the Wife's character. These two parts can be, logically speaking, in contradiction. In the passage quoted she is

---

[1] D 878   Wommen may go now   saufly up and doun
In every bussh   or under every tree
Ther is noon oother incubus   but he [a Friar]
And he ne wol doon hem   *but* dishonour
(my italics)

glorying in her freedom from 'daunger', but over the page she
gives her own version of 'daunger' in practise:

D 409
I wolde no lenger   in the bed abyde
If that I felte   his arm over my syde
Til he had maad   his raunson unto me[1]
Thanne wolde I suffre hym   do his *nycetee*   silliness, simplicity

So, too, there is more than a hint that she is tidying up her experience to fit her case. The first thing she remembers of her fifth
husband, the one she loved, is that he was

D 505
            to me the mooste shrewe
That feele I on my ribbes   al by rewe

but she later presents herself as having got a final victory over him
(D 812ff.) after which the marriage was happy. The impression one
gets is that really it was the best marriage of the five, because the
contestants were evenly matched. The tale is just wish-fulfilment,
not convincing about the Wife's case at any level.

The contradiction might seem to be between the parts of the
Wife's character that are lovable and the others that are terrifying. She is enormously attractive as a human character when she
is remembering her 'yowthe and jolitee' (D 470) before going on,
with characteristic dauntlessness, to refuse to regret their loss:

D 476
Lat go   farewel   the devel go therwith

She is also predatory and scarifying. (How *did* her last two husbands meet their ends, by the way? – and why aren't there any
children?) It is of this second aspect that Blake says truly:

Chaucer has been equally minute and exact; because she is also a scourge
and a blight. I shall say no more of her, nor expose what Chaucer has
left hidden; let the young reader study what he has said of her: it is
useful as a scarecrow. There are of such characters born too many for the
peace of the world.[2]

But the contradiction is within the Wife of Bath's case, not her
character. The gods have sent her the impulse to love and to

---

[1] 'Daungere' is a military as well as a courtly love term:
A 1849   Frely   withouten raunson or daunger
and the hint is that 'daunger' can be overcome by the payment of 'raunson'.
[2] From William Blake's *Descriptive Catalogue*, quoted in C. F. E. Spurgeon,
Five Hundred Years of Chaucer Criticism and Allusion (Cambridge, 1925),
Part II, p. 45.

dominate: the splendid liveliness comes from her successful expression within the same character of both sets of impulses. There is no reason why a woman can't be both loving and combative, perhaps at the same time; and the Wife is very much both when she is most herself. But equally there is no reason why women must or ought to join these attributes. The Wife says as much herself in the astrological passage which Chaucer may have added to a second edition of the poem.[1]

> D 609
> For certes   I am al Venerien
> In feelynge   and myn herte is Marcien
> Venus me yaf my lust   my likerousnesse
> And Mars yaf me   my sturdy hardynesse
> Myn ascendent was Taur   and Mars therinne

Venus, as we may agree in this language, gave her her delight in life ('lust') and lecherousness, and Mars gave her what she more euphemistically calls 'sturdy hardinesse'. But this is the end of the Wife's claim to speak for all women. She likes using the first person plural for her assertions, and her parting prayer (to, of all possible deities, Jesus Christ) is made on behalf of all women:

> D 1258
>   Jhesu Crist us sende
> Housbondes meeke   yonge and fressh abedde
> And grace   toverbyde hem that we wedde
> And eek I praye Jhesu   shorte hir lyves
> That wol nat be   governed by hir wyves
> And olde and angry   nygardes of dispence
> God sende hem soone   verray pestilence

But the passage about Venus and Mars admits that the Wife's character is unusual. There is no general inevitability in the conjunction of Mars and Venus (*The Knight's Tale* is all about a 'debate' between them) even though, as Blake said, 'there are of such characters born too many for the peace of the world'. The Wife's success is a personal one, then, in fusing qualities that don't necessarily belong together. Her drive to prove the world is *so*,

---

[1] The variations in the mss. suggest that he took a great deal of trouble over the Wife's Prologue, perhaps, even, that he shared some of our puzzlement about how to take her. The editions print as lines 44a–f a very Wife-like saying which Chaucer may have suppressed as likely to turn the reader against her at the wrong moment: similarly some mss. give either *The Shipman's Tale* or *The Merchant's Tale* to the Wife (*The Wife of Bath's Prologue* and *The Merchant's Tale* have an unusually large number of common lines), either of which would fit some aspects of her but would denigrate her.

that happiness *must* come from the subjection of husbands, is no more an argument (which is not to say that nothing she says is strong as an arguable proposition) than Iago's or the Miller's different drives to prove the nastiness of love.

The Wife's achievement is to make sense not of her case but of herself, to take herself seriously. She is perhaps a better woman than the Prioress[1] who in trying for a style of femininity which is impossible to her physique condemns herself to a kind of unwholeness of life. The Wife lives splendidly the life suggested to her by the inclinations the gods have sent her, and may perhaps be in *that* limited sense an example to be held up to the admiration of youth. But this, and what Blake says, can only bring us back to our questions about how the poem is significant, by way of making us remember that it can't be significant as moral – or immoral – *exemplum*. That would in this case be a way of being *in*significant.

We take *The Wife of Bath's Prologue* seriously as a comic poem of – not an argument about – love. We can also say the poem is a criticism of life if Chaucer in it sees a thing steadily and whole. But here again I feel the urge (which is equally difficult to justify or subdue) to ask whether we are meant to judge the Wife and if so how, and whether Chaucer was committing himself to anything in creating her. Is our enjoyment of the poem serious if it is only enjoyment? (If the poem is to be serious we must certainly enjoy it, but may not 'enjoyment' save us the trouble of asking how the poem might matter to us?)

Chaucer is here trying to understand an instance of a style of love: the creation is the understanding. He takes whatever personal risks and makes whatever personal commitments are implied thereby. Does he know at first hand the kind of life she describes so vividly? Could he write so well if he had never himself been in the lioness's den? These are not factual questions about Chaucer's life but alternative ways of continuing our discussion of how we are to take his comic poetry with the seriousness it deserves. We know next to nothing about Chaucer's private life: what we know (because we read) is that he can use the language of the Wife of Bath's life; and language is at least not disconnected from experience. He imagines the language and (since 'to imagine a language means to imagine a form of life'[2]) that is excellent evidence of his understanding of the way of life expressed. We live the same

---

[1] I here follow the view of Mr David Sims more closely than usual.

[2] L. Wittgenstein, *Philosophical Investigations* (Oxford, 1958), p. 8e.

life, in the imagination, as we read. But to what kind of seriousness does that commit us? At present all I want is to show that the more we admire Chaucer's 'pure poetry' the more strongly we have to ask that and questions like it.

III

At any rate what we admire in *The General Prologue*, the fabliaux, the Wife's Prologue, and *The Nun's Priest's Tale*, is a life of language which is found in the context of a range of well-defined other styles. Perhaps if *The Wife of Bath's Prologue* had been Chaucer's only surviving poem it would seem just as splendid as it does now; perhaps not. It is at any rate sure that it finds its place in the whole collection, and that the place depends on our sense of the rest of the whole.

The obvious case of the interdependence of Chaucer's styles is the mock-heroic. It is not absolutely true that the mock-heroic needs the real heroic: most of our contemporary comics make a living out of varieties of mock-heroic without there being anything heroic in evidence. But that is a peculiarity of the modern world that goes with our difficulty in saying anything that requires overt seriousness. In Chaucer *The Nun's Priest's Tale* depends on *The Knight's Tale* and *vice versa* – or, to take the briefer example, *The Envoy to Scogan* depends on *Trouthe* and *Gentilesse*. Throughout its first eighteen lines, *Scogan* builds up a mock-heroic structure of imposing grandeur, which it then lets down into a kind of commonsense horror.

1   Tobroken been the statutz   hye in hevene
     That creat were   eternally to dure

Chaucer begins magnificently, and goes on to explain with equal splendour of diction that the Gods can 'wepe and wayle and passioun endure' as is proved by Venus's weeping on to the earth, and exclaims,

13   Allas Scogan   this is for thyn offence
      Thow causest   this diluge of pestilence

      Hastow not seyd   in blaspheme of the goddes
      Thurgh pride   or thrugh thy grete *rekelnesse*   rashness
      Swich thing   as in the lawe of love forbode is?

The 'lawe of love' has just the comic solemnity one would expect in a citing of Andreas Capellanus. But what Scogan is accused of is

18   That for thy lady   sawgh nat thy distresse
      Therfore thow yave hir up   at Michelmesse

– where it seems unmistakable that the ordinary phrase 'yave hir up' should be spoken with grotesque emphasis, an exaggeration of the ordinary iambic movement. If so the tone descends from the mock-heroic to something more like our 'you did *what?*' It seems to me improbable that Chaucer could have done that mock-heroic so finely if he hadn't also been able to command the simple heroic, in those equally splendid moral ballades, *Trouthe* and *Lak of Stedfastnesse*: I quote a stanza of the latter.

15   Trouthe is put doun   resoun is holden fable
      Vertu hath now   no dominacioun
      Pitee exyled   no man is merciable
      Through covetyse is *blent* discrecioun   blinded
      This world hath mad   a permutacioun
      Fro right to wrong   for trouthe to fikelnesse
      That al is lost   for lak of stedfastnesse

The connections of *The Wife of Bath's Prologue* with the rest of Chaucer are less straightforward; but for the full enjoyment of the Wife we need also, at least, the rest of Chaucer's love-poetry, his whole language of love.

Just so, our tricky questions about the Pardoner and the Summoner arise in the context of the great range of attitudes found in *The General Prologue*. We considered the extreme cases separately, but the ordinary way of taking them where they belong is perhaps a better way of understanding them. There is also in the Prologue, as well as the comic clarity of vision I talked about, the downright sentimentality about the Plowman (below, p. 203), the straight but not uncritical approval of the Parson, the more equivocal liking of the Clerk,[1] and the neutrality of the portrait of the Knight (who is just a 'verray parfit gentil knight'); and this is before we think of the characters Chaucer adversely criticizes as part of the crea-

---

[1] Chaucer conveys, I think, plainly enough, his liking of the Clerk; but it is only after he has shown the Clerk's eccentric passion for philosophy and after he has allowed himself to be funny about it

(A 286   That unto logyk   hadde longe ygo)

that Chaucer gives him that line which ought to be – now more even than in the fourteenth century – on the wall of every don's 'office':

A 308   And gladly wolde he lerne   and gladly teche

This is as much as the Wife's line quoted above an instance of the force of Middle English 'wolde'.

tion – in different ways the Prioress, the Monk (so liberal as to have made religion altogether unnecessary), the Shipman and, to complete the scale, the Pardoner and Summoner.

The comic sanity of the 'pure poetry' is the centre, but a centre that must be completed by other parts which may be equally important for one's sense of Chaucer – and of what is central to Chaucer. Perhaps Chaucer is a really great comic poet only to those who also see him as a great tragic writer.

8

The Tragic Canterbury Tale

I

The claim made for *The Knight's Tale* at the end of the last chapter and in the title of this one may be thought extravagant. Many find the tale tedious or uninterestingly obscure. To fit the Knight it has to be a courtly romance (a kind of medieval Western without the thrills); and we may feel that there is little in the Knight's view of the world to interest Chaucer or, *a fortiori*, ourselves. The story is slow; except between the gods there are no credible conversations; and except at odd moments that have been thought inappropriate there is none of that vitality of language which I have already called Chaucer's pure poetry. The critics, moreover, tend to take sides between Palamon and Arcite and prove conclusively that one – or the other, as the critic's taste inclines – is the hero, and that the tale accordingly enacts poetic justice (or injustice as the case may be[1]); and this controversy taken as a whole can only confirm one's impression that Palamon and Arcite are indistinguishable. (It is fairly obvious that one of the changes Chaucer makes in Boccaccio's story is to flatten the distinctions between the two.) If so the bored reader may feel that the question of justice or injustice will not save the tale. So perhaps he may go to the most brilliant of the Chaucer critics and read that '*The Knight's Tale* is essentially neither a story nor a static picture, but rather a sort of poetic pageant. Its design expresses the nature of the noble life.'[2] This is a formulation which I am grateful for and shall use; but one might be forgiven if the first reaction to it was a certain sinking of the heart. So what? we might ask. Of what possible concern is the nature of the noble life to Chaucer or to me?

Such is a common response which the first three parts of the poem make understandable enough. (Or, if this cap doesn't fit

---

[1] For Palamon and poetic justice see William Frost, 'An Interpretation of Chaucer's Knight's Tale', *The Review of English Studies* xxv (1949); for Arcite and injustice see A. V. C. Schmidt, 'The Tragedy of Arcite', *Essays in Criticism* xix (1969).   [2] Muscatine, *Chaucer and the French Tradition*, p. 181.

and like Ford Madox Ford you are entranced with *The Knight's Tale* from the beginning and all the way through,[1] I will confess that it took me several years of admiration for Chaucer before I could see the tale as more than the lengthy gesture towards literary decorum which he felt he had to make before settling into his true strength, the fabliaux and the Marriage Group.)

But there are certainly, at the very least, some passages of strikingly powerful poetry in *The Knight's Tale*. It is when we come to *this* that we are forced to stop wondering idly what the poem is all about, and begin to be 'carried away':

A 1995
   Ther saugh I first   the derke ymaginyng
Of Felonye   and al the compassyng
The crueel Ire   reed as any *gleede*
The pykepurs   and eek the pale Drede
The smylere with the knyf   under the cloke
The *shepne* brennynge   with the blake smoke
The tresoun   of the mordrynge in the bedde
The open werre   with woundes al bibledde
Contek with blody knyf   and sharp manace
Al ful of *chirkyng*   was that sory place
The sleere of hymself   yet saugh I ther
His herte blood   hath bathed al his heer
The nayl ydryven   in the *shode* anyght
The colde *deeth*   with mouth gapyng *upright*
Amyddes of the temple   sat Meschaunce
With *disconfort*   and sory contenaunce
Yet saugh I Woodnesse   laughynge in his rage
Armed Compleint   *Outhees* and fiers Outrage
The careyne in the busk   with throte ycove
A thousand slayn   and nat of *qualm* ystorve
The tiraunt   with the pray by force yraft
The toun destroyed   ther was no thyng laft
Yet saugh I brent   the shippes hoppesteres
The *hunte* strangled   with the wilde beres
The sowe *freten* the child   right in the cradel

gleede, red-hot cinder; *shepne*, sheep-fold; *Contek*, strife; *chirkyng*, chattering, twittering; *shode*, temple; *deeth*, corpse; *upright*, flat out; *disconfort*, discouragement; *Outhees*, hue and cry; *qualm*, plague; *hunte*, hunter; *freten*, munch.

That *ought* to startle anybody not too far gone in lethargy. Mr Speirs finds just the right word for this description of the temple of

---

[1] 'When you read *Palamon and Arcite* you are so carried away by the story that you have no time to bother your head about what manner of man the author was. You are enveloped in an affair. That is the quality of great art.' F. M. Ford, *The March of Literature* (1939), p. 378.

Mars when he says, 'It is concentrated, intense vision, as authentic-ally *vision* – on its smaller scale – as the *Inferno* itself.'[1] Yet the visionary force comes to the reader with a coherence and signifi-cance characteristic more of art than visions. The emotion is obviously strong, but the passage is not simply shocking. The image of a sow munching a child right in its cradle must shock if it is realized, but Chaucer is not emphasizing the shock. The feeling is kept under control by the repeated distancing 'Yet saugh I' within a passage which is itself formally a description of paintings. The lines are not saying (with Shelley in *The Cenci*) 'O my God can it be possible...' but, 'Mars is so...' Chaucer's power of seeing the object steadily is here more terrible than any loss of the poet's nerve could be. The success is comparable with *The General Pro-logue*'s power to make comedy out of the sordid or horrid without pretending they are otherwise than sordid or horrid. But this is a tragic grand style.

The Mars passage works rather like the Miller's description of Alison, but at a slower pace, and more deliberatively. It is not only a series of impressions and not only a collection of generalities, but a compound of the two which creates what Chaucer means by 'Mars'. This may be briefly shown from the first four lines of the passage quoted, where the abstract nouns 'feloyne' and 'ire' are followed by the first poetic surprise; for how does one react to anger's being not merely red but as red as a red-hot cinder? Not, at any rate, by seeing a visual image. Or even if you do see a red-hot cinder it is not labelled IRE. The way of connecting the quality and the image is more creative. The force of the image of the coal, however felt, is taken with the general term and the general term gives direction and meaning to the image, so that the two are more than either separately. In the next two lines we have an abstract noun, 'drede', qualified by 'pale', a noun substantive, 'pick-purse', and then a highly particular though succinct image, 'the smiler with the knife under the cloak'. Each adds a touch to a whole (a Gothic whole – I am not arguing that there is much importance in the order of images or that a few more or less would matter much) which could not be called either general or particular. There are various degrees of personification of the abstract nouns, depending to some extent on whether we decide to give them capital letters. This compound of general and particular is a more solemn version of what we often find in *The General Prologue*

---

[1] *Chaucer the Maker*, p. 125.

where, for example, the concentrated particularities about the Prioress (A 146ff.) are rounded off by the term 'conscience' (A 150) so that the details 'embody and animate' 'conscience' and the general word focuses the sense of the particular observations.

The unfakeable rhythmic life of the Mars passage is another sign of continuity with the styles of the comic poetry; the urgency is communicated in ways we do not need metrical expertise to admire. As in the conversations of *The Miller's Tale* the speech-phrases are spontaneous-sounding and yet made so by a command of metre. The typical line is again

> The crueel Ire reed as any gleede

where the more freely we allow the line to divide into its balancing, troubled-sounding halves – the further we get from any simple notions of what pentameters ought to be – the stronger the line is. The barely-sounded final -*e* on 'pale' gives another effectively halting phrase:

> The pykepurs and eek the pále Dréde

I call this a tragic grand style: but it is very unlike Milton. Its power is that of a concentration of spoken English, even where it is very close to the Italian original. Chaucer is often at his most original, most himself and most English, when he is translating quite closely. Boccaccio's version of the lines discussed is:

> videvi l'Ire rosse come foco
> e la Paura pallida, in quel loco.[1]

Chaucer's 'reed as any gleede' is characteristically more vivid and closer to speech – but as much as tragic style? Boccaccio, with the genius of his language, is decorous, melodious – and a little thin. The pick-purse is a Chaucerian innovation which completes the alteration of tone, and goes far beyond what the Italian would consider as 'epic dignity'.[2] Chaucer is more urgent, visionary, and also more down to earth than Boccaccio; if he is writing a tragic tale it is an un-Italian kind of tragedy; if this is a grand style it is a grand style very unlike Dante's. These are considerations we must recur to. (See below, pp. 146, 253 ff.)

The Mars vision makes one prick up one's ears, and that leads to noticing that all the gods in *The Knight's Tale* are more interesting

---

[1] *Teseida*, ed. Roncaglia (Bari, 1941), VII, 33–4: 'I saw Anger, red as fire, and pale Fear, in that place.'

[2] 'The catastrophes here mentioned, some of them scarcely of epic dignity...' F. N. Robinson in Chaucer's *Works*, p. 677.

than Palamon or Arcite or Emelye, and that all the gods except
Jupiter are powerful, mysterious, and almost unrelievedly cruel and
malign. The exception, Jupiter, who plays no part in the tale's
action, is the subject of another passage which stands out in early
readings – and which for me remains the centre of the poem. This
last speech by Theseus works in a similar way to the Mars vision,
but on an extended plan, so that instead of that chaotic-looking
compound of images and generalities we get a formal *sentence*
followed by the *exempla* which enforce it. My immediate point is
how well this is done. To consider at present only a few lines –

A 3011
And therfore   of his wise *purveiaunce*   providence
He hath so wel   biset his ordinaunce
That speces of thynges   and progressiouns
Shullen enduren   by successiouns
And nat eterne   withouten any lye
This maystow understonde   and seen at ye
   Loo the ook   that hath so long a norisshynge
From tyme   that it first bigynneth to sprynge
And hath so long a lif   as we may see
Yet at the laste   wasted is the tree
   Considereth eek   how that the harde stoon
Under oure feet   on which we trede and *goon*   walk
Yet wasteth it   as it lyth by the weye
The brode ryver   somtyme wexeth dreye
The grete tounes   se we wane and wende
Thanne may ye se   that al this thyng hath ende
   Of man and womman   seen we wel also
That nedes   in oon of thise termes two
This is to seyn   in youthe or elles age
He moot be deed   the kyng as shal a page
Som in his bed   som in the depe see
Som in the large feeld   as men may see
Ther helpeth noght   al goth that ilke weye
Thanne may I seyn   that al this thyng moot deye

Here, too, one can say that this is an English grand style, a style
conspicuously absent from early Chaucer; but here, too, the
emphasis must be on 'English'. For, with all its unmistakable
formal weight, the passage works with what Miss Daunt calls
'pieces of language';[1] the half-line phrases all belong very much to
poetry but could all have been spoken elsewhere. With all its
sombre dignity – which seems to me as unmistakable evidence of

[1] Marjorie Daunt, 'Old English Verse and English Speech Rhythm', *Trans-
actions of the Philological Society* (1946).

poetic power as anything in *The Miller's Tale* – the appeal is all
the time to experience, 'this you can understand and see with
your eyes'.

One way of bringing out Chaucer's distinction is to compare
him with his 'translators' into modern English. I forbear to quote
Professor Coghill's Penguin Classics version, which even con-
trives to make the passage jolly: but Dryden, too, who admired
The Knight's Tale very much and for broadly (I think) the right
reasons,[1] fails to convey the moving solemnity of the original.

> The Monarch Oak, the Patriarch of the Trees
> Shoots rising up, and spreads by slow Degrees;
> Three Centuries he grows, and three he stays,
> Supreme in State; and in three more decays:
> So wears the paving Pebble in the Street,
> And Towns and Tow'rs their fatal Period meet:
> So Rivers, rapid once, now naked lie
> Forsaken of their Springs; and leave their Channels dry.

This is done with the plainness of which Dryden is a master, but
his easy neatness gives a matter-of-fact air and removes the
feeling of significance. And with the feeling goes the significance
itself, for the passage's quality cannot depend on its paraphrasable
prose sense, which is commonplace enough. The commonplaceness
is what Dryden brings out – which means that this version is at
once less solemn and less realized than Chaucer's. Dryden's pebble
is not as hard as Chaucer's stone; and people tread on Chaucer's
stone but not Dryden's pebble.

If we come on things as striking and as mysterious as these
passages, the poem in which they are found acquires as a whole the
beginnings of an interest. We may well try again in the hope that
these features which at first stand out of the mist will eventually
become connected into a landscape.

II

If one is shocked by the gods into trying to take *The Knight's Tale*
whole, the first trap to be avoided is the view of the tale as a neatly
final account of 'the nature of the noble life'.

It will not even do to take the tale as an evaluation of the Knight's
view of the world, but that will perhaps serve as a way in. For the
tale certainly does, as Muscatine says, 'express the nature of the

---

[1] Cf. the Preface to *Fables Ancient and Modern*.

noble life' – and, I would add, it certainly criticizes it. To see how will take us back to the insufficiency of the account and the need to ask other questions.

The tale is full of the things knights were supposed to be interested in – battles and tournaments, set pieces of royal condescension, banquets, rich buildings, ceremonies of various kinds, and love at its most painful and courtly. Perhaps in places it is simply a neutral account of what goes on in the mind of a verray, parfit, gentil knight. Emelye is certainly an example of what the knight could find amiable in woman.

A 1033

This passeth yeer by yeer and day by day	
Till it fil ones in a *morwe* of May	morning
That Emelye that fairer was to sene	
Than is the lylie upon his stalke grene	
And fressher than the May with floures newe	
For with the rose colour stroof hire hewe	
I noot which was the fyner of hem two	
Er it were day as was hir wone to do	
She was arisen and al redy *dight*	dressed up
For May wol have no slogardie anyght	
The sesoun priketh every gentil herte	
And maketh hym out of his slep to sterte	
And seith 'Arys and do thyn observaunce'	
This maked Emelye have remembraunce	
To doon honour to May and for to ryse	
Yclothed was she fressh for to devyse	
Hir yelow heer was broyded in a tresse	
Bihynde hir bak a yerde long I gesse	
And in the gardyn at the sonne upriste	
She walketh up and doun and as *hire liste*	was pleasing to her
She gadereth floures party white and rede	
To make a subtil gerland for hire hede	
And as an aungel hevenysshly she soong	

Mr Speirs records his admiration for the passage and Emelye: 'The freshness and naturalness of the clear visualization of the young girl springs from the comparisons with the flowers; the conversational tone ensures an entire freedom from conventional stiffness and accords the picture human warmth.'[1] I think this is on the whole true, but the way of putting it may be misleading. In one sense a 'clear visualization' of Emelye is just what this passage is not. (What is she wearing? What is her face like?) The 'visualization' is 'clear' only to the extent that it is very

[1] *Chaucer the Maker*, p. 122.

114

stylized and indeed a 'picture'. The clearness is that of clear outlines and simple colours, which is as much as to say that the Knight sees his heroine much less sharply than the Miller sees Alison. There are, after all, things that a gentleman doesn't notice; and Emelye is at an opposite extreme from those of Chaucer's characters like the Wife of Bath who would be instantly and individually recognizable. Emelye is introduced by the comparison with lilies and roses which, whatever it may say of the Knight's feelings and tastes, tells us nothing individual about her: the only approach to particularization is in the comparatives – she is more beautiful than the lily, fresher than May, because her complexion vies with the rose's. Even when we come to details, the few things we are told of Emelye are all from the dead centre of medieval fashion rather than anybody's sight of a real woman. The flowers, of no species, are the right colour, and so is her hair. The urge to call her singing ('hevenyssh' – but soprano or contralto?) a 'last touch' records one's feeling that the whole is framed and stylized. It is essential to the way Emelye is presented that she should be generalized: the season stirs *every* civilized heart. So the extreme opposite of Mr Speirs's position can be argued reasonably enough: 'Emelye herself, the last of the four central characters, is even less an individual than the other three. We know nothing whatsoever of her character...'[1]

All the same I don't want to leave it there with Mr Spearing or to say with some other critics that Emelye is positively unreal. I share Mr Speirs's feeling that the passage gives a sense of life – even a feeling that is free from 'conventional stiffness'. But I have to say at the same time that whatever life there is is of a thoroughly conventional kind. To call it conventional need not be to make it dead: and that is the advance of this passage over Chaucer's other conventional courtly beauty, the lady Blanche of *The Book of the Duchess*. Both are exactly what is to be expected. Yet Mr Speirs is right to say that Emelye's 'freshness' is given as something alive, by the flowers and the delicate rhythmic movement which, though, I think 'conversational' is not the right word for. The rhythmic movement has the kind of closeness to speech which does not deny the formality I find in the passage.

Emelye is the true knight's idea of what is loveable in a woman;

[1] A. C. Spearing (ed). *The Knight's Tale* (Cambridge, 1966), introduction, p. 30. Mr Spearing here takes the flimsy opportunity of the introduction to a school edition to make one of the few serious attempts to get to grips with the tale.

in order to fall in love a true knight has to see a woman like, or even *as*, Emelye. It is a living but limited ideal, and Emelye is somewhere between unreal idealization and lively realization, as she has to be if the tale is the Knight's view of life. And here, in the view of Emelye, *The Knight's Tale* does seem to be just an expression of 'the nature of the noble life' with, apparently, no comment beyond what the limitation and liveliness of the creation imply.

Emelye is as it were the first degree of Chaucer's evaluation of knightliness, as neutral as the portrait of the Knight in the Prologue. But there are other degrees. I think Chaucer is all the time, even when the tale is at its most tragic, asking what this style of life, this way of looking at the world, is really worth. In the case of Emelye the question doesn't demand a very profound effort of him. But elsewhere he takes things more seriously, and if we follow this scale of seriousness it will lead us back to the gods and the question of what it is to take *them* seriously.

There are plenty of signs that Chaucer isn't simply endorsing the Knight's style, but at first they might seem to indicate that the tale is not very deep, that Chaucer is not much involved with it. This is true where the Knight's view of the world is seen to be naive:

> A 2110
> For if ther fille tomorwe   swich a cas
> Ye knowen wel   that every lusty knyght
> That loveth *paramours*   and hath his myght   passionately
> Were it in Engelond   or elleswhere
> They wolde *hir thonkes*   wilnen to be there   willingly

The 'cas' is the tournament, and the mention of England together with the rather boy-scout enthusiasm is a reminder that tournaments were often enough the last places where real knights would wish to be, and that Richard II sometimes had difficulty in filling his lists. Or there is this, which – addressed to an audience including the Wife of Bath – needs no comment:

> A 2822
> For in swich cas   wommen have swich sorwe
> When that hir housbondes   ben from hem ago
> That for the moore part   they sorwen so
> Or elles fallen   in swich maladye
> That at the laste   certeinly they dye

Here the Knight's attractive simplicity may not seem very much more than the Prioress's.

I think the tale rises well above this level in its treatment of Theseus, the true knight *par excellence* and the only mortal *character* (if he is mortal) in the poem. The importance of Theseus in the tale is obvious enough. The language used of him would often fit Providence equally well. I do not think that this is explicit enough to make it necessary to speak of 'allegory' or to launch into fourfold interpretations: but look for instance at the form of the prayer to Theseus of Hippolyta and the Ladies:

> A 1756
> And alle crieden   bothe lasse and moore
> 'Have mercy Lord   upon us wommen alle'
> And on hire bare knees   adoun they falle

Theseus announces the tournament in almost the form of speech used at the end of the tale about Destiny:

> A 1842
>   ech of yow   shal have his destynee
> As hym is shape   and herkneth in what wyse
> Lo heere youre ende   of that I shal devyse

Theseus appears on the day of the tournament

> A 2528
>   at a wyndow set
> Arrayed right as he were   a god in trone
> The peple presseth   thiderward ful soone
> Hym for to seen   and doon heigh reverence

Soon afterwards the herald begins the proclamation

> A 2537
>   The lord hath   of his heigh discrecioun
> Considered...

and he ends the same speech

> A 2560
> Gooth now youre weye   this is the lordes wille

– not, one notices, 'this' lord's will.

But if Theseus, incarnate knighthood, is a Destiny-like power, controlling the action of the tale, he is also human, and limited not only by his short temper and kind heart but by the lack of insight sometimes very noticeable in the use he makes of his power. If he is Destiny, Destiny is neither omniscient nor even, on the surface, very wise. This is shown very clearly by the opening episode of Theseus's war on Thebes – an episode which has been thought superfluous but which certainly matters for one's sense of how the tale is judging the courtly way of life.

The *narracio* begins by introducing a group of courtly ladies who have come to ask a boon of Theseus. The ladies present themselves (A 898–904) with ostentatious propriety, arranged two by two, dressed in black, and making an enormous clamour (propriety in the Middle Ages not being so far removed from Nature as it is now). The eldest lady speaks and, having first asked (A 920) for 'pitee' (which 'renneth soon in gentil herte') she explains her right to it. First she shows that all the ladies are qualified by social standing to deserve 'pitee'

> A 922
> For certes lord   ther is noon of us alle
> That she ne hath been   a duchesse or a queene

– why should that have seemed less snobbish to Chaucer than to us? But perhaps Chaucer found it easier not to be distracted by dislike of duchesses from seeing that though they're all snobs they deserve pity nonetheless. A little later we come to the details of the ladies' misfortune:

> A 938
> And yet now   the olde Creon   weylaway
> That lord is now   of Thebes the citee
> Fulfild of ire   and of iniquitee
> He for despit   and for his tirannye
> To do the dede bodyes   vileynye
> Of alle oure lordes   whiche that been yslawe
> Hath alle the bodyes   on an heep ydrawe
> And wol nat suffren hem   by noon assent
> Neither to been yburyed   nor ybrent
> But maketh houndes   ete hem in despit

It is not the death of their husbands they complain of: death comes to all (as Egeus later remarks, quite happily) and they can accept it with the relatively mild 'cursed be that day.' What they cannot bear is that their husbands should not receive the burial due to their rank. 'Vileynye' is the opposite of 'gentilesse'; 'vileynye' is the behaviour and style proper to low people, and *The General Prologue* tells us that the Knight himself has never in his life spoken 'vileynye' to anybody (A 70–1). 'Vileynye' – strongly emphasized by the verse movement – is now suffered by the dead bodies.

This is purely an offence against courtliness. What the ladies complain of is, to put it reductively, a breach of manners. Of course 'manners' are the expression of the whole courtly life, and an insult to this part peculiarly denigrates the whole: yet part of one's response is that this is not a *political* problem. The situation of the ladies can't, we think, affect the result of the war in Thebes, and the non-burial of the bodies has (unlike the similar case at the beginning of the *Antigone* of Sophocles, which may seem separated from us by less of a gulf of history than Chaucer's tale) no religious significance. The ladies have *only* (we might say) suffered an affront to public decency.

But the response of Theseus, perhaps as politically surprising to Chaucer as to us,[1] is that of the ideal knight as king. A real politician might have sympathized – would have expressed compassion, anyway – and might have set on foot negotiations for a War Graves Commission, meanwhile relegating the ladies to decent obscurity at minimum cost to the exchequer.[2] But the ideal knight pities the ladies:

> A 952
>   This gentil duc   doun from his courser sterte
> With herte pitous   whan he herde hem speke
> Hym thoughte   that his herte wolde breke
> When he saugh hem   so pitous and so maat
> That whilom weren   of so greet estaat

Being in control of society, Theseus can act on his pity and wipe out this affront to 'gentilesse' which challenges the noble life, without a thought of the consequences (and being a romance *The Knight's Tale* can tell us he did so without the slightest preparation).

---

[1] Froissart's *Chronicles*, full of situations like this one, are far more starry-eyed about politics than Chaucer ever is. For Chaucer on politics see *Lak of Stedfastnesse*, also his *Compleynt to his Purs*.

[2] The seventeenth-century stage version in which Shakespeare may have had a hand, *The Two Noble Kinsmen*, tries to make the episode dramatically credible:

> I, i   He will not suffer us to burne their bones,
>   To urne their ashes, nor to take th'offence
>   Of mortall loathsomenes from the blest eye
>   Of holy *Phoebus*, but infects the windes
>   With stench of our slaine Lords

Here a religious suggestion joins with a fear of plague and also a concern, well-grounded in seventeenth-century life, for adequate waste-disposal. This doesn't really *explain* the expedition to Thebes: my point is, however, that Chaucer carefully avoids any reasons of this sort; he shows the offence as an offence purely against 'gentilesse'.

This is splendid – and it will never do. Chaucer shows in the following passage both the magnificence of this ideal and its unintelligent arbitrariness, the connection in Theseus between the order of the noble life and bloody chaos.

A 975
    The rede statue of Mars   with spere and targe
So shyneth   in his white baner large
That alle the feeldes   glyteren up and doun
And by his baner   born is his penoun
Of gold ful riche   in which ther was ybete
The Mynotaur   which that he slough in Crete
    Thus rit this duc   thus rit this conquerour
And in his hoost   of chivalrie the flour
Til that he cam to Thebes   and alighte
Faire in a feeld   ther as he thoughte to fighte
But shortly for to speken   of this thyng
With Creon   which that was of Thebes kyng
He faught   and slough hym   manly as a knyght
In *pleyn* bataille   and putte the folk to flyght   pitched
And by assaut   he wan the citee after
And rente adoun   bothe wall and sparre and rafter
And to the ladyes   he restored agayn
The bones   of hir housbondes   that were slayn
To doon obsequies   as was tho the gyse

The first three lines are for Chaucer unusually sinister, and may send a thrill down the spine: the direct consequence of Theseus's 'pitee' is the entry of Mars into the poem. And, of course, we learn all about Mars later. After the thrill of Mars and the magnificence of the Athenian host, the campaign itself is treated with the severest brevity. But a point is strongly made: the pity of the true knight leads to the destruction (done, of course, in an entirely proper manner) of Thebes, whose 'waste walles wide' echo through the rest of the poem: and the kindness to the ladies is the catastrophe to the innocent Palamon and Arcite that begins the story. In one line at least the irony looks to me unmistakable:

And to the ladyes   he restored agayn
The bones...

The most natural reading is surely to put a slight ironic stress on 'bones', to suggest something like 'all this for *bones*!' And soon afterwards this comment is reinforced by a glimpse of real war, when we meet Palamon and Arcite as they are discovered by the pillagers stripping the corpses.

This episode is both a creation and critique of the courtly ideal. Anyone interested in courtliness will find it repays endless pondering: it contains layer on layer of admiration and limiting judgment. All the same, perhaps it answers the question of what the true knight is worth a little too easily. The criticism might be thought to be of a Lytton Strachey kind, brilliant but external, leaving the critic untouched. Chaucer is perhaps making the eternally true bourgeois comment on aristocratic statesmen: How magnificent they are – and how dangerous! How badly they need educating! The episode reminds me of Arnold on the Barbarians or of those whose admiration for Churchill was, more recently, mingled with fear of what he would do if he got the chance. But if this is all there is to Chaucer's criticism it still need not go very deep: we could still be left wondering what there is in the tale of more than antiquarian interest.

The first step towards a vindication of Theseus is the next along our path towards seeing what is tragic in the poem. For whatever his limitations may be, Theseus does succeed in making something of the love that has reduced Palamon and Arcite to chaos.

Palamon and Arcite are men who are fatally determined to make the worst of things. As they frequently explain, they suffer their torments because of the gods, and we must soon consider what this means; but without thinking about the gods at all we can see that there is no need for them to suffer as they do. Palamon and Arcite are sworn brothers and, at first, are loyal to each other. One part of the courtly life, comradeship in arms, sustains them in adversity. But they are ruined by another part, rivalry in love. (Or, in the tale's theological terms, their loyalty to Mars preserves them but they are undone by Venus.) As soon as love comes they forget their vows, and their brotherly affection is replaced by a hatred so rancorous that at one point Palamon (on whose moral superiority to Arcite one interpretation of the tale depends) is reduced to an exact inversion of the proper plea to 'kill me but let my brother go' and says, after betraying Arcite to Theseus,

A 1721
But sle me first   for seinte charitee   only
But sle my felawe eek   as wel as me

The love they feel is always deadly, its effects always and simply those of a serious illness. Love is not without its pains, as was known to medieval as well as more modern poets; but for Palamon and Arcite and Emelye there is *nothing* in love but pain and woe; the acuteness of the feelings is *only* that of a sudden wound:

> A 1077
> He cast his eye   upon Emelya
> And therwithal he *bleynte*   and cride 'A'   blenched
> As though he *stongen* were   unto the herte   stabbed

(Mr Speirs's comparison of this with Criseyde's 'Who yaf me drinke?' neglects the difference between intoxication and death.) Arcite fares no better:

> A 1114
> And with that sighte   hir beautee *hurte* hym so   wounded
> That if that Palamon   was wounded sore
> Arcite is hurt   as muche as he or moore

What he says concentrates on the deadliness of the wound:

> A 1118
> The fresshe beautee   sleeth me sodeynly
> Of hire that rometh   in the yonder place

and this has followed an even more explicit affirmation from Palamon that

> A 1098
> The fairnesse of that lady   that I see
> Yond in the gardyn   romen to and fro
> Is cause   of al my criyng   and my wo

These are all ways of speaking that belong to the troubadour tradition (Chaucer can himself begin a lyric 'Your yen two wol slee me sodenly'[1]) but there is more here than the use of these figures to express the intensity of the experience: compared with the damage done by love the merely military wounds the knights have suffered are as nothing. And this is the nature of love all the way through the story. Arcite even seems to think that Emelye, not the Furie Infernal, is the causer of his death. His 'peynes stronge' are still at the end those of love:

> A 2771
> Allas the wo   allas the peynes stronge
> That I for yow have suffred   and so longe
> Allas the deeth   allas myn Emelye [!]
> Allas departynge   of oure compaignye

[1] *Merciles Beaute*, line 1. It is true that the same poem ends with Chaucer's announcement that he counts the God of Love not a bean. (F. N. Robinson's classification of this poem as 'of doubtful authorship' is a *stylistic* absurdity.)

Allas myn hertes queene   allas my wyf
Myn hertes ladye   endere of my lyf   *heroes*

and his last words are not 'Far weel Emelye' but (A 2808) 'Mercy
Emelye'. We do not need to believe that love is always ennobling
to see that there is something wrong with this love.

Palamon and Arcite make the worst of their misery for themselves. They cannot decide not to be in love – Venus sends them
this hopeless passion – but they certainly could have made of the
experience something less uninterruptedly disastrous, and Venus
couldn't have stopped them.

> A 1670
> For certeinly   oure appetites heer
> Be it of werre or pees   or hate or love
> Al is this reuled   by the sighte above

But *only* appetites are so ruled. We cannot decide not to have an
appetite; but it may be resisted or it may be indulged in an infinite
variety of ways.[1] I imagine that during a long spell in prison a
hopeless passion, however painful, could be a way of staying
human, and there are comparable cases in medieval poetry where
the imprisoned knight comes close to feeling gratitude for the
passion. Yvain remains in captivity even when he could escape,
'detained by love',[2] and the narrator of *The Kingis Quair* is also
made happy by a similarly imprisoned love.

But Palamon and Arcite are not able 'to take it well'. Arcite
announces as his belief,

> A 1182
> Ech man for hymself   ther is noon other

and even after he has made the impressive speech beginning

> A 1251
>   Allas why pleynen folk so   in commune
> On *purveiaunce* of God   or of Fortune   providence

he is quite unable to apply it to himself, and misses his own point
by saying

> A 1268
> Thus may we seyen alle   and namely I
> That wende   and hadde a greet opinioun
> That if I myghte   escapen from prisoun
> Than hadde I been   in joye and perfit heele
> Ther now I am exiled   fro my wele

[1] Cf. the doctrine of Dante in *Purgatorio* XVIII, 19ff.
[2] Chrestien de Troyes, *Yvain*, line 1531.

Syn that I may nat seen you   Emelye
I nam but deed   ther nys no remedye

Palamon says

A 1309
For slayn is man   right as another beest
And dwelleth eek   in prison and arreest

So the question with which the Knight ends the first part is rather tricky:

A 1347
Yow loveres   axe I now this questioun
Who hath the worse   Arcite or Palamoun?

This is a trap that leads straight to the critical pursuit of distinguishing between these two who are as like as two peas. The real question is whether they are both right to take love like this: and that covers the other and deeper question, whether they are right to complain of the injustice of the gods.

The self-pity of Palamon and Arcite is closely linked with the frequent misunderstandings – almost, the theme of misunderstanding – in the poem. It seems extraordinarily difficult for all the characters to understand their own and each other's motives. In the first episode Theseus quite mistakes the purpose of the group of courtly ladies:

A 905
'What folk been ye   that at myn homcomynge
Perturben so my feste   with criynge?'
Quod Theseus   'Have ye so greet *envye*
Of myn honour   that thus compleyne and crye?'
                    * wishing evil to others

When Palamon screams 'A!' as though he had been stabbed to the heart (A 1078), Arcite assumes that his trouble is that prison has driven him to despair, and before he can be corrected preaches a little sermon about submission to fate, which we later remember ironically. Palamon and Arcite are each mistaken about the other's comparative happiness after Arcite has escaped to Thebes, and their common neglect of Emelye's feelings makes it come as a surprise when she tells Diana that she doesn't want to marry at all (A 2304-5). Mercury delivers a deceptive oracle (A 1391) and near the end of the tale 'thise wommen' make the very odd mistake of supposing Arcite has died on purpose:

A 2835
'Why woldestow be deed'   thise wommen crye
'And haddest gold ynough   and Emelye'[1]

('Why did you insist on dying...')

Palamon and Arcite's determination to be miserable may be
seen to belong with these misunderstandings if we put both
alongside one of the tale's central preoccupations, the problem of
how to know one's place in the world and how to see any justice in
it. The two main statements are given one to Palamon and one to
Arcite in speeches we have already glanced at: Arcite's is the 'Allas,
why pleynen folk so' passage (A 1251ff.) and Palamon's is:

A 1303
        O crueel goddes that governe   FORTUNE
This world with byndyng   of youre word eterne
And writen   in the table of atthamanut
Youre parlement   and youre eterne graunt
What is mankynde   moore unto you holde
Than is the sheep   that *rouketh*   in the folde?   cowers
For slayn is man   right as another beest
And dwelleth eek   in prison and arreest
And hath siknesse   and greet adversitee
And ofte tymes   giltelees pardee
   What governance   is in this prescience
That giltelees   tormenteth innocence?

This question is at the heart of the tale, and it means, with the
heroes' misery and all the mistakes, that the courtly view of the
world is failing for some characters to make any sense of the world.
For Palamon and Arcite the world is (in Egeus's words) a malign
'thurghfare ful of wo'; and the only wisdom Arcite takes to his
grave is this baffled pathos:

A 2777
What is this world?   what asketh men to have?
Now with his love   now in his colde grave
Allone   withouten any compaignye

Theseus does not immediately answer this question, but one of
his achievements in the tale is to create out of the love which
reduces Palamon and Arcite to subhuman misery the human and
civilized order of the tournament. He shows them that their love

---

[1] The oddity of this couplet stuck in Pope's memory, and his last recorded verse
is a parody of it:
   Ah Bounce! ah gentle Beast! why wouldst thou dye,
   When thou had'st Meat enough, and Orrery?

need not be what they make of it; and the courtly life which seems to be destroyed by love is made by Theseus the means of accommodating love.[1] In this way Theseus shows that, whatever its limitations or stupidities, there is something creative about the noble life. Theseus, limited Destiny, saves Palamon and Arcite at least from their first fate by worshipping, bringing within the noble life, those forces (called Venus and Mars) that are destroying them. 'To fighte for a lady' (A 2115) is better than what Palamon and Arcite were doing in the grove (that was fighting over a woman) because it organizes the love.

But anything that Theseus creates is always at risk, always, so to speak, a near thing. I can call the tournament 'civilized' but Theseus only decides on it after retracting his first intention to execute Palamon and Arcite immediately, and its civilization (in a world where the gods are on the loose) is never to be guaranteed. Anything civilized or human is there because Theseus never quite lets the tournament get out of hand. But from another viewpoint it is not much removed from barbarity. Numerous commentators have remarked on the prevalence of wild-animal imagery in this part of the poem; and the line between true knight and wild animal might not be easily drawn by a casual observer either of the tournament or of the earlier fight. Still, Theseus limits the action within the bounds of law – but, again, only just. It is right that one of the crowning details of the Mars vision should be the insecurity of the conqueror

> A 2029
> With the sharpe swerd   over his heed
> Hangynge   by a soutil twynes threed

which so obviously reminds us of the mighty conqueror who controls the action of the tale.

Yet with all his limitations of vision Theseus can make more of the courtly life than Palamon or Arcite can. And it is tempting to remain at this level and see the tale as a moral fable about making the best of things, patting oneself on the back, meanwhile, for seeing that it isn't about poetic justice of the primitive sort in which the right (or wrong) man gets the girl. In a sense I do think that *The Knight's Tale* is about 'taking wel that we may nat eschue' –

[1]   Onde, pognam che di necessitate
      surga ogni amor che dentro a voi s'accende,
      di ritenerlo è in voi la potestate.
               Purgatorio XVIII, 70–2

but the trouble with any account like the present, which could give no reason for calling the tale 'tragic', is that it virtually leaves out the gods. It also leaves unanswered Arcite's and Palamon's questions about justice and sense. These two concerns fall together. The gods kept pushing their way in even as I was conducting the above discussion, and it is high time we considered them.

III   IMPORTANT

To show that Chaucer's criticism of the nature of the noble life has not gone the way of all academic evaluations of dead ideas we have to return to the gods, because it is the presence of the gods that forces me to see the tale as tragic. If the Thebes episode could be seen as detached criticism of the noble life, and if the arrangements culminating in the tournament seem a kind of higher commonsense, the parts where the gods enter both implicate the poet and turn his work, in ways it is my business to explain, into a criticism of life, of permanent power and significance.

Why are all the gods who are characters in *The Knight's Tale* so convincingly malevolent? With the terrible Mars passage we discussed we are far from any mood of calmly detached comment. The passage has the impact, coming directly from an involvement with life, of a mind that has recognized something of the terror of life. I said that the Mars vision is not merely shocking, but it certainly has that quality of pulling the reader up short, of making him realize that life may be like *this*, which has (in this other context) the force of the kind of shock that can change a man's sense of life. And Mars is not alone: Diana and Venus are equally godlike and hardly more likeable (though it is true that all three show qualities that make their worship not merely and not necessarily subhuman). Why does Chaucer put the gods in the tale? What difference do they make to our view of Palamon, Arcite and Theseus?

It would be the wrong question to ask 'Does Mars exist?' and worse to ask 'Did Chaucer believe in Mars?' – though in both cases if the questions were put the answer would have to be *yes*. The gods are one way of organizing the world. Saturn is a way of making a category, and if I say I do not believe in Saturn I would have to say I do not believe in *infortuna major*, the kind of misfortune to which Saturn lays claim:

A 2456
Myn is the *drenchyng*   in the see so wan   drowning
Myn is the prison   in the derke *cote*   cell
Myn is the stranglyng   and hangyng by the throte
The murmure   and the cherles rebellyng
The groynynge   and the pryvee empoysonyng

It would be absurd to say that these misfortunes never happen, and very unimaginative to say that they cannot be seen as belonging together. If I say I believe in Saturn I mean I see the point in making that class of events.

But of course in *The Knight's Tale* Saturn is far more than merely a category. The powers of Saturn, Mars, Venus are felt by the reader as divine powers which are not to be explained away by such classification as the above. These two observations together, that the gods are coherent categories, and that they're *gods*, may suggest why Chaucer needed to make them so important here. Here, too, is one sign of the magnitude of the tale's achievement, for the resuscitation of dead gods is notoriously difficult – witness D. H. Lawrence's attempts in *The Plumed Serpent*, which give so much more a sense of striving for the divine than of any actual presence of the gods.

Chaucer's material, moreover, was hardly promising. When a religion has cooled down far enough to be calmly talked about, its gods already have one foot in that grave of all the religions, scholarship – from ritual to myth to Mr Casaubon is an irreversible process[1] – and Chaucer gets his gods from a thoroughly self-conscious and intellectualized tradition. When Christianity drove out the gods some went underground,[2] others became safe as saints, others retired to the yet more safe academic respectability of the heavens, where they became the star gods of the medieval astrologers and were not even considered rivals of Christianity. It is these star-gods who appear in *The Knight's Tale* and elsewhere – often enough, as we have seen, as the subjects of Chaucer's

---

[1] Cf. 'Now, as we know from psychotherapeutic experience, projection is an unconscious, automatic process whereby a content that is unconscious to the subject transfers itself to an object, so that it seems to belong to that object. The projection ceases the moment it becomes conscious, that is to say when it is seen as belonging to its subject. Thus the polytheistic heaven of the ancients owes its depotentiation not least to the view first propounded by Euhemeros, who maintained that the gods were nothing but reflections of human character.' *The Collected Works of C. G. Jung*, Vol. IX, Part I (1959), p. 60.

[2] On this subject see Jean Seznec, *The Survival of the Pagan Gods*, 2nd edn (New York, 1953).

frivolous fun. Astrology as known to Chaucer is more a philo-sophical system than a religion; it is difficult to imagine anything less chthonic.

Yet in *The Knight's Tale* Mars, Saturn and Venus are all too lively: the reader feels that the poet is very far from falling into mere academic discussion of them. The setting of the poem in the distant past gave Chaucer his opportunity of taking the gods seriously without insulting the church; but the life of the gods is very much of the present. Mars lives with the life of his terror; Venus is alive for Chaucer so long as there is uncontrollable love. The achievement is to see the love as the goddess, as well as *vice versa*. The gods are only categories in so far as they retain and make solemn all the life of the passions they categorize. Chaucer has this great creative achievement, that he has used the gods to describe some of the things to be met with in life – which is to say in our life – without depriving the gods of their divinity.

Even gods as terrible and in some aspects as evil as Mars and Saturn are two of the necessary conditions of human life. Without the possibility of the sudden violence of Mars or the different, coldly senseless violence of Saturn, or the inexplicable passions of Venus and Diana, there could be no human life as we know it. The difficulty that monotheistic religions have always had in account-ing for this state of affairs may be another pointer to why Chaucer needs polytheism. For, if there is one God and he is good why did He design a world in which we plainly see the senseless malignity of Saturn? Why is it necessary for Christians to pray for deliver-ance from 'sudden death' – which could well be understood as a prayer for protection against Saturn? If there is one good God it requires, at least, some subtlety of argument to show that we do not deserve all the misfortunes that occur to us. Christ would not endorse the view that anyone to whom an accident occurs is justly punished: 'Or those eighteen, upon whom the tower in Siloam fell, and slew them, think ye that they were offenders above all men that dwelt in Jerusalem? I tell you, Nay...'[1] But this is only because we all deserve such punishment. The passage con-tinues, '...but, except ye repent, ye shall all likewise perish'. This leaves unanswered the question of why the tower fell on those sinners in particular. Who is responsible for natural causes? It would make a kind of sense to say that the tower fell because Saturn made it fall:

---

[1] Luke xiii, 4–5.

A 2463
   Myne is the ruyne   of the hye halles
The fallynge of the toures   and of the walles

If we attribute such events to Saturn that would be a way of con-
veying the meaninglessness and the aura of pointless malignity we
might well associate with them.

Mars and Saturn succeed in the tale because they are ways of
allowing Chaucer to perceive at once and deeply what would
otherwise have been only scattered impressions. This is part of
what I meant by calling the Mars vision a whole: it is more than a
series of images because they cohere into the god.[1] Since the
possibility of these misfortunes is an inescapable part of the human
condition, they are capable of a religious treatment. It is even
possible, without approving of their actions, to bring these gods
into a sort of morality. Part of the Mars passage I did not quote
mentions 'the butcher and the smith' who make use, morally, of
the powers of Mars. Theseus himself is a worshipper of Mars, and
Mars is properly one of the gods of the tournament. Even Saturn
is the god of just as well as of senseless misfortune. He says

A 2461
   I do vengeance   and pleyn correccioun
Whil I dwelle   in the signe of the leoun

and the 'fallynge of the toures and of the walles' is in fact

A 2465
Upon the mynour   or the carpenter

The walls come in upon the miner's tunnel *because* he has not
done the work properly. Saturn, too, is the god of contrivances to
meet disaster as well as the god of disasters themselves: it is not out
of character that he should patch up, after some catastrophe he has
been the patron of, the kind of compromise we have to make often
enough in life.

The gods allow Chaucer to bring to bear a religious, or tragic,
depth of feeling, without having to pretend that they are really
nice characters. Mars and Saturn are as bad as they seem, and the
tale depends on the directness of their shock to a reader; yet at the
same time the poet creates a religious awe of them.

[1] (This is unlike Larkin's 'Church Going' where our 'compulsions meet' and
are 'recognized and robed as destinies', because in Chaucer the recognition of
Saturn as God is inseparable from his recognition as 'compulsion' – Saturn is
an infliction only in so far as he is also Destiny.)

A 1918
    First in the temple of Venus   maystow se
    Wroght on the wal   ful pitous to biholde
    The broken slepes   and the sikes colde

This Venus is much more terrible than the goddess of *The Parliament of Fowls*, but the terror allows Chaucer in the next line also to use the word 'sacred':

    The sacred teeris   and the *waymentynge*   lamenting

So, too, the statue of Venus is (A 1955) 'glorious for to se'; and when Chaucer ends the Mars vision with the word 'glory' he is not being simply ironical:

A 2049
    With soutil pencel   depeynted was this storie
    In redoutynge of Mars   and of his glorie

Everything, of course, depends on what is done with the gods, what is made of this way of speaking and feeling. They are not in themselves any guarantee of the tale's success. But through the gods Chaucer not only makes his final comments on courtly life, he generalizes them into a tragic criticism of any life fit to be called human. The gods are one of the tests that civilization – any civilization – has to pass.[1] Mars is given his particular place in the courtly life because as god of War he is worshipped by Theseus: but any human life has to find *some* place for Mars, Venus and Saturn. The place Theseus gives to Mars makes the comment I elaborated above about the inseparability in Theseus of 'gentilesse' and destructiveness.[2] Mars and Venus are then both inalienably part of 'the noble life', and the Mars vision draws no veil over what is here being worshipped. Venus, too, is as unclassifiable as either 'good' or 'bad' as she is in *The Parliament of Fowls*. Chaucer seems to be putting the case at its worst and asking whether the noble life, that includes the worship of Mars, Venus and Diana, can survive this worship as something civilized and valuable. Saturn, of course, is not worshipped in the poem; he is recognized

---

[1] For a comparable discussion of *Sir Gawain and the Green Knight*'s treatment of 'natural forces' see below, pp. 226ff.

[2] The failure to see this connection is the weak point of Muscatine's essay in *Chaucer and the French Tradition* and allows him to be neater and shallower than the poem demands. If his scheme of the poem (in which Theseus as order is opposed to disorder) were to stand, Theseus would have to hate Mars, the deification of disorder. But Mars is in the tale because Theseus worships him.

as 'wys Saturnus the olde' but has no temple. Perhaps Saturn is as near as the poem comes to recognizing a devil, a divine force to be wholly shunned. But I shall show that the course of the tale makes even this untrue and says, in so far as it says anything explicit, that Saturn too ought to be worshipped – but under the guidance of the god we have not yet discussed, Jupiter.

The way that courtly life can survive the gods is shown at first when Theseus, as limited destiny, manages to civilize the force of love – Venus – which is destroying Palamon and Arcite, as I argued above. Theseus lives with these gods; which doesn't mean that he understands them or tames them. But his courtly life gives him at least a *modus vivendi* with Venus and Mars, which means recognizing and wondering at them, and not being daunted. What Theseus says of love is strongly reminiscent of the Chaucer *The Parliament of Fowls*:

> A 1785
>   The god of love   a benedicite
> How myghty and how greet a lord is he
> Ayeyns his myght   ther gayneth none obstacles
> He may be cleped a god   for his myracles

> *PF* 10
> Yit happeth me ful ofte   in bokes reede
> Of his myrakles   and his crewel yre
> There rede I wel   he wol be lord and syre
> I dar nat seyn   his strokes been so sore
> But 'God save swich a lord'   I can na moore

And by these I put two lines of *Troilus and Criseyde* to which I shall have to recur:

> V 1749
> In ech estat   is litel hertes reste
> God leve us   for to take it for the beste

Theseus is not guaranteeing anything: it isn't that he has got Venus on a lead – any more than Troilus can guarantee that Venus will bless him and Criseyde. Theseus is not offering Palamon and Arcite, with the hubris of the Book of Common Prayer, 'forgiveness of sins to all them that with hearty repentance and true faith turn unto him'.[1] But he is like Troilus giving Venus a chance to show her favourable aspect by giving her her due place: whereas, left to themselves, Palamon and Arcite can only see the malevolent aspects of Venus. Similarly he draws Mars into the courtly world

---

[1] The Order for the Administration of the Lord's Supper.

when he makes war 'manly as a knight' (A 987) and Diana when 'after Mars he serveth now Diane' (A 1682).

So with all his limitations of intelligence Theseus can erect and maintain in the world of Venus, Mars and Diana, which is to say, in the human condition, the structure of the noble life. He can show in his own person its true nobility; and he embodies the reason for continuing civilized life, although it is a civilized life with terrible shortcomings.

Mars, Venus and Diana are not, however, the final trial. After the tournament Theseus seems to have got everything under control; and as decent, unintelligent destiny, he pronounces judgment:

> A 2656
> He cryde 'Hoo namoore   for it is doon
> I wol be trewe juge   and no partie
> Arcite of Thebes   shal have Emelie
> That by his fortune   hath hire faire ywonne'

But Saturn, who is in this respect subhuman, decides differently; and the final trial of the Knight's vision of life is Saturn's worst, *infortuna major*. Saturn's formal statement of his powers is steadier and more chilling than the Mars vision. His is the god-like force of 'mere anarchy'. One of his more recent literary appearances is as the god of the Marabar Caves, who reduces everything to the same dull BOUM.[1] He is also some relation of Shakespeare's witches. And when we get to Saturn the very triviality of the gods makes its point. The anthropomorphic tradition allows Chaucer to make Venus and Mars squabble, Venus to weep ridiculously into the lists (A 2666),[2] and various minor deities to run absurdly around when their woods are felled to provide materials for Arcite's pyre (A 2925). In their more terrible way, the gods of *The Knight's Tale*, except Jupiter, are as absurd as those of *The Book of the Duchess*. They are all within the orbit of the trivially malign Saturn, who himself begins his main and very blood-chilling speech with the oddly homely

> A 2453
> 'My deere doghter Venus'   quod Saturne

---

[1] E. M. Forster, *A Passage to India*, Chapter XIV. 'What had spoken to her in that scoured-out cavity of the granite? What dwelt in the first of the caves? Something very old and very small. Before time, it was before space also. Something snub-nosed, incapable of generosity – the undying worm itself.' *Ibid.*, Chapter XXXIII.

[2] Cf. *Scogan*, lines 8–14.

133

Saturn's plot which decides the action of the tale is the final challenge to Theseus. As well as the god of senseless disaster, Saturn is the god of the contrivances by which, between disasters, men patch things up.[1] He causes accidents and keeps things going afterwards. The joining of these two functions in one god seems to me a real insight: they *have* to be joined in life, and the contrivances may be as senseless as the disasters.[2] So Saturn pleases the gods with his contrivance – but at the expense of the wholly senseless death of Arcite. The contrivance to restore peace on Olympus is itself the human disaster. Saturn's function, plotting or being violent, is to destroy significance; and the point of Arcite's death is the impossibility of seeing any justice in it. (It is of course often argued that what Saturn dispenses is *justice*: that both Arcite and Palamon get what they pray for, Arcite victory and Palamon Emelye, and that therefore they have no complaint against divine justice: to which I will only say that this is the kind of justice one expects from Saturn.)

So Arcite meets a death of which he can make no sense at all and which, in its cold factuality, is one of the most striking things in the poem. Some critics who shall be nameless take this as an unfortunate outburst of comedy at an inappropriate moment (but some people *do* find violent death amusing).

A 2743
    Swelleth the brest of Arcite   and the *soore*
Encreesseth at his herte   moore and moore
The clothered blood   *for* any lechecraft
Corrupteth   and is in his *bouk* ylaft
That neither veyne blood   ne *ventusynge*
Ne drynke of herbes   may ben his helpynge
The *vertu expulsif   or animal
Fro thilke vertu   cleped natural*
Ne may the venym   voyden ne expelle
The pipes of his longes   gonne to swelle
And every *lacerte*   in his brest adoun
Is *shent* with venym   and corrupcioun
Hym gayneth neither   for to gete his lif
Vomyt upward   ne dounward laxatif

Soore, wound; *for,* despite; *bouk,* trunk; *That,* so that; *ventusynge,* cupping; *vertu...natural* (in our physiology) nervous system, liver; *lacerte,* muscle; *shent,* done for.

[1] Madame Beck is thoroughly Saturnian, 'Wise, firm, faithless; secret, crafty, passionless; watchful and inscrutable; acute and insensate...' *Villette,* Chapter VIII.
[2] Chaucer reaches this traditional position despite himself for he says that Saturn's intervention to 'stynten strif' is 'agayn his kynde' (A 2451).

> Al is tobrosten   thilke regioun
> Nature hath now   no dominacioun
> And certeinly   ther Nature wol nat wirche
> Fare wel phisik   go ber the man to chirche
> This al and som   that Arcita moot dye

This passage works by sometimes delicate changes of tone, but none of them, not even the last lines, can be called comic. There is detailed and apparently scientific commentary ('vertu expulsif' and 'lacerte'), a homely version of the same material at the beginning, the sudden change to a highly but generally emotional tone with the word 'shent', and the formal philosophical statement about Nature leading to the wry commonsense (comic only in form – the commonsense tone in which we do sometimes recognize the unspeakable) of the end. The last line sums up the whole,

> This al and som   that Arcita moot dye

– Chaucer can say so with such succinct finality because he has created the fact in what goes before. It *is* almost a 'fact' that is created. Arcite's death is ordinary and clinical and, as befits a victim of Saturn, has no more nobility than a death certificate. It is as far from the solemnity of Theseus's closing speech as it is from the terrors of the temple of Mars. The problem it sets Theseus is made explicit in the already quoted final question of Arcite:

> A 2777
> What is this world?   what asketh men to have?
> Now with his love   now in his colde grave
> Allone   withouten any compaignye

This death and this question are asking Theseus what he can make of Saturn, and that is the central tragic concern of the tale.
 We may begin with this clue:

> A 2722
> For fallyng nys nat   but an aventure

This is applied to those wounded in the tournament, but it fits Arcite's case equally well. Even that sense-destroying event is only an event. By omitting Saturn from his pantheon, Theseus allows Arcite's death to upset his justice; but this forced recognition of Saturn is not necessarily a sign that Theseus is forced into chaos – any more than he has been by Mars, Venus or Diana. The end of *The Knight's Tale* is a triumphant vindication of Theseus.

The noble life can survive even the infortune of Saturn. To see
how this is so demands an explanation of why the great final speech
about Jupiter – the god we have yet to consider – takes the shape
it does.

The ground is prepared for the introduction of Jupiter by Arcite
himself. Although in his final words Arcite is as far as ever from
making the world either comprehensible or bearable, although in
his last desolate speech his concern is with the pointless misery of
life – with Saturn – Arcite has changed, and can find at the end a
manner quite different from anything we have heard from him
before:

A 2783
I have heer   with my cosyn Palamon
Had strif and rancour   many a day agon
For love of yow   and for my jalousye
And Juppiter *so wys*   my soule gye   as surely
To speken of a servaunt   proprely
With alle circumstances   trewely
That is to seyen   trouthe   honour   knyghthede
Wysdom   humblesse   estaat and heigh kynrede
Fredom   and al that longeth to that art
So Juppiter   have of my soule part
As in this world   right now ne knowe I non
So worthy to ben loved   as Palamon
That serveth yow   and wol doon al his lyf
And if that evere   ye shul ben a wyf
Foryet nat Palamon   the gentil man

Arcite has here attained a degree of self-knowledge. He is no
longer (like Landlord Bunce in *Mr. Weston's Good Wine*) blaming
God for everything; he now realizes his responsibility for his own
life, and that takes the form of wanting help from Jupiter and
recognizing that need as the most certain thing he has left. At
last, at this moment of Saturnian final disaster, Arcite is able, in
part, to 'maken vertu of necessitee'. Even of this situation something can be made. What he can do is to sound the knightly
virtues in a noble list – the tone, and the weight of the tale is the
guarantee of the nobility – to conquer his jealousy, after calling it
by its name, and commend Emelye to 'Palamon the gentil man'
in a touchingly courteous and tender way. Then follows, before the
Theseus speech, Arcite's uncourtly death, the remarks of Egeus,
and the ceremonies of Arcite's funeral.

The funeral is sometimes thought one of the tale's superfluities:
Chaucer did not manage to abridge the *Teseida* as severely as he

should have done, and his embarrassment is shown by the very odd example of his favourite device, *occupatio*, surely the longest on record, where for nearly fifty lines (A 2919–66) he says in detail exactly what he is not going to say about the funeral. The funeral is certainly in a way insubstantial, despite its detailed splendour. The ceremonies are performed with proper dignity, but they have nothing of the force and immediacy of the death they mark, and may be felt as inadequate to the occasion – the noble life looking here rather thin compared with 'life'. Still, the funeral is conducted properly. I wish to contend that both the proper performance and the inadequacy of the funeral are essential for the success of the end of the tale. The ceremonies need the Theseus speech, without which they are inconsequential; but without the proper celebration of the funeral and without Arcite's preceding change of heart Theseus would be set a very much harder task.

So we return to the consideration of the last speech of Theseus, and such is the unity of this non-novelistic tale that the speech can make or break it. Most of the recent commentators who have seen the speech's importance think it fails. (The most distinguished exception is Professor Muscatine; but he does not show how the speech succeeds.)

It is first necessary to see that the Theseus speech is not the series of logical lapses Professor Salter takes it to be.

The eloquence of the passage is beyond doubt: what is debatable is the wisdom of invoking 'the Firste Moevere of the cause above', with its inevitable Christian associations, to cover the activities of Mars, Venus and Saturn in this particular poem...A return to Boethian argument (ll. 3035–8) is not sustained; Theseus's reasoning descends to a practical sphere. The injunction

> 'To maken vertu of necessitee,
> And take it weel that we may nat eschue...'
> (3042–3)

represents good sense rather than wisdom: it is not simply wrong but 'folye' to rebel against 'hym that al may gye'. A list of useful points takes the speech further and further away from philosophic matters. We are asked to rejoice that Arcite died 'in his excellence and flour' (l. 3048) and then that he has escaped 'out of this foule prisoun of this lyf' (l. 3061)... only the confident flow of the poetry disguises the basic illogicality of the appeals.[1]

But this objection to Theseus's logic need be relevant only if he is trying to speak logically – which is not reasonably to be expected of a

---

[1] Elizabeth Salter, *Chaucer, 'The Knight's Tale' and 'The Clerk's Tale'*, Studies in English Literature Series, no. 5 (1962), p. 35.

man who is both a soldier and a ruler. And conversely the 'confident flow of the poetry' may carry more weight than any logical flaw can destroy, if this creation is a poetic one. Professor Salter offers no comment on the most glaring illogicality of all, the contradiction between the Boethian (and Aristotelian) opening about the 'fair chain of love' (A 2988) and the later section about the 'foule prison of this lyf' (3061). The latter is Chaucer's innovation on his sources. If every part derives from its whole and if the whole is the fair chain of love it is not easy to see how the parts, though finite, could be wretched, much less a 'foule prison'. In the other great passage where the same Boethian thought is expressed, the end of Book III of *Troilus and Criseyde*, there is no hint of the world's wretchedness. *Of course* the passage can be demolished as formal philosophical argument.[1] But the important contradiction, the one that counts for the reader of Chaucer's poetry, is in the nature of the world not the logic of Theseus. Palamon knows by the experience of the poem that the world is a prison. Theseus cannot deny it, but he knows equally well from his experience of the same story that love is also to be found ordering the world – knows, that is, that a life of nobility is possible. Johnson answered Boswell's request for reassurance about the certainty of the proofs of Christianity with a similar contradiction:

Sir, you cannot answer all objections. You have demonstration for a First Cause: you see he must be good as well as powerful, because there is nothing to make him otherwise, and goodness of itself is preferable. Yet you have against this, what is very certain, the unhappiness of human life.[2]

Mrs Salter seems to want Chaucer to say that a world which includes Venus, Mars and Saturn has no place for Jupiter. It is not Theseus who is here being simple-minded: he has had to learn the contrary in the course of the tale.

The Theseus speech falls into two sections, the first a discussion of mutability and in particular human mortality, the second a discussion of and decisions about the particular problems raised by the death of Arcite. It is at first surprising that Theseus should be concerned with death in general, and death in its widest context of life and the conditions of life. (That he is makes ludicrous the account of this part of the tale as the neat and tidy ending

---

[1] Though there is no necessary contradiction between seeing the world as a prison and believing that human life in the prison may yet have 'excellence and flower'. Cf. Dickens, *Little Dorrit, passim*.

[2] Boswell, 19 April 1778.

made by a Theseus anxious to get things arranged.[1]) By generalizing the problem of Arcite's death Theseus states it, in one way, at
its most difficult; but that is his way of making the death possible
to accept. The death of Arcite has been shocking, but it is a shocking
instance of what must happen to us all; and if Theseus can manage
to accept death, the place of an individual death, even one as
shocking as this, may follow naturally. But any 'acceptance' of
death must be a religious feeling, not a demonstration that all is
for the best in the world. Theseus has to take the same path as
Charlotte Brontë later follows after another terrible death:

I cannot forget Emily's death-day; it becomes a more fixed, a darker, a
more frequently recurring idea in my mind than ever. It was very terrible.
She was torn, conscious, panting, reluctant, though resolute, out of a
happy life. But it *will not do* to dwell on these things.[2]

That was written while Anne Brontë was dying. But almost the
next letter Mrs Gaskell quotes ends: 'Oh! if it would please God to
strengthen and revive Anne, how happy we might be together:
His will, however, be done!' It is by generalizing Arcite's death
that Theseus can dwell upon it and say 'His will be done'. Here
Egeus makes an instructive contrast (*pace* those numerous critics –
and Boccaccio – who take his speech as the positive wisdom of the
poem). Egeus seems to think that *because* death comes to all it
doesn't matter much. He begins with a fallacy beside which the
Theseus speech seems as tight as Bertrand Russell:

A 2843
  'Right as ther dyed nevere man'   quod he
  'That he ne lyvede in erthe   in some degree
  Right so ther lyvede never man'   he seyde
  'In al this world   that som tyme he ne deyde'

– which is contradicted by our continued existence – and he continues with those lines of Polonius-like wisdom on which Chaucer
records the opinion implied by the line I italicize:

A 2847
  'This world nys but   a thurghfare ful of wo
  And we been pilgrymes   passynge to and fro

---

[1] See, for instance, the otherwise interesting essay in which I find: 'And his
'[Theseus's] watchword is: politics as usual. Hence his philosophical reflections are enlisted rhetorically in the service of his marriage plans for Palamon
and Emily.' R. Neuse, 'The Knight: The First Mover in Chaucer's Human
Comedy', *University of Toronto Quarterly* XXXI (1962); reprinted in *Geoffrey
Chaucer, a Critical Anthology*, ed. J. A. Burrow (1969), p. 250.
[2] Quoted in Mrs Gaskell's *Life of Charlotte Brontë*, Chapter XVII.

> Deeth is an ende   of every worldly soore'
> *And over al this   yet seyde he muchel moore*

This is 'a low-spirited stoicism compounded of fear and resignation'.[1] By contrast Theseus's effort to say 'God's will be done,'
– or to say it better – comes from the strength of the poem, from
what makes me want to call it tragic.

The first part of the Theseus speech shows death as a necessary
condition of something worthwhile, which is, I think, why he
begins with life rather than death. 'All this thing moot deye' – but
one feels in the verse the worth of the mortal as well as its frailty.
Theseus knows that in Jupiter's universe the end is part of the very
idea of existence: we cannot live except in so far as we are also
doomed to die. Without death there could not be our life; and so
the acceptance of death need not be a defeat for life. The finality of
death is one of the conditions of any significance we may find in
life: if nothing is final everything can be altered. Theseus's
acceptance of death is the final extension of his power to worship
Venus and Mars in the noble life: they are all conditions of a
life that can be splendid. But as far as prose sense goes this position
is much like that of Egeus: the difference is in the conviction and
the depth of feeling expressed by the poetry. The speech is no
more to be judged as a logical exercise than Charlotte Brontë's
letters are; and if the reader shares my respect for the *poetry* of the
Theseus speech (above) he will also see that the speech is a fitting
climax to the tragedy.

Jupiter represents Theseus's sublime conviction that Saturn is
not the only or the final truth about the world; and he can refer to
Jupiter more convincingly because Arcite has already twice done
so. And this generalization of Arcite's death is the final sign that
the poem is not restricting its criticism to courtly life but is about
human life itself. The tests to which the noble life is subjected
turn out to be those any human life must pass.

But what of the death of Arcite? Theseus manages to pick up the
words Arcite himself has used, and to bring out the meaning of the
funeral ceremonies. Nothing Theseus says tries to alter the mere
senseless fact of Arcite's death. But he does alter its senselessness;
for even that death can now be seen as the occasion of Arcite's
final irreversible establishment in honour – in a sense, of his last
judgment and admission to glory. 'Honour', beautifully emphasized in Theseus's poetry, can be attained even by a man whose

---

[1] Conrad, *Victory*, Part I, Chapter VI.

death is as absurd as that. Falstaff could have profited by the passage – though one may sometimes also sympathize with his comment, 'I like not such grinning honour as Sir Walter hath.'[1] It is because I find Theseus's creation of honour out of the death of Arcite wholly convincing that I cannot agree with Mr Spearing's final comments: 'The twentieth century can perhaps legitimately see in this fourteenth-century poem a view of the human condition as neither comic nor tragic but absurd – a view of life similar to that expressed by a modern writer such as Samuel Beckett.'[2] Mr Spearing's remark could be true only if 'the human condition' were the same as 'life', which fortunately it is not. Even if one agreed that for the Knight the human condition is absurd it would not follow that he is saying that human life is absurd. The human condition includes Venus, Mars, Saturn (and swich rascaille) but human life is what we, perhaps in humble co-operation with Jupiter, make of the human condition. Hence I find Chaucer, whether or not like Samuel Beckett, the opposite of absurd at least in the sense that he is deeply engaged with the tragic *significance* of life.

By finding honour in the unintelligible death of Arcite, Theseus shows his life to be strong enough to continue, as Palamon marries Emelye. Mr Spearing makes a similar observation into a damning comment: 'Theseus has moved from unconvincing philosophical speculation to sensible practical advice; he has not shown that all is for the best in the world of the poem, but he has shown how to go on living in a world ruled by Saturn.'[3] But how intolerable it would have been if Theseus had tried to pretend that all *is* for the best in the world of the poem! 'How to go on living in a world ruled by Saturn' is precisely the tragic question the tale raises, and if Theseus answers it the courtly life had passed its final trial. Moreover, 'showing how to go on living in a world' could never be a petty achievement.

Theseus speaks the religious feeling of the whole tale when he says that wisdom is

---

[1] *1 Henry IV*, v, iii. A knowledge of *The Knight's Tale* might have led Byron, too, beyond the wonderment of his gloss on Falstaff:

> I wonder (although Mars no doubt's a god I
>   Praise) if a man's name in a *bulletin*
> May make up for a *bullet in* his body?
>   *Don Juan*, VII, st. xxi

[2] Spearing (ed.), *The Knight's Tale*, p. 79.
[3] *Ibid.*, p. 78.

SOME OF CHAUCER'S STORIES

A 3042
To maken vertu   of necessitee
And take it weel   that we may nat eschue

This emerges as much more than the lapse into commonsense
Mr Spearing and Professor Salter think it. There is something
strongly positive in this resignation, unlike Egeus's, something that
allows for the creation of honour. But, again, the strength is in the
movement of the poetry, not in the prose sense. (Cf. 'For since by
man came death, by man came also the resurrection of the dead'[1]
which also looks like an argument, but whose force depends
(whatever Paul intended) on the quasi-poetic movement repre-
senting a feeling. It is this, not any crazy logic, that Handel's
setting brings out.) To be able at last to

A 3069
thanken Juppiter   of al his grace

is a triumph, though not of logic. Chaucer here makes ideas we
associate with renunciation and negation a centre of strength from
which one may look Saturn in the face and continue life. 'The
reference to Jupiter', says Mr Spearing, 'again rings hollow; what
"grace" of his has been displayed in the story we have been
following?'[2]

This is a good question, if only because it is virtually the same as
the one asked by the dying Arcite. One way of answering it would
be to continue the critical commentary, trying further to show that
the 'ring' of the speech is far from 'hollow'. But I will answer
instead with the two already-mentioned lines that condense, much
more than the 'Palinode', the religious feeling of *Troilus and
Criseyde*:

V 1749
In ech estat   is litel hertes reste
God leve us   for to take it for the beste

– 'God grant us the power to make the best of it.' The capacity to
'take it for the best' is the grace of Jupiter in *The Knight's Tale*.
Even after the machinations of the other gods, Jupiter can grant
Theseus the power to continue the noble life not senselessly but
with acceptance and hope. We see the power of Jupiter at work in
the change in Arcite (the groundwork of the achievement of
Theseus) and in the way Theseus can show Arcite's honour.

[1] I Cor. xv. 21.
[2] *The Knight's Tale*, p. 78.

Jupiter is true to the life of the tale: it is Jupiter, not the Knight's liking of happy endings[1], that gives Theseus the chance to create at the end

A 3071   of sorwes two
O parfit joye   lastynge everemo[2]

As for the theology of Theseus, his expression of belief in terms of a first mover superior to Saturn, I can only say that I am unphilosophical enough to think his argument a very strong one. Saturn boasts about the wideness of his orbit, that his power includes that of the other gods. But there is still a way in which Jupiter comes before Saturn. The oak does end, as Theseus says; it ends because, in this mythology, Saturn, the 'bringer of old age',[3] makes it die. But who made the oak? The creation must come before the destruction even though we could not imagine the oak immortal: you or I can, like Saturn, destroy an oak tree, but we can't make one. Jupiter may be superior to Saturn even if Saturn is powerful and uncontrolled.

Theseus rescues the tale from determinism even in a world (as ours is) within the orbit of Saturn, but in a radically unmodern way. (If the phrase 'the medieval mind' could ever be made sense of it would be with regard to *The Knight's Tale*.) The deliverance, like that in Chaucer's *Trouthe*, comes only to those who receive what is sent 'in buxumnesse'. The Knight puts this deliverance before us with the clarity and power only a great tragic poet could command.[4]

[1] Cf. the Knight's very naive interruption of the Monk – a justifiable response but not a convincing literary theory – at B 3957ff.
[2] It is the absence of any such notion as 'Jupiter' that makes Mr Koonce's account of the two Venuses (above p. 56) so unconvincing. The aspects of Venus cannot be ruled: we can only pray to another God to allow us to 'take her wel': if the prayer is granted and we are not destroyed by Venus we have cause for gratitude not only to the goddess herself but also to Jupiter.
[3] Holst, *The Planets*.
[4] This 'deliverance' is of the order of Silas Marner's, though more solemn and tragic. I mention George Eliot's novel because like Chaucer's poem it is commonly both underrated and misunderstood. George Eliot is thought to tamper with the scales of providence, in the interests of sentimentality. *Silas Marner* is certainly full of convenient coincidences: Eppie arrives just at the right moment, after her mother has died at just the right spot for her to be able to wander past Silas, Silas happening to be in a cataleptic trance at his open door. But what makes this 'the right moment'? It is mistaken to see benevolent gods dictating the action in the same way as it is mistaken to see *The Knight's Tale* as deterministically controlled by Saturn. The lots drawn in Lantern Yard proclaim Marner's guilt – but only in that language: it is obvious enough that the drawing of lots can't *force* anybody to do or think anything (though one can see how

One offshoot of the tale's worship of Jupiter is that it reflects back on the more social criticism of the noble life we discussed earlier. For these lines about Jupiter represent Chaucer's achievement of final trust in Theseus – whose failings he knows very well. This is part of

A 2482
The grete effect   for which that I bygan

that Chaucer, the most intelligent and sceptical man of his century, works in *The Knight's Tale* to a position of trust in the military aristocracy. If Theseus shows how to go on with life, that is the life in question. Here Chaucer shows an utter freedom from literary eccentricity that marks his final emergence from the style of *The Book of the Duchess*. Chaucer knows all about the shortcomings of Theseus but he *doesn't* want the philosophers to be kings.

IV

We need at least to understand the kind of religious language Theseus speaks, to see why the death of Arcite can be tragic as well as squalid, if we are to make anything significant of our own lives and deaths.

So I would like to call *The Knight's Tale* a tragedy and Chaucer a tragic poet. But tragedy is an enactment, and Chaucer's story is not enacted even to the extent possible in a novel: as a story it has little of the impact of tragedy. The gods are a kind of substitute for enactment: they give the reader the kind of direct involvement with the tragic depths (the facing what is terrible and perceiving it as divine) which a novel gets by telling or a play by enacting a story. But if the noun is too much to swallow here perhaps I may be permitted at least the adjective. The sense in which the tale is tragic is a real one, not merely the sense often attributed to Chaucer

natural it is for Marner's faith to collapse as a result of the lots, how providential that they should be *wrong*, so showing Marner that God doesn't manipulate us in the way he wants to believe). But especially there is nothing determined in what Marner does when he finds Eppie. ('BOSWELL. "If, Sir, you were shut up in a castle, and a new-born child with you, what would you do?" JOHNSON. "Why, Sir, I should not much like my company."' (26 October 1769.)) The last thing that would occur to me if I found a child on the hearth would be to try to keep it: I would telephone the police at once. But Marner naturally (the naturalness is one of the book's triumphs) keeps Eppie. There is no conscious decision; it is because he 'finds himself able' (the phrase is Mr David Sims's) to make *this* of the situation that one can see a grace of God in the tale, very like the power of Jupiter Theseus celebrates.

and in fact that of one of his least intellectually reliable characters, the Monk.[1] For the Monk tragedy is the kind of enjoyment of sentiment in which to this day his style of 'manly man' may often be found indulging. But Chaucer's description of *Troilus and Criseyde* as a 'tragedye' (v 1786) gives his sense of the word. *The Knight's Tale* is about fate in the same way as *Troilus and Criseyde*, and much more successfully.

Tragedy is always about the interaction of a man with the gods, often when he defies or fails to recognize them. 'In Shakespeare or Sophocles the greater, uncomprehended morality, or fate, is actively transgressed and gives active punishment.'[2] But to call Venus or Mars in *The Knight's Tale* moral in any sense whatever would be ridiculous. 'Out of greed for adventure, a desire to be off, Agamemnon sacrifices Iphigenia: moreover he has his love-affairs outside Troy: and this brings on him death from the mother of his daughter, and from his pledged wife. Which is the working of the natural law.'[3] It is true that tragedy may often make that kind of sense: we live (thank God) in a world where there is nothing very surprising in Macbeth's coming to a bad end. But *The Knight's Tale* shows the opposite, the failure of divine justice or 'the natural law' in human affairs; and that too is something that is observable in the world.

Had Œdipus, Hamlet, Macbeth been weaker, less full of real, potent life, they would have made no tragedy; they would have comprehended and contrived some arrangement of their affairs, sheltering in the human morality from the great stress and attack of the unknown morality. But being, as they are, men to the fullest capacity, when they find themselves, daggers drawn, with the very forces of life itself, they can only fight till they themselves are killed.[4]

The Knight's Tale, however, makes a distinction which Lawrence might have found useful, and which may suggest the tale's place in *our* world. The achievement of Theseus is certainly a contrivance, as much a contrivance as Saturn's plot, but of a quite different kind. The tale shows the importance of distinguishing the manoeuvrings of the latter from Theseus's patient waiting upon 'Jupiter the

---

[1] B 3163   Tragedie is to seyn a certeyn storie
               As olde bookes maken us memorie
               Of hym that stood in greet prosperitee
               And is yfallen out of heigh degree
               Into myserie and endeth wrecchedly.
[2] D. H. Lawrence, *Study of Thomas Hardy*, Chapter III; *Phoenix*, pp. 419–20.
[3] *Ibid.*, p. 439.
[4] *Ibid.*, p. 420.

king'. If Theseus with Jupiter is contriving a life that can do little more than survive in the world of the gods, his contrivance is at least as fully and tragically aware of what we find in 'life itself' as Lawrence. Chaucer may show in this tale a tragic truth that we need to complement Lawrence, or Shakespeare, or Sophocles.

The Knight's Tale can do so only if it develops – for the first time in our language – a tragic style; and it is sad that Arnold could not recognize parts of the tale as a style of high seriousness, even in his sense of the phrase. Arnold's difficulty was perhaps in the peculiar Englishness of Chaucer's tragic style: it is, I argued, not restricted to the decorous, and it has strong links with spoken language, unlike Virgil or Arnold's image of Homer. (Theseus's speech is convincingly a speech to a parliament.) What such observations mean for our relative valuation of Chaucer and Dante is the subject of a later chapter: here I will just suggest that *The Knight's Tale* shows there can be medieval poetry of full tragic seriousness which is yet not committed to any philosophical programme or to any continuous literary decorum – which can be exploratory and tentative rather than, with Dante, assured and determined to be assured, and which can recognize the injustice as well as the sense in life.

So when Mr Speirs says, '*The Knight's Tale* is continually on the point of moving beyond itself (as *par excellence* a courtly romance) into a substantiality that would be that of comedy or tragedy; yet it never completely does move beyond courtly romance, as does *Troilus and Criseyde*',[1] I do want to go a little further and see it as 'moving beyond itself' into a seriousness we can properly call tragic. And *The Knight's Tale* is as important for our sense of what is truly great in Chaucer as *The Wife of Bath's Prologue* or *The Miller's Tale*.

---

[1] *Chaucer the Maker*, p. 123.

9

The Religious Tales

'Bookes of legendes of seintes and omelies and moralitee and devocioun' (H 1088) form a surprisingly large part of *The Canterbury Tales*, but only three of them are of very much interest. *Melibee* is Chaucer's demonstration that he can write precious prose; *The Parson's Tale* is his proof that he can write a sermon as dull as the real thing can be; *The Second Nun's Tale* is Chaucer's membership card of that flourishing fourteenth-century guild, the manufacturers of saints' lives. Apart from *The Physician's Tale* (a minor success of a not very profound kind) the possibly interesting religious tales are those of the Prioress, the Man of Law and the Clerk; and about these three there is a dominant tradition of criticism which I believe mistaken and misleading in its central assumption that they are all three much the same sort of thing.

It is because this assumption is believed by some of the best critics that I think it worth refuting. Mr R. O. Payne, for instance, whose book has helped me in several ways, writes of Chaucer's Saints' Legends 'In only one of these is the protagonist literally a saint, but in form and effect, as well as in the characters of the protagonists, they are so alike that the distinction is doctrinal rather than literary.'[1] This makes me want to protest on behalf of *The Clerk's Tale*.

Going with the belief that the tales are 'so alike that the distinction is doctrinal rather than literary' one often finds (though not in Mr Payne's work) exasperation with what is thought to be the sentimentality of all three. The 'litel clergeoun' of *The Prioress's Tale*, Constance, and Patient Griselda, are all felt to be representatives of a sickly-sweet goodness, all white and sweet and pure, a style of virtue admired in its century but simply of its time and place and with nothing to say from the past in our world. In other words the moral and religious feeling of all three tales is thought to be stone dead. They all appear to share an unreal

[1] R. O. Payne, *The Key of Remembrance* (New Haven, 1963), p. 157, footnote.

sentiment about mothers and infants that may make the reader
want afterwards to go and rinse his mind in something like *The
Miller's Tale.* A variation on this common view is to see Chaucer's
sentiment as effective but the enemy of real religious depth and of
artistic control.[1]

It seems to me that these three tales are quite different, that the
reactions I have described are fully appropriate to none of them,
and that *The Clerk's Tale* stands out as one of Chaucer's most
finely and daringly exploratory poems, the opposite of sentimental. A feeling that *The Clerk's Tale* is not to be lightly dis-
missed comes out in the work of our two best critics in a similar
tentative way. Mr Speirs is here at his most tantalizing, making
remarks which he doesn't follow up, the most interesting coming
in his section about *The Man of Law's Tale*: 'There is the same
quality of tenderness for Griselda and her child in the *Clerk's
Tale.* The natural human feeling has acquired a peculiar sanctity
and grace which we should hesitate to find sentimental.'[2] But he
doesn't say *how* the sanctity and grace have been acquired or
what difference it makes to our thinking about the poem. Professor
Muscatine records this impression, with which I heartily agree:
'[*The Clerk's Tale*] requires rereading; and with successive readings
one's indifference turns to tolerance, then to admiration.'[3] But
apart from a few hints which I shall gratefully use he too does not
explore very far how the tale works to create the admiration.

I

The Prioress's Tale is the easiest to grasp of the three, though
critics have not always found it so. In the fifteenth century the
tale was occasionally detached from the other Canterbury Tales
and bound up with pious collections, so it must have been acceptable to some people as an ordinary Miracle of the Virgin, presumably to be read aloud for the edification of the devout. If so
the devout were imposed upon, and the tale has occasionally been
seen by later critics as simply a satire. F. N. Robinson comments
in his edition that the latter view is 'certainly mistaken'.[4] I agree:
but how do we know? To answer that question would be to see
that the real mistake is in supposing these are the alternatives.

---

[1] The most widely influential modern statement of this last view is Professor
Salter's *Chaucer, 'The Knight's Tale' and 'The Clerk's Tale'.*
[2] *Chaucer the Maker,* p. 135.
[3] *Chaucer and the French Tradition,* p. 191.   [4] P. 734.

It is mistaken to try to decide whether Chaucer is for or against the Prioress's kind of piety. What strikes one is that he is superior to it: he condescends to the Prioress by humouring her.

Much of what the Prioress says, both in her Prologue and her tale, has a touching beauty and even, sometimes, more strength than one might expect. Her Prologue links her own tender feelings with a more seemingly powerful god than the one she worships in *The General Prologue*.

> B 1643
> 'O Lord oure Lord   thy name how merveillous
> Is in this large world ysprad'   quod she
> 'For noght oonly   thy laude precious
> Parfourned is   by men of dignitee
> But by the mouth of children   thy bountee
> Parfourned is   for on the brest soukynge
> Somtyme shewen they   thyn *heriynge*'   praising

The condescension is not cheap; Chaucer is allowing her religion whatever power and her emotion whatever religious depth it can achieve. Again,

> B 1745
> The swetnesse   hath his herte perced so
> Of Cristes mooder   that to hire to preye
> He kan nat stynte   of syngyng by the weye

– that does express to me a touchingly beautiful religious senti- ment, though even here there is a hint that the child never knows when to stop. So I find it hard to sympathize with the view that one's complete response to the Prioress should be a sneer.

Nevertheless the tale is not to be taken at face value as a Miracle of the Virgin, for the religious feeling is shown to be damagingly limited and, in some ways, perverse. The limitation comes out clearly enough in, for instance, the Prioress's use of her favourite word 'litel'. The school is 'litel' (though it contains (B 1687) 'children an heep'); the child is a 'litel clergeon, seven yeer of age' (B 1693) and a 'litel' son (of a widow, of course) (B 1699). Even his grammar is a little one:

> B 1706
> This litel child   his litel book lernynge

and when, long after he should have died 'by weye of kynde' (B 1840) he at last lies down,

B 1871
 in a tombe of marbul stones cleere
Enclosen they his litel body sweete

There can be surely no doubt about the sweet but limited emotion of these lines; and a similar feeling (*pace* Professor D. W. Robertson) is in the Prioress's use of 'innocent'. It is true that 'innocent' is a respectable theological term which the Prioress uses correctly, but what she expresses are the sweet emotions that her story attaches to the word.

One way of showing the limitation of this style is to point out that very often the Prioress is on the very edge of unintentional comedy. She is so securely cut off from the world that she has no idea when the worldlings might find her funny; the *ridiculousness* of the last half-line of the Abbot's question to the half-dead child is as much part of the verse as the sentimentality:

B 1837
Tel me what is thy cause for to synge
Sith that thy throte is kut to my semynge

And if one is in the wrong mood it can make good sense to take the child's reply as successful black humour:

B 1839
'My throte is kut unto my nekke boon'
Seyde this child

The way we enjoy the Prioress's sentiments establishes her devotion as itself 'litel'. She is tenderly sentimental about the martyr in much the same way as she is about her dogs in *The General Prologue*: and we may go along with and enjoy this without making it very important. Perhaps 'charming' is the word for this style of religion. What is not so charming is the Prioress's attitude to the Jews. There the sentimentality is so thoughtless as to be wicked; the tenderness is seen to be connected, by way of unintelligence, with something the opposite of tender. The Prioress's view of the Jews is, as one might expect, a very naive one.

B 1678
 Ther was in Asye in a greet citee
Amonges Cristene folk a Jewerye
Sustended by a lord of that contree
For foule usure and lucre of vileynye
Hateful to Crist and to his compaignye

This is the ordinary medieval Christian party line. Chaucer, unlike Ezra Pound, is not given to first person denunciations of

Usura: but whether or not he approved of it, the force of these lines is surely in the unintelligence of the Prioress's emotion. The question why usury is so villainous and if so why a lord should sustain it cannot occur to her: she prefers to enjoy the hatred. So it follows for the Prioress, whose 'conscience' has nothing to do with intelligence, that the Jews (in general) should as a matter of course commit out of mere hatred of Christianity a murder likely to produce (as in fact it does in the tale) disastrous reprisals. At the end of the tale the pious tenderness about the martyr comes into surprising adjacence to the rancour and injustice towards the Jews. Both these things are equally part of the Prioress's religion.

B 1811

This child   with pitous lamentacioun
Up taken was   syngynge his song alway
And with honour   of greet processioun
They carien hym   unto the *nexte* abbay   nearest
His mooder swownynge   by the beere lay
Unnethe myghte the peple   that was theere   hardly
This newe Rachel   brynge fro his beere

With torment   and with shameful deeth echon
This provost dooth thise Jewes   for to *sterve*   die
That of this mordre wiste   and that anon
He nolde   no swich cursednesse   observe
Yvele shal have   that yvele wol deserve
Therfore with wilde *hors*   he dide hem drawe   horses
And after that   he heng hem by the lawe

The transition between the two sets of emotions is made as abrupt as possible by the way the languishing half-lines of the first quoted stanza are immediately followed by the inversion 'With torment. . .' – this is abrupt for us but not for the Prioress because for her there is *no* transition; the two emotions are inseparable. In the second stanza not only the murderers but everyone who is supposed to have known of the murder are lynched – the proceedings cannot be called even 'savage and summary justice'[1] since death precedes trial.

Any apology for the Prioress here must be a way of showing the unreality of her religion, its discontinuity with any real world. It might be said that her hatred of Jews is unlike and less dangerous than modern anti-Semitism. Perhaps some notion of the history of the Jews in medieval England is necessary if we are not to respond with inappropriate modern reflexes. (F. N. Robinson does

---

[1] G. H. Russell, 'Chaucer: The Prioress's Tale', *Medieval Literature and Civilization*, ed. D. A. Pearsall and R. A. Waldron (1969), p. 223.

not supply the necessary note.) The Jews were closer to coming over with the Conqueror than most of the aristocratic English families who like to think they were in that dubious boat. The Jews were indispensable to the advanced feudal system of Norman times, which condemned usury but could no longer manage without it: the contempt of a landed aristocracy for the suppliers of credit was overcome by the need for credit; so for a time the Jews were tolerated. Their separateness of religion and race fitted their role as people doing necessary work too dirty for Christians. The difference between their situation and that of the coloured immigrants who do the dirty work in modern Britain was, of course, that the Jews were rich, which gave a particular edge to anti-Jewish sentiment. During the thirteenth century the Jews of England were subjected to a series of violent and mean persecutions the general effect of which was to kill Jews while preserving their property for those whose orthodoxy was proved by the killing. This 'cursedness' could be 'observed' because by the thirteenth century alternative sources of credit were becoming available. (So it was that when Edward III repudiated his debts in 1339 the sufferers were Christians, albeit Italians.) The Jews made several unsuccessful applications to be allowed to leave England, and in 1290 their request was granted, on the condition of the forfeiture of their non-portable property. (Some of this is reputed still to stand in Lincoln, the home town of the 'yonge Hugh' of line B 1874.) So the Prioress, a provincial Englishwoman who wanted to be fashionable, was speaking a hundred years after the departure of the Jews, of whom Chaucer's audience would have had little personal knowledge except on their travels.

But if the hatred is not of real Jews it must be as unreal and limited as the love of the martyr. This means in turn that what matters is the feeling defined within the tale. We are not called upon to judge it with reference to the 'real life' of Chaucer's times or our own, but as a tradition of feeling, made available directly to us by the tale. What Chaucer himself 'really' thought about the Jews we don't know, though it would be surprising in a responsible public servant if he were as simple-minded and savage as the Prioress. Whether Chaucer liked or disliked the Jews, he uses the Prioress's feeling about them to show up the unreality of her religion.[1] That the stupidity of her hatred is now

[1] Cf. Langland's attitude to the Jews in *Piers Plowman* B-text passus XVIII–XIX. Langland as usual is simpler than Chaucer and closer to the Prioress.

archaic will not rescue her religion as religion. We might view it with the disinterested fascination of Frazer inspecting savage rituals, but that is a way of no longer taking it seriously on its own terms. At best we might say that the Prioress is a gentle lady given to savage opinions about what she knows nothing of. (During the Second World War the gentlest old woman I knew, whom the war hardly touched, was strongly of the opinion that all German prisoners of war ought to be burned to death.) But in that case the Prioress's religion is a sort of private luxury, hardly a religion at all. Her religion could not be a strength in adversity, and it could say nothing about God. It is insufficient for a woman who was as near as any woman could come to being entrusted with a cure of souls.

The Prioress's Tale is perfect, and in the way in which *The Canterbury Tales* are often thought to have most strength. If Chaucer's procedure is to view the different life-styles of the pilgrims from some serene untouched centre, then *The Prioress's Tale* is of the essence of Chaucer. We see the Prioress's religion with perfect clarity and detachment, in all its charm and depravity. Nevertheless the tale's perfection is a minor perfection. Chaucer can clear up this area of religion in a couple of hundred lines, and there is no reason to suppose it mattered more deeply to him than it does to us. The value of the tale is perfectly in the precise degree of seriousness the evaluation of the Prioress calls forth from the poet. I cannot see the tale as one of Chaucer's greatest, because the subject cannot go deep enough with him, or with us. It is perfect but, as D. H. Lawrence remarked, 'For me, give me a little splendour and I'll leave perfection to the small fry.'[1]

The Physician's Tale is the complementary minor perfection. It is perfectly uncritical: everything is clear and decent and there is no irony and no exploration at all. All the values are given, and the tale refers to them rather than creating them or exploring them. And so like *The Prioress's Tale*, *The Physician's Tale* is perfect – but minor because, for the opposite reason, it is taking no risks. It is not a great work because there is no deep imaginative involvement in it. Both these tales take their place as decidedly less interesting than the great poems that characterize the Canterbury Tales – the ones I have called 'pure poetry', *The Knight's Tale*, *The Franklin's Tale* – and *The Clerk's Tale*.

---

[1] A comment on Edwin Muir's phrase 'There remain [Lawrence's] gifts, splendid in their imperfection...' 'Accumulated Mail', *Phoenix*, p. 804.

II

The Man of Law's Tale and *The Clerk's Tale* are more difficult and more interesting than *The Prioress's Tale* because in them Chaucer is committing himself further. In *The Man of Law's Tale* he is committed *not* to 'place' the piety in such a detached way – and to attempt a more substantial and important moral feeling than we have in *The Physician's Tale*. But the lack of criticism is at the same time the great weakness of *The Man of Law's Tale*. In the interests of seriousness Chaucer seems to be trying to stifle his critical intelligence, which occasionally breaks out, with results disastrous to the poem and its notion of seriousness.

In *The Man of Law's Tale* Chaucer seems to be trying to create the aura of magical significance sometimes to be found at that end of the range of Saint's Life which continues without a break into folk tale. Shakespeare can bring ghosts and witches into plays but where can Chaucer – whose world in some ways is more rational – go for any comparable sense of mystery? I have argued that the gods of *The Knight's Tale* are convincingly divine, but their style of speaking is not at all numinous. For that one might expect Chaucer to go to folk ballads – things like

> O they rade on, and farther on,
>   And they waded through rivers aboon the knee,
> And they saw neither sun nor moon,
>   But they heard the roaring of the sea.

> It was mirk mirk night, and there was nae *stern* light,   star
>   And they waded through red blude to the knee;
> For a' the blude, that's shed on earth,
>   Rins through the springs o' that countrie.[1]

But Chaucer the courtly poet is more effectively cut off from folk poetry than Alexander Pope (which is not to say that his language is as discontinuous with the language of folk poetry as Pope's). If Chaucer is trying for a sense of the numinous, there may seem good reason why he should not be trying to 'place' the sense. It is one thing to put the Prioress's religion in perspective, another to do the same thing for a ghost in a literary tradition which does not permit ghosts. A criticized miracle collapses: only Shakespeare can laugh at a ghost without destroying its ghostliness.[2] The equi-

---

[1] 'Thomas the Rhymer.' I quote the most poetic version I know, from *Border Ballads*, ed. William Beattie (1952), p. 225.
   Hamlet, I, v.

valent of the ghost here is the aura of miraculous sanctity surrounding Custance, which Chaucer seems to be attempting quite
uncritically. The best moments in the tale are those where he
brings it off.

B 551
That oon of hem was blynd   and myghte nat see
But it were with   thilke eyen of his mynde
With which men seen   after that they ben blynde

There are some few successful moments of this kind, but they are a
small fraction of what seems a long tale. (Is *The Man of Law's Tale*
longer than *The Clerk's Tale*? It seems – and therefore *is*? – longer,
but in fact *The Man of Law's Tale* has the smaller number of
lines.) Chaucer fills out *The Man of Law's Tale* with whatever more
or less suitable material comes to hand. The tale gives him a
chance to indulge at length the sentiments about mothers and
children which we noticed in *The Prioress's Tale*. Chaucer seems
to enjoy this emotionality and here too it is beautiful enough,
though it would have been stronger if he could have judged it as
part of the creation – or if it had not been feeble (to make the obvious
comparison) beside Dante's account of Ugolino of Pisa.[1]

But Chaucer seems under a strain to keep up the right feelings.
Several different pieces of celestial machinery are switched in. As
well as God we have Fortune, Satan and several of the astrological
deities; but they all seem dragged in to inflate the sense of significance: the astrology is present, apparently, very unlike the gods
of *The Knight's Tale*, only to impress the reader into taking the
tale with a seriousness it doesn't really deserve. The result is that
the tale may misfire by provoking as to answer the rhetorical
questions *wrong*.

B 309
Imprudent Emperour of Rome   allas
Was ther no *philosophre*   in al thy toun?   (here), astrologer
Is no tyme bet than oother   in swich cas?
Of viage is ther   noon eleccioun
Namely to folk   of heigh condicioun?
Noght whan a roote   is of a burthe yknowe?
Allas we been to lewed   or to slowe

Certain times are certainly better than others for alliances and
marriages, and a thorough understanding of characters and

---

[1] *Inferno* XXXIII; used by Chaucer well enough, but with less power and more
sentiment, in *The Monk's Tale*.

circumstances is necessary; but NO, 'philosophres' are not the people to consult; if they *are* consulted any sense they may achieve has nothing to do with roots of births; and the line about 'high condition' is just a characteristic bit of snobbery which we can again answer NO to.

The other kind of rhetorical question, the one without an answer, is found for instance here:

B 939
Who yaf Judith   corage or hardynesse
To sleen hym Olofernus   in his tente?

– which we might answer, 'Who indeed?' There are several like this.

A sign of the same strain is the frequent resort to apostrophes in the grand manner, whether it be to vices (B 925 O foule lust of luxurie...) or the hypothetical audience (B 562 O queenes lyvynge in prosperitee) or those villains, whether Satan, the Sultaness or the careless messengers, who are never allowed to do anything wrong without a solemn high style denunciation:

B 358
O Sowdanesse   roote of iniquitee...

B 365
O Sathan   envious syn thilke day...

B 771
O messager   fulfild of dronkenesse...

There are whole strings of these, stanzas at a time, and I don't see why I should take them seriously in the work of a poet who elsewhere shows us real poetic seriousness.

The final sign that Chaucer can't keep up the mysterious holiness comes in the occasional lapse into the manner of the Wife of Bath which is, in this context, very like giggling in church:

B 272
Housbondes been alle goode   and han ben yoore
That knowen wyves   I dar sey yow na moore

B 708
    They goon to bedde   as it was skile and right
For thogh that wyves   be ful hooly thynges
They moste take in pacience   at nyght
Swiche manere necessaries   as been plesynges
To folk that han ywedded hem   with rynges
And leye a lite   hir hoolynesse aside
As for the tyme   it may no bet bitide

This, like the occasional lapses in *The Parson's Tale* (for example, I, 422ff.), destroys the atmosphere. *The Knight's Tale*, on the other hand, can include a good deal of comedy; which is a sign that its seriousness is altogether more robust. But in *The Man of Law's Tale* one remembers *this* 'pacience' more easily than the solemn virtue the tale is supposed to be exemplifying: the tale cannot live in the world of Chaucer's other, stronger styles. The result is that it fails to make its morality: in a way the tale takes its revenge on the morality. When we come to these lines we are plainly meant to feel a strong moral, embodied by the whole tale:

> B 824
> But nathelees   she taketh in good entente
> The wyl of Crist   and knelynge on the stronde
> She seyde 'Lord   ay welcome be thy *sonde*'   sending

In *The Clerk's Tale* these lines might have been convincing; in *The Man of Law's Tale* they fall flat; which is one of the signs that the tale has to be more than a convenient cloak for the moral. So too the great villainess of the piece, the Sultaness, looks to me a relatively heroic figure, defending what she believes in against the weak caprice of her son.

The Man of Law's Tale is Chaucer's nearest approach to Lydgate. It seems to be not the creation of anyone's belief – the Man of Law's[1] or Chaucer's – but the result of a mechanical determination to practise the art of religious tale-telling which is only occasionally justified by convincingly mysterious feeling.

III

Even before facing the central problems of *The Clerk's Tale* we can see that it is much better written than the Man of Law's. The openings of the two poems make a revealing contrast. In *The Man of Law's Tale* the poet's emphases are in all the wrong places and one's attention tends to wander. The verse form does little beyond commanding us, by being rhyme-royal, to take the poem with a seriousness not created in the verse.

> B 134
> In *Surrye* whilom   dwelte a compaignye
> Of †chapmen† riche   and therto ‡sadde‡ and trewe
>
>   * Syria   † merchants   ‡ serious

---

[1] One of the minor objections is that the tale seems to be told by three different characters: the amusing critic of Chaucer's works (B 47–95) who could be the Man of Law of *The General Prologue*; the odd speaker of the tale's disconnected Prologue; and the sentimental teller of the tale itself.

These rich merchants are of no importance to the tale but are introduced with a solemn emphasis sufficient for the tale's hero; the heroine, however, slips in almost unawares in a careless-looking subordinate clause:

B 148
   Sojourned han thise merchantz   in that toun
A certein tyme   as fil to hire plesance
And so bifel that   thexcellent renoun
Of thEmperoures doghter   dame Custance
Reported was   with every circumstance
Unto this Surryen marchantz   in swich wyse
Fro day to day   as I shal yow devyse

That is second-rate verse. It is thrown down carelessly: there is no fit between form and sense – as if this were the first way of putting it that occurred to Chaucer and he thought, 'Oh well, that will have to do'. Chaucer's padding lines and half-lines often serve to emphasize some intense statement at their side, but I can think of no good reason why the sense of this stanza should stop, as it does, two and a half lines before the end.

The Clerk's Tale begins:

E 57
   Ther is   right at the west syde of Ytaille
Doun at the roote   of Vesulus the colde
A lusty playn   habundant of vitaille
Where many a tour and toun   thou mayst biholde
That founded were   in tyme of fadres olde
And many another   delitable sighte
And Saluces   this noble contree highte

   A markys whilom   lord was of that lond
As were his worthy eldres   hym bifore
And obeisant   ay redy to his hond
Were alle his liges   bothe lasse and moore
Thus in delit he lyveth   and hath doon yoore
Biloved and drad   thurgh favour of Fortune
Bothe of his lordes   and of his commune

This has long been, in connection with its tale, one of my favourite passages of Chaucer, and I do not think I am only following a whim. But it is not easy to say why this opposite extreme from the Wife of Bath's plunge into her subject is as attractive as *The Wife of Bath's Prologue*. The attractiveness is a function of tone, but that is not distinct from the very careful way the passage gets the subject on the move. The first stanza does not introduce any of the tale's major figures but it does establish very well the scene's feeling in its tone. The quiet definitenesss expresses right from the start a tone that is later seen to be specifically the Clerk's, and which is maintained throughout the poem with none of the Man of Law's lapses. (Muscatine, *Chaucer and the French Tradition*, Chapter 6, part 2 (ii) writes well of this style of the Clerk's.) Chaucer is here getting the rhythm so right, giving each word just the weight it needs, that the passage is as fully itself as anything said by the Wife of Bath, though slower and more formal. Despite what Professor Muscatine calls the style's 'frugality' it is not thin. When Walter is introduced in the second stanza it is in this already established tone, with an emphasis suitable to his place in the tale. In parallel with 'Saluces' he is named in the last line of the third stanza. (Griselda is introduced in a very similar way at the beginning of Part II.) And for all the restraint of this style it is not divorced from the life of the spoken language – which is not the monopoly of those who use it like the Miller. The rhetorical balances within and between lines are a heightening of speech; and for instance the parallel phrases of the last quoted couplet give a real concentration of feeling and sense.

The Prologue and the first two parts of *The Clerk's Tale* may be found attractive by readers who cannot take the rest. There is a Wordsworthian willingness to recognize truths calmly (perhaps a better way round would be to say there is a streak of the Clerk in Wordsworth) in lines like

E 36
But deeth   that wol nat suffre us dwellen heer
But as it were   a twynklyng of an ye
Hem bothe hath slayn   and alle shul we dye

The materially poor life of Janicula and Griseld is spiritually and emotionally attractive: the chastity of style is an obviously appropriate medium for describing this pleasing temperance of life, which may remind one of the opening of *The Nun's Priest's Tale*, done with less particularity. We are not told the name of Griselda's sheep, but unlike Custance she lives in a world from which sheep need not be excluded. And the description of Griselda, though it concentrates on her morality, is far from suggesting that she is unattractive or sexless:

E 211
    But for to speke   of vertuous beautee
    Thanne was she oon   the faireste under sonne

For povreliche   yfostred up was she
No *likerous lust*   was thurgh hire herte yronne
Wel ofter of the welle   than of the tonne
She drank   and for she wolde vertu plese
She knew wel labour   but noon ydel ese

   But thogh this mayde   tendre were of age
Yet in the brest   of hire virginitee
Ther was enclosed   rype and sad †corage†

    * sensual desire   † the bent of the heart

This is the opposite of the separation in Custance of holiness from 'swich maner necessaries' as pertain to marriage. Griselda's beauty is 'vertuous', certainly, but this way of putting things makes her virtue and her beauty interdependent: she is virtuous in so far as she is beautiful. One need not be surprised at Walter's choice from any point of view.

Then again one may like the Clerk's way of handling the Wife of Bath when he makes the vassals assure Walter (E 114) that marriage is not slavery and Walter insist on picking his own wife; also when at the end of the tale he hits the right nail squarely on the head by calling her doctrine that of a 'secte' (E 1171).[1] We may even admire the subtlety of his answer to the Wife which while appearing to be about marriage really transfers the discussion to the question of patience, the virtue which she conspicuously lacks.

But of these compliments, however well-merited, only the last will take us into the real problem of *The Clerk's Tale*; by the real problem I mean, of course, how we are to take Griselda as a moral heroine. The obvious difficulty in so doing is that in one way she is the opposite of moral, and in several places the Clerk has to disclaim any intention of making her a model for wives. A wife who allows the children to be carried off apparently to violent death could not in life be morally defensible. I have heard in conversation attempts to say that in the Middle Ages women were expected to be meek and to submit to their husbands, so that Griselda's course of action is (or was?) all right. But the Clerk says,

E 1142
   This storie is seyd   nat for that wyves sholde
Folwen Grisilde   as in humylitee
For it were inportable   though they wolde

– 'this story is told not to make wives imitate Griselda in humility, for that would be *intolerable* – even if they wanted to...' But it is

---

[1] 'Secte' could mean 'sect' or 'sex': I think the Clerk knows this as well as editors.

equally clear that in some other sense Griseld is offered as a moral example. The Clerk continues

E 1145
But for that every wight   in his degree
Sholde be constant   in adversitee
As was Grisilde   therfore Petrak writeth
This storie   which with heigh stile he enditeth

For sith a womman   was so pacient
Unto a mortal man   wel moore us oghte
Receyven al in *gree*   that God us sent   goodwill

But *how* can that follow if Griseld ought not to have been so patient to a mortal man? She can only be a moral example if at certain crucial moments we can forget her wickedness: but it at least requires some thought to see how that might be possible.

The first part of *The Clerk's Tale* could hardly announce more plainly that we are not reading a novel. The characters, if they can be called 'characters', are no more naturalistic than the action: both are obviously intended to suggest some further significance. There are, of course, some naturalistic touches which as I shall show have their place in the tale, but they don't affect the general proposition. *The Clerk's Tale* is somewhere among the realms of folk tale, fable, parable and allegory.

Let us see what happens if we opt for this last term. Consider, out of context, some of the things Griselda says to Walter.

E 358
Wondrynge upon this word   quakynge for drede
She seyde 'Lord   undigne and unworthy
Am I to thilke honour   that ye me beede
But as ye wole youreself   right so wol I
And heere I swere   that nevere willyngly
In werk ne thoght   I nyl yow disobeye
For to be deed   though me were looth to deye'

E 501
She seyde 'Lord   al lyth in youre plesaunce.
My child and I   with hertely obeisaunce
Been youres al   and ye mowe save or *spille*   destroy
Youre owene thyng   werketh after youre wille

Ther may no thyng   God so my soule save
Liken to yow   that may displese me
Ne I desire   no thyng for to have
Ne drede for to leese   save oonly yee
This wyl is in myn herte   and ay shal be
No lengthe of tyme or deeth   may this deface
Ne chaunge my corage   to another place'

E 645

'I have' quod she 'seyd thus   and evere shal
I wol no thyng   ne nyl no thyng certayn
But as yow list   Naught greveth me at al
Though that my doughter   and my sone be slayn
At youre comandement   this is to sayn
I have noght had no part   of children tweyne
But first siknesse   and after wo and peyne

Ye been oure lord   dooth with youre owene thyng
Right as yow list   axeth no reed at me
For as I lefte at hoom   al my clothyng
Whan I first cam to yow   right so' quod she
'Lefte I my wyl   and al my libertee
And took youre clothyng   wherfore I yow preye
Dooth youre plesaunce   I wil youre lust obeye

And certes   if I hadde prescience
Youre wyl to knowe   er ye youre lust me tolde
I wolde it doon   withouten necligence
But now I woot youre lust   and what ye wolde
Al youre plesance   ferme and stable I holde
For wiste I that my deeth   wolde do yow ese
Right gladly wolde I dyen   yow to plese

Deth may noght make   no comparisoun
Unto youre love'

Outside the situations in which they occur these all seem quite clearly addresses by the Christian soul to God. They would not have been out of place in Richard Rolle or Dame Julian of Norwich, and perhaps are stronger than anything Rolle wrote, in the restraint and dignity with which a deeply-felt submission to the divine will is expressed. It cannot be mere fortuity that Griselda's words make this sense so well. Language is never accidentally ambiguous for so long, hence the impossibility of finding the perfectly apt quotation of more than the length of a line of two.

Once one starts looking it is easy to find plenty of hints in the tale that Griselda is either the Christian soul or the church in her union with Christ, and that Walter is God.[1] This is how Janicula phrases his reply to Walter:

E 319

'Lord' quod he 'my willynge
Is as ye wole   ne ayeynes youre likynge
I wol no thyng   ye be my lord so deere
Right as yow lust   governeth this mateere'

---

[1] I find that Mr Trevor Whittock writes rather similarly of *The Clerk's Tale* in his *Reading of the Canterbury Tales* (Cambridge, 1968), p. 145.

At Griselda's first meeting with Walter,

> E 292
>   doun up on hir knes   she gan to falle
> And with sad contenance   kneleth stille
> Til she had herd   what was the lordes wille

(not 'this' lord's will). In answer to the question 'Where is youre fader   O Grisildis?' (E 297) she

> E 298
>   with reverence   in humble cheere
> Answerde 'Lord   he is al redy heere'

And much later in the tale when Griseld exclaims

> E 852
> O goode God   how gentil and how kynde
> Ye semed

it would make good grammatical sense to take 'ye' as 'God'.

Above all, the terms of the marriage to which Griselda agrees and which for the rest of the tale we have to accept as something given, are much more like what a Christian may think of God as demanding than what any wife could ever have thought proper to concede to a husband.

> E 351
> 'I seye this   be ye redy with good herte
> To al my *lust*   and that I frely may   pleasure
> As me best thynketh   do yow laughe or smerte
> And nevere ye to grucche it   nyght ne day?
> And eek when I sey *ye*   ne sey nat *nay*
> Neither by word   ne frownyng contenance?
> Swere this   and heere I swere oure alliance'

Griselda – contemporary with the Wife of Bath – does swear this: she is swearing to

> E 1151
> Receyven al in gree   that God us sent

not to enjoy the caprices of a husband.

But Walter is in another way very obviously not God; and the Clerk has repeatedly to say or imply as much, insisting that in so far as the story concerns a wife and a husband the husband is in the wrong, to escape picturing God as a husband with an unfortunate *idée fixe*. This could suggest that the tale can only make its point if the passages that express the moral are removed from their contexts, and that would be a way of calling the tale a failure. Yet there has to be some separation of the meaning from the figure that expresses it. On the other hand there must be some connection: the story must give to the idea of the soul's patience some strength of particularized life that even as the finest general statement it must miss. So the story and the moral must be at once connected and disconnected? The difficulty of the task the Clerk has set himself comes clear enough in that formulation – but then, philosophers are tricky fellows, and perhaps the Clerk is not as lost as I seem to be suggesting.

God's relation with the human soul must be shown to be *like* Griselda's with Walter. If there is no force in the likeness the Clerk is wasting his time. But the likeness must be restricted to and by the word 'pacience'. The religious passages have to be detached from their contexts in the tale in every way but one, leaving only the thread of 'pacience' to connect tale and moral; but with that thread the emotional poignancy of the tale has to be drawn across to the doctrine to charge it with an undoctrinal power. (That is the kind of definition of 'pacience' this philosopher chooses to make.) The tale, then, needs to generate an emotion and to bear it across to an otherwise separate doctrine. I have shown the separation by quoting passages out of context; there remain the questions of the tale's pathos and the connection of that with the moral idea.

Some people cannot tolerate the emotions of *The Clerk's Tale*. I find especially when discussing Chaucer with undergraduates that young women can rarely forgive or forget that Griselda fails to stand up to her husband in the proper way. But it does seem to me possible to follow the Clerk along his tightrope. If the situations are too real Griselda, as a real woman, will be disgusting. On the other hand if the tale is too unreal it will fail to add anything to the doctrine. For success it must keep a perfect, difficult balance between the two. It seems to me that Professor Salter is missing this point when she writes that 'the more vividly [Griselda] emerges as a sentient being, the less will be her power to move and instruct as a pure religious symbol'.[1] To make Griselda more than a pure religious symbol is certainly dangerous, but it is the attempt to make the tale more than a versified sermon.

[1] *Chaucer, 'The Knight's Tale' and 'The Clerk's Tale'*, p. 50. Cf. 'The purity of Griselda's innocent, submissive words and gestures is contaminated by nearness to this world of sublunary passions. We are asked to hate, to pity, to judge on her behalf, when we should only have to admire and learn' (*Ibid.*, p. 60).

Certainly we need some delicacy and flexibility of response to move between the tale's different levels; but to do so it is only necessary to follow the tale. The objections to Griselda's wifehood are a refusal to co-operate with the Clerk for, at the moments when objection would be appropriate, she is not a wife but the Christian soul. On the other hand if we try to take her as a pure symbol we miss the emotional power which her other status as a wife gives to the symbolism.

The model of what we have to do is given by the episode of Walter's proposal. Here the tale is close enough to its folk origins to allow us to swallow the terms of the marriage without making the objections the same words would force out of us in a novel; and, as I argued, we later realize that the contract is not that of an earthly marriage at all: but at the same time the situation is realized strongly enough for us to sympathize warmly and without qualms when it comes to Griselda that she is the chosen one. This feeling is channelled into the other context, the religious. This presents no great difficulty once we get used to the way the tale goes.

Generally speaking the pathetic scenes throughout the tale are overwhelmingly successful in their creation of poignant emotion, and very careful in the way they apply it to the real subject.[1] When the children are in turn so callously removed by the Fell Sergeant, some critics have found Griselda's calm a sign of coldness, but the very opposite seems to me to be the case: we respond with strong compassion, at its strongest when Griselda must allow herself no murmur. In fact I find the end of the tale, where she can permit herself the ordinary marks of her feeling, comparatively weak. But it is part of my case that this response is at the same time an objection to the doctrine of the end of the tale. When all turns out to have been for the best the difficulty of seeing Griselda and Walter as real husband and wife is at its strongest – for what wife could forget the past and transform her husband into a 'benygne fader' so easily? – but this is *also* the moment at which the Clerk's presentment of patience is least persuasive, for he has to argue as an orthodox Christian that God is not *really* cruel. And that, I

---

[1] This discussion is in part an attempt to answer the view of Mr Robert M. Jordan (in *Chaucer and the Shape of Creation*, pp. 198ff.) which I have not the space to consider in detail. But he says (p. 198), for instance, 'In the Clerk's Tale Chaucer founders dangerously on one of the besetting problems of inorganic narrative – the maintenance of continuity and a minimum degree of integration among individuated structural elements.'

suspect, somewhat devalues Griselda's earlier patience. But this adverse comment is not very weighty – at least not until we confront ourselves with the question of what we learn from *The Clerk's Tale*. The tale is not perfect but it is very splendid. In Griselda's early silences Chaucer profited more from his reading of Dante than in any of the places where he is translating or guying Dante.

So too *The Clerk's Tale* gives us the best of the tender mother-and-child situations that so appealed to Chaucer and the taste of his century – best in themselves and also because here, at last, Chaucer is making them part of his poem's exploration rather than just enjoying them and criticizing them as in *The Prioress's Tale* or wallowing in them with the Man of Law.

> E 554
> And thus she seyde   in hire benigne voys
> 'Fareweel my child   I shal thee nevere see
> But sith I have thee marked   with the croys
> Of thilke Fader   blessed moote he be
> That for us deyde   upon a croys of tree
> Thy soule litel childe   I hym bitake
> For this nyght shaltow dyen   for my sake'

We take the particular emotional force of these words and bear it across to the idea of 'pacience'.

So with the whole range of styles and feelings in the tale. The scenes I have mentioned are as near as it comes to the novelistic, but there are also the many 'human touches' (if the phrase is still possible) which contribute to the soil of an ordinary world out of which 'pacience' grows. The tale works, unlike *The Man of Law's Tale*, in so far as the religious feeling is *not* wholly disconnected from the ordinary world.[1] Before Griselda can fall on her knees before the Lord she has to put down her water-pot. The ladies who are to array the bride do not like to handle her old clothes – because they are, one supposes, not dirty but unfashionable. The multitude welcoming as they think Walter's second wife are as fickle as any of Shakespeare's and remark that the new wife is more beautiful and younger than Griseld. Griselda's faint is so

---

[1] That is what is wrong with Raleigh's otherwise useful remark that Griselda is 'not a patient woman; she is Patience'. (Walter Raleigh, *On Writing and Writers* (1926), p. 106.) Yes – but Patience only as she is also a woman. Raleigh has just had to say, 'Every kind of apology has been offered for Griselda. But they won't wash.' Certainly – in so far as she is a woman. This leads straight back to our discussion.

real that the children have to be torn from her grip. Janicula is enough of a real peasant to have expected all the time that the marriage would go wrong. And so on.

IV

The comparison I have made between the three religious tales is like the one between the various layers of *The Knight's Tale*: the judgment of courtliness in the latter's opening episode is perfect and detached, like the criticism of religion in *The Prioress's Tale*. *The Clerk's Tale* comes from somewhere as deep as the gods and the Theseus speech.

But even if this is conceded, is it not still true that the Clerk's *exemplum* is a very bad one? With that plot, it may be objected, thoughts of the unsatisfactoriness of Griselda are bound to intrude. He might have found another example that showed patience equally well without stretching our imaginative agility in this way and involving us in these difficulties.

The Clerk delights in subtlety as philosophers are prone to, and it may be that he wants this story to tickle some of his listeners and bamboozle others. He *wants* the absurdity of the marriage: the very inappropriateness of the figure has attractions for the scholastic mind. (Cf. Wittgenstein's delight in outrageous extreme cases.) But I think the real defence of the Clerk will be to show that he is not being as straightforwardly didactic as perhaps he wishes to be.

This story allows the Clerk to put patience before us with an extreme shockingness that is at the same time an extreme clarity. Our submission to God is as if a husband requires this of a wife: patience demands responses as impossible in ordinary terms as Griselda's. The Clerk has to run his dangers in order to make his point with its full, startling force. For all his pointing of a moral the Clerk is not, or at least not simply, preaching to us: part at least of what the tale does is closer to our common notions of art or philosophy: it creates an idea and makes that idea clearer than it could otherwise be. But it cannot dictate what we should do with the idea.

The tale at its best is not about consequences. The quality of Griselda's patience would not have been impaired if the tale had ended with her retirement to obscurity and Walter's second marriage – which is why I see the specifically Christian happy ending as a weakness. The value of Griselda's response to adversity is not proved because it is at last rewarded; the value lies in the thing itself, in the capacity (as in *The Knight's Tale*) to

A 3043
       take it weel   that we may nat eschue.

E 1156
[God] suffreth us   as for oure excercise
With sharpe scourges   of adversitee
Ful ofte to be bete   in sondry wise

and there is no need to insist that God is really a 'benyngne fader' (E 1097) before understanding the value of the 'exercise'. It lies in the submission itself, the '*voluntary* acceptance of *unavoidable* suffering'[1] which cannot be made valid or invalid by any subsequent event. Or, as Muscatine puts it, 'Walter's lack of motivation is an advantage in presenting this theme. This is *pure* chastening, *pure* correction. Griselda's trial is a trial because there is no reason for it.'[2] No doubt the Clerk would demolish this drift of thought with scholastic ease, and argue that patience makes sense only in the world of a loving heavenly father who guarantees that no suffering faithfully borne is in vain because He will make everything good. But the tale would disprove him: its greatness is in the suffering. Griselda is only truly heroic if there is no such guarantee. (The Book of Job seems to me similarly most strong where Job's patience is absolutely without hope of reward: but that is no defence of the Clerk against the flaw in his tale.)

I would say though that however flawed *The Clerk's Tale* is, it puts patience before us – that unmodern virtue – with an immediacy we are unlikely to find in a more modern writer.[3] The suggestion that God may require of us something like Walter requires of Griseld is the force that the Clerk gives to the idea of patience by telling this story about it. 'Patience clearly does exist',[4] but Chaucer's tale gives us the realization of the existence, the shock about the possible ways of making something deep of life, that is one of the marks of a great poet.

The tale makes its point in a way that can challenge us, as well

---

[1] Peter Winch, 'Can a Good Man be Harmed?', *Proceedings of the Aristotelian Society* LXVI (1965–6), 67. Professor Winch's whole essay is most germane to this discussion.

[2] *Chaucer and the French Tradition*, p. 194.

[3] The most telling comparison would be with another medieval poem, the *Patience* of the Gawain ms.

[4] Winch, 'Can a Good Man be Harmed?', p. 68.

as that legendary group of eccentrics, the fourteenth-century audience. And perhaps the idea of patience, so much more at home in the Middle Ages, is one of the things we need Chaucer to say to us. By putting Christian patience to us so sharply the Clerk challenges us to make up our minds about it.

If the reader feels something monstrous in Griselda's patience, something demanding rebellion against such a god and such a world, that is at least a possible answer to the Clerk's challenge to see clearly. We might reject the idea, having understood it fully for the first time. It is not necessary to *agree* with the Clerk to see the depth and power of his conception.

But this in turn is too facile. The Clerk certainly thinks he has told the tale in order that 'every wight in his degree Sholde be constant in adversitee' (E 1145-6). The tale is a model of the *imaginative* discovery and understanding that can be given by poetry. It makes us imagine patience as we follow this story. But what does that imply for our lives – or for Chaucer's? Must we raise those impossible questions of what literature can teach and what difference it can make to life? *The Clerk's Tale* is by a man who has lived with the questions he is treating: the quality of the tale is the guarantee. But how 'lived with'?

I do not mean to assert that Chaucer was himself a patient man. We just don't know, though from what we do know it seems, if anything, unlikely. (We don't even *know* – and the question has been much discussed – whether or not Chaucer was a confessed rapist.) He may not have practised patience; but he is certainly here creating a language of patience – and where is language used if not in life? Chaucer is thinking about patience in this poem – really and deeply thinking; and that means he is committing himself and anyone who reads him, in imagination. The connections between what happens in our imaginations and the rest of our lives are of great importance, of course, but are unlikely to be clarified here. My point, the real compliment to *The Clerk's Tale*, is that it forces one to raise these questions as seriously as one can. It takes us as far down amongst what we take for granted as to make us wonder whether we are right in our usual ideas about what literature is and can do.

At any rate I will say that if a poet takes us to these depths in the imagination he will affect in some ways the whole man. Shakespeare was not himself necessarily wicked because he expresses the evil of *Macbeth* – but it would be equally misleading to think of him as a disinterested observer. He is extending the language to include this monstrosity of evil, and so changing our picture of the world.

The imaginative commitment on which depends the kind of knowledge art can give can be dangerous. Within the magic circle of his poetry's sanity, Chaucer conjures up spirits, here the spirit of heroic patience. But the spirit could only materialize in life. If we sympathize with patience we imagine *as if* we were living it. (Art is a metaphor of life.) And to sympathize is risky; for if we make patience part of our language we make it potentially part of our experience. (And conversely, of course, the Clerk could make no sense to us unless we knew in life something comparable with what he describes.) Chaucer tells us what 'pacience' means – but only by showing us what it is like to live patiently. So *The Clerk's Tale* is at least the opposite of 'living, our servants can do that for us' – the possibilities it shows can only be possibilities for living and can only be understood by those capable of asking where patience belongs in life. (That is another implication of saying that Chaucer is creating a language of patience.)

But the critical effort, the saying that there are things wrong or unsatisfactory about the Clerk's idea, is also a connection of the poetry with 'life'. Poetry is characteristically about our beliefs and values – but not credally: it is not 'I believe in patience...' but

A 859
Whilom   as olde stories tellen us...

Nevertheless I do say that *The Clerk's Tale* is a deeply sincere poem, evidence that its author, whatever his temper, was not 'a man with a paltry, impudent nature'.[1] In the tale Chaucer really asks himself what patience is and what it is worth. A man who has really asked himself those questions – whether in living, or writing a poem, or reading it – will not be the same as he was before.

I am afraid we shall have to recur to questions like these, but immediately I will instead come towards them from another point of view. *The Merchant's Tale* presents a view of the world that is at once powerful and very cynical. In showing this I shall ask whether this means that the tale ought to be kept away from the young and impressionable and reserved for hardened academics. It does go

---

[1] 'A critic must be able to *feel* the impact of a work of art in all its complexity and its force. To do so, he must be a man of force and complexity himself, which few critics are. A man with a paltry, impudent nature will never write anything but paltry, impudent criticism. And a man who is *emotionally* educated is rare as a phoenix', D. H. Lawrence, 'John Galsworthy', *Phoenix*, p. 539.

several stages further towards raising that question than, for instance, the portraits of the Pardoner and the Summoner that we considered earlier; and I do not take it for granted that we should answer the question by the modern liberal NO.[1]

Meanwhile I can at least claim that the greatness of *The Clerk's Tale* is in its profound exploration of patience, and that that is the kind of achievement that is paid for at great cost, demanded of more than the intellect. *The Clerk's Tale* is more than *The Prioress's Tale* because it is more of an adventure in life, which Chaucer could not have made, and which we cannot follow, without discovering things about the soul. It is this quality of risky exploration and truthfulness that makes the Clerk's the best of the religious tales and amongst the deepest of Chaucer's poems.

Even so, *The Clerk's Tale* is such an incomplete extreme that if it had been Chaucer's only surviving poem we might have thought of him as a brilliant but wayward contemporary of Langland. The tale needs things like *The Wife of Bath's Prologue* as a balancing opposite, and that too is one of the ways of taking it seriously. *The Clerk's Tale* needs the famous Envoy with which Chaucer breaks the Clerk's spell and brings us back into a more ordinary world.

---

[1] Cf. the views of the Arts Council Working Party about contemporary British obscenity laws. It takes a body of professional littérateurs to believe so easily in the powerlessness of literature.

10

Malignity and 'The Merchant's Tale'

The Merchant's Tale, one of Chaucer's most powerful works, is the most sinister of *The Canterbury Tales*. It shows signs of un-finished revision (being at one stage notoriously intended for a priest, see line E 1251) and one can find flaws in it: for instance, Justinus does not get a fair crack of the whip; he is sidetracked into an attack upon his own wife and instead of making his case joins in the tale's theme of detraction, which gives Placebo too easy a victory. But this does not restrict the malign force of the tale's comedy.

The Merchant's Tale pours very convincing scorn on the love not only of old January but also of the young Damyan and May. The contempt is marked right from the beginning. The narrator has no need to argue against January's ideas (they are certainly not worth arguing against: he appears to believe, for instance (E 1840), that a man cannot cut himself with his own knife); all he does, in this most Swiftian of Chaucer's stories, is to state January's ideas about marriage and demolish them with occasional revelations of scorn. For example the tale begins with a coldly factual account of January's lascivious ways and his wish to legalize them in one of those marriages which Camus somewhere calls *des débauches bureaucratisées*: then we come to the single scornful line which annihilates the old fool:

E 1263
'Noon oother lyf' seyde he 'is worth a bene
For wedlock is so esy and so *clene*   clean, chaste
That in this world it is a paradys'

then

Thus seyde this olde knyght that was so wys

'Knyght' here has the force of an opprobrious term.

The tale reminds me of *Troilus and Cressida* in the coldness of its animus against love. So much would have been too obvious to need saying had there not been a recent fashion for seeing its comedy as lighthearted and for taking one or more of its characters as standing positively for life and creativity.[1]

But the method of the tale (the strategy and tactics of the on-slaught) is far from obvious. *The Merchant's Tale* is one of the most complex of Chaucer's works in what Henry James calls its 'doing' and David Garrick 'the concoction'. By illustrating this I hope to raise the questions of how its malignity manages to be comic, and whether we can take it properly without becoming as soured as the Merchant.

The story itself is told with the annihilating plainness of the last line I quoted, and this plainness is in the end its most powerful weapon. But its power comes from its place, surrounded as it is by a range of literary artifice. I will list a few of the non-naturalistic elements.

When January (one of the numerous ticket-names) seeks 'conseil' from his friends it is given not naturalistically but in a formal disputation between Placebo and Justinus. At the wedding Bacchus and Venus are amongst the guests. The dénouement is brought on because May's plot happens to be discovered by the King and Queen of Fayerye (whose domestic disharmony resembles that of the other characters). Amongst the authorities cited by name are the Wife of Bath and *The Romance of the Rose*. (Here the rose-garden is the place where the nasty old man goes for his sex: the Merchant takes the chance of reminding us that Priapus is the god of gardens.)

With this last we come to the tale's funniest and most malign device: misused quotation. Out of context would one know that this paraphrase of the Song of Solomon is not beautiful?

E 2138
Rys up my wyf my love my lady free
The turtles voys is herd my dowve sweete
The wynter is goon with alle his reynes weete
Com forth now with thyne eyen columbyn
How fairer been thy brestes than is wyn
The gardyn is enclosed al aboute
Com forth my white spouse out of doute

---

[1] Cf. the chapter on the tale in T. W. Craik, *The Comic Tales of Chaucer*, (1963) and Malcolm Pittock, 'The Merchant's Tale', *Essays in Criticism* XVII (1967). The latter is a good essay which says, however, that the sin of May and Damyan is 'treated with a mitigatory light-heartedness' (p. 32).

Thou hast me wounded   in myn herte O wyf
No spot of thee   ne knew I al my lyf
Com forth and lat us   taken oure disport
I chees thee for my wyf   and my confort

This is a good example of the truism that the meaning of any
piece of language depends on its situation. There are subtle hints
of something wrong with this way of speaking (my division of line
2147 gives the rhythm of one such place) but in the mouth of
Troilus any of the possibly dubious things could be ignored. It is
when we realize the kind of 'disport' it will be, with the lecherous
old man and the disillusioned girl (imagine what January means by
'confort') that the passage becomes obscene in a way that is only
underlined by the Merchant's characteristic line of scornful
demolition,

E 2149
Swiche olde lewed wordes   used he

The uncleanness of this quoting out of context depends for its full
force on a knowledge and preferably a love of the originals; but in
the most telling case the original is Chaucer. One of Chaucer's
favourite sentiments occurs in a line repeated with minor variations half a dozen times in the course of *The Canterbury Tales*:

Pitee renneth sone   in gentil herte

Theseus forgives Palamon and Arcite like this:

A 1756
And alle crieden   bothe lasse and moore
'Have mercy Lord   upon us wommen alle'
And on hir bare knees   adoun they falle
And wolde have kist his feet   ther as he stood
Til at the laste   aslaked was his mood
For pitee renneth soone   in gentil herte

In *The Merchant's Tale* this beautiful line is the witheringly
contemptuous comment on the way May 'succumbs':[1]

E 1982
'Certeyn' thoght she   'whom that this thyng displese
I rekke noght   for heere I hym assure
To love hym best   of any creature
Though he namoore hadde   than his sherte'
Lo pitee renneth soone   in gentil herte

---

[1] I borrow Muscatine's witty and true sentence: 'Criseyde succumbs to the
combined power of Troilus' "worthynesse" and Pandarus' energy. Alisoun
succumbs to Nicholas' pleasant violence. May, on the other hand, just
succumbs', *Chaucer and the French Tradition*, p. 233.

Immediately following is a related device, a piece of the bogus sententiousness frequently inserted by the Merchant and as often as not glossed 'Auctor' (the sign that the author is saying something particularly memorable) by good manuscripts. The passage continues,

> Heere may ye se   how excellent franchise
> In wommen is   whan they hem narwe avyse

Amongst the other gems of solemn wisdom we find

> E 1859
>   but fresshe May
> Heeld hire chambre   unto the fourthe day
> As usage is of wyves   for the beste
> *Auctor*   For every labour   somtyme moot han reste
> Or elles longe   may he nat endure
> This is to seyn   no lyves creature
> Be it of fyssh   or bryd   or beest   or man[1]

So, too, we have apostrophes like those of *The Man of Law's Tale* – but leading to such favourite puns as those of the last two lines of this passage:

> E 2057
> O sodeyn hap   O thou Fortune unstable
> Lyk to the scorpioun   so deceyvable
> That flaterest with thyn heed   whan thou wolt stynge
> Thy tayl is deeth   thurgh thyn envenymynge
> O brotil joye   O sweete venym queynte

Literature and love are demolished at the same time. A few minor themes are also exposed to the Merchant's treatment. As well as love he deflates 'conseil', respect for age, joy in youth, and the old image of blindness as lack of self-knowledge. These traditional motifs are all devalued.

Through this background of ironic artifice the plain tale runs its sense-destroying course. January is not the only repulsive character. Indeed, after making him (however funnily) disgusting in the first half – swigging aphrodisiacs on his wedding-night to stimulate his very would-be lust – Chaucer even engenders some sympathy

---

[1] The 'Auctor' here is Jean de Meun in the passage where, more extreme than the Wife of Bath, he urges the barons to

> Remuez vous, tripez, sailliez,
> Ne vous laissiez pas refredir
> Par trop voz membres entedir.

See *Le Roman de la Rose*, lines 19696ff.

for January in the second half. (This is rather like the way we develop some sympathy for old John the Carpenter in *The Miller's Tale*.) January is after all not as bad as May and Damyan.

The symbolism is the desire of May's creative body for the awakening phallus of her lover...The picture is of a youthful vigour which contrasts with January's desperate skin-rubbing sensuality...life will out, and January's garden is entered by the vigorous fertile Damian, and by love, albeit surreptitious and adulterous love, up in a tree. The power of sexual vitality as a manifestation of life is here poetically expressed...[1]

Mr Holbrook's essay is much more interesting than the work of most Chaucer specialists, but here I feel like saying with Millán Astray, if this is life '¡*Viva la Muerte!*' Youthful vigour is not necessarily even attractive, let alone admirable. Think of Donne's string of adjectives for the reformed church:

> plaine, simple, sullen, yong,
> Contemptuous, yet unhansome. As among
> Lecherous humors, there is one that judges
> No wenches wholsome, but course country drudges.[2]

The language of courtly love is certainly applied to May and Damyan.

E 2092
> fresshe May
> That loveth Damyan   so benyngnely
> That she moot outher   dyen sodeynly
> Or elles she moot han hym   as hir leste
> She wayteth   whan hire herte   wolde breste

But this 'love' is simply her decision that she must 'han hym'. Their love – this language – is reduced to plain, simple, sullen, young sex. Love for these three becomes the factual question of whether or not the male organ has entered the female organ. Chaucer is usually quite reticent about the details of sex (in comparison with Dunbar he is reticent here, too – see below, Chapter 14) but he shows quite finally that this is what love means to these people. Mr Holbrook: 'It takes Damyan to give May what she needs.'[3] But what she needs and what she gets is defined by the charge that January makes, that 'in it went'; and it is against this charge that May defends herself with lies bold enough to justify

---

[1] David Holbrook, *The Quest for Love* (1964), p. 108.
[2] *Satyre III. Poems by J.D.* (1633), p. 334.
[3] *Quest for Love*, p. 109.

one of the Wife of Bath's contentions.[1] The circumstances are aggravated. January is not merely cuckolded, but cuckolded before his (sightless) eyes, having been climbed over by May on her way into the tree. The language is aggravated, too:

E 2331

'I moste han   of the peres that I see
Or I moot dye   so soore longeth me
To eten   of the smale peres grene
Help for hir love   that is of hevene queene
I telle yow wel   a womman in my plit
May han to fruyt   so greet an appetit
That she may dyen   but she of it have'
  'Allas' quod he   'that I ne had heer a knave
That koude clymbe...'

This passage is full of *double-entendre*. For 'peres' see Partridge's article on 'Poperingh Pear' in *Shakespeare's Bawdy* (1955). 'Clymbe' is perhaps given a sexual meaning only by the context, but the complicated use of 'fruit' is lexically demonstrable. Here May is being all things to both men. 'Fruit' is an ordinary word for 'offspring' in the contemporary homilies which argue that progeny and not delight is the true end of sexuality. The *Middle English Dictionary* cites (4(a)) 'Þou usyst þi wyif most for lust & noȝt for fruyte.' This is a sense May conveys to January: it follows from her reason (for him) for climbing into the tree, that is, to satisfy the craving of a pregnant woman for (vegetable) fruit. But for Damyan she uses 'fruit' to refer to the satisfaction of a quite different craving: to him she uses the word like the Wife of Bath, for whom 'fruit' is the sexual act itself:

D 113

I wol bistowe   the flour of al myn age
In the actes   and in fruyt of mariage

For Damyan her 'plit' is that she is guarded by her husband. There must also be surely some loading of the word 'dyen', but I have not fathomed it: the traditional later pun would not make sense here.

But to say that January is 'cuckolded' is to give the tale jolly literary associations (all those lighthearted Elizabethan jokes about horns) that Chaucer avoids. Right at the end here there is still literary artifice, but it is again parody of Chaucer. Of the climactic passage Mr Jordan says, 'Far from savage, the speaker is gauche and

---

[1] D 227   For half so boldely   kan ther no man
Swere and lyen   as a womman kan

obsequious.'[1] But the apparent gaucherie with which the Merchant delays the one line that matters looks like something quite different if we put it beside any one of half a dozen of Chaucer's own apologies to the ladies – the one I choose being a remarkable flaw in Book v of *Troilus and Criseyde*:

> V 1772
> Bysechyng every lady   bright of hewe
> And every gentil womman   what she be
> That al be that   Criseyde was untrewe
> That for that gilt   she be nat wrooth with me

The proper comment on this kind of apology is the Merchant's parody – which also has the effect of emphasizing the one plain line more than if he'd just said it. The gaucherie is really deliberate nastiness.

> E 2348
> He stoupeth doun   and on his bak she stood
> And caughte hire by a twiste   and up she gooth
> Ladyes I prey yow   that ye be nat wrooth
> I kan nat glose   I am a rude man
> And sodeynly anon   this Damyan
> Gan pullen up the smok   and in he throng

The rich organization of *The Merchant's Tale*, as much as the plain course of the story until 'in he throng', is devoted to the destruction of any significance any of these characters may have found in sex. They are simply left with the act (or not the act, which for January is the question). The vices are the opposite of 'jovial and generous'[2] ones. So May succeeds in deceiving January and all ends happily for all concerned – unlike *The Miller's Tale*. January can see; May and Damyan have had their sex, however momentarily, and escaped unpunished. Even the King and Queen of Fayerye have both had their way. So much for genial old Chaucer?

Perhaps I can bring the critical problem to a focus by putting together two critical extremes which I believe equally mistaken.

The Franklin's is one of the gentlest, most gracious, smiling tales ever spoken with unhumorous dignity, and the Merchant's one of the most savagely obscene, angrily embittered, pessimistic and unsmiling tales in our language.[3]

---

[1] *Chaucer and the Shape of Creation*, pp. 149–50.
[2] Macaulay on Sunderland; *History of England*, original edition, vol. II, p. 64.
[3] C. Hugh Holman, in *Chaucer, Modern Essays in Criticism*, ed. Edward Wagenknecht (New York, 1959), p. 241.

The cynicism of the Merchant's Tale is seen to be in no way surprising, and... in no sense expressive of Chaucer's own sentiments, or even of Chaucer's momentary mood. The cynicism is the Merchant's. It is no more Chaucer's than Iago's cynicism about love is Shakespeare's.[1]

Kittredge's trenchant commonsense won't quite do. It is obviously unfair to attribute the sentiments of characters in plays to the author, and much bad Chaucer criticism has been the result of confusing author and characters. Nevertheless there is one obvious way in which Iago's cynicism is Shakespeare's: Shakespeare imagined and wrote Iago. It is queer to say a thing happens 'only' in the imagination – as if we lived somewhere else. And a corrupted imagination brings us close to the terminology of religion: if a man habitually imagined like Iago he would be damned. If Iago was a dramatic monologue Shakespeare would at least have a case to answer – as he has in a play so unrelentingly destructive as *Troilus and Cressida*. The difference between *Othello* and *The Merchant's Tale* is that the former 'places' the various wickednesses of Othello and Iago – whereas the latter is, as it were, from Iago's point of view. To have written it Chaucer must have felt sympathy with the Merchant, and if we enjoy the tale we sympathize with him too.

Yet Holman won't do either. *The Merchant's Tale* is positively and consistently funny – there is a positive joy in its destructiveness. This could not be unless there was something to destroy. It is as if Chaucer, having spent his life on the creation of a language of love, should sometimes enjoy saying 'Ah, to hell with it.' In a way the tale does express Chaucer's mood, and not just a momentary one; he has to experience and express it to be able to judge it. Taking the tale seriously – enjoying its wickedness to the full – is our recognition of something similar in ourselves.

Nevertheless the tale is judged by its context. Iago has his place in *Othello* and *The Merchant's Tale* in *The Canterbury Tales*. It is placed by reference to the Wife of Bath and the Miller on the one hand and the Knight, the Clerk and the Franklin on the other. Chaucer is the whole, not the parts; the tale is a possibility only in a world of other and far better possibilities. But even this may be an escape, for it could go as well in reverse: the love of *The Franklin's Tale* is possible – but only if we recognize the sex of *The Merchant's Tale* as well. In other words, Chaucer is still exploring, with a disturbing power that is the sign of his maturity, the aspects of Venus we met with in *The Parliament of Fowls*.

[1] G. L. Kittredge, 'Chaucer's Discussion of Marriage', reprinted *ibid.*, p. 203.

All the same, however squarely we try to recognize the malignity of *The Merchant's Tale*, however much we take it to heart as a reason for forswearing the idea of nice old uncle Chaucer, there is a great difference between the tale and the work of Dunbar with which I shall later compare it: Dunbar is unable to feel anything else than what Chaucer gives to the Merchant; but Chaucer could write *The Franklin's Tale* too. Chaucer's language of love has to include the Merchant's malignity, but the alternative statement is that the Merchant finds a place and is judged within Chaucer's language of love.

I I

'The Squire's Tale' and
'The Franklin's Tale'

I

The Squire's Tale is to the Franklin's as *The Prioress's Tale* is to
the Clerk's. Like the Prioress's, *The Squire's Tale* is the perfect
placing of something quite limited, and done, it appears, without
the effort Chaucer needed for the comparable achievement of his
early poems. The Squire and the Franklin together set a characteristic pair of traps. *The Squire's Tale* looks unfinished and chaotic
and *The Franklin's Tale* golden, elderly and genial; both first
impressions are the opposite of the truth.

The Squire's Tale is not unfinished. Its subject is the Falcon's
lament, surrounded by the charming naivetés that characterize the
Squire. The Falcon herself is not merely charming but beautiful
(I insist that I mean no harm to the tale by calling it perfect): she is
as much purely courtly love as the first Tercel of *The Parliament of
Fowls*.

F 621
  'So ferde this tercelet   allas the day
  Though he were gentil born   and fressh and gay
  And goodlich for to seen   and humble and free
  He saugh upon a tyme   a kyte flee
  And sodeynly   he loved this kyte so
  That al his love   is clene fro me ago
  And hath his trouthe   falsed in this wyse
  Thus hath the kyte   my love in hire servyse
  And I am lorn   withouten remedie'
  And with that word   this faucon gan to crie
  And swowned eft   in Canacees *barm*   bosom

This is the old troubadour accent, perfectly created, but given a
certain prettiness, reduced from anything very deeply serious, by
the mere fact that the 'falsyng' is done by a falcon chasing a kite.
(There is no similar insistence on the birds *as birds* in the declara-

181

tions in *The Parliament of Fowls*; but this is half-way to the love of Chantecleer for Pertelote because

B 4351
'Ye been so scarlet reed   aboute youre yen')

What ought to follow this delicate lament? The Squire promises that the Falcon is to get her love again (F 654), but that is not the subject of the poem. The subject is this courtly-love sadness itself, and nothing need follow it. But if I was right to call *Troilus and Criseyde* Chaucer's attempt to settle courtly love once and for all by considering it alone, *The Squire's Tale* is *Troilus and Criseyde* in reverse. It is the only Canterbury tale about pure courtly love, and the judgment made by placing courtly love in *The Squire's Tale* and then *The Squire's Tale* just before the Franklin's is an example of the way Chaucer makes the tales dramatically limit and evaluate each other. It is plain enough that this love in itself, how-ever beautiful, is not of the utmost significance in the world of the Marriage Group. It is confined by context in the same way as the rose-garden description of *The Parliament of Fowls*, which I called so beautiful – and so limited.

All the same, the Franklin has got his work cut out to justify the amiably patronizing tone with which he interrupts the Squire. It is, after all, no easy matter to justify a confidence that one is superior to perfection, even of the Squire's limited kind. The Franklin says,

F 675
                    considerynge thy yowthe
So feelyngly thou spekest   sire I *allowthe*   allow thee
As to my doom   ther is noon that is heere
Of eloquence   that shal be thy peere
If that thou lyve

But meanwhile the Franklin can condescend to such eloquence:

F 719
I lerned nevere rethorik   certeyn
Thyng that I speke   it moot be bare and pleyn

How far does his tale justify his attitude of indulgence towards the minor perfection of the Squire's youthful rhetoric?

II

It is easy enough to like *The Franklin's Tale*, with its pleasant mellowness of tone and evenness of temper, but coming as the

natural end of the series of tales Kittredge called the Marriage
Group, it runs some danger of seeming merely *nice* and, perhaps,
even a little senile, the work of a man (whether the Franklin or
Chaucer) too far past the problems he offers to solve to be taken
very seriously. I want to ask how justified we are in ourselves
condescending to the tale which may well have Chaucer's last
poetic words on human love.

The Franklin is sometimes close both in his moral style and his
attitude to the past to some poems in which Chaucer speaks in his
own person. The Franklin's

> F 777
> Lerneth to suffre   or elles so moot I goon
> Ye shul it lerne   *wher so* ye wole or noon   whether

is close in content and feeling to these lines of the moral ballade
Trouthe:

> 15   That thee is sent   receyve in *buxumnesse*   obedience
> The wrastling for this world   axeth a fal

Similarly, the tone which predominates through at least the first
three-quarters of the tale is typical of Chaucer's own softer mood. It
is found straight away in the brief Prologue:

> F 709
> Thise olde gentil Britouns   in hir dayes
> Of diverse aventures   maden layes
> Rymeyed   in hir firste Briton tonge
> Which layes   with hir instrumentz they songe
> Or elles redden hem   for hir plesaunce
> And oon of hem   have I in remembraunce
> Which I shal seyn   with good wyl as I kan

This, as well as reminding us of Marie de France, sets the story at
once in the hazy golden past of 'thise olde gentil Britouns', who
are evidently contemporaries of the people of Chaucer's own
Former Age. But this softer side of Chaucer (though a few find it
pleasant enough) is not the reason for the survival of his works;
and if all we could find to say for the Franklin were that he is
'gentil' and close to Chaucer, it might be right to sympathize
with Harry Bailly:

> F 695
> 'Straw for youre gentillesse'   quod oure Hoost

Yet the Franklin is made to join in the discussion of the other
tales of the Marriage Group in a way that can leave no doubt of his

intended importance. He answers the Wife of Bath and the Clerk directly, if mildly, and the whole trend of his tale is a rebuke to the Merchant. For the Clerk there is

F 768
Wommen *of kynde* desiren libertee   by nature
And nat to been   constreyned as a thral

and for the Wife he immediately continues

And so doon men   if I sooth seyen shal

For the Merchant the Franklin makes a direct statement of the value of marriage which is also implied by the whole tale, a statement as free from irony (at least on the part of the teller) as anything in Chaucer:

F 803
Who koude telle   *but* he hadde wedded be   unless
The joye   the ese   and the prosperitee
That is   bitwixe an housbonde   and his wyf?

The Franklin also puts in its place the Squire's connection of love with wonders and marvels by introducing the illusions of the Magician.

But we have to ask whether the tale is strong enough to make a fitting end to the series. And my dominant impression of the opening of the tale is of the benign uninvolvement of the Franklin with his story of the courtship of Dorigen and Arveragus and the terms of their marriage contract. The courtship is presented in a bare outline that keeps the reader's attention by its economy but which is at an opposite extreme from the immediately exciting plunge into her subject of the Wife of Bath. The Franklin's interest seems to be in his advice about love and marriage. Between lines F 741–802 he solves to his own satisfaction all the problems raised by the earlier tales, beginning with the Wife's theme of 'maistrye', the question of who is to be boss.

The Franklin's advice is not avuncular or woolly-minded. It is a series of daring paradoxes (not a compromise): he says that 'maistrye' drives out love (F 765) but also that each party must 'obey' (that is, grant 'maistrye' to) the other (F 762). Patience is necessary but not the voluntary suffering of 'maistrye'. The husband must be both in lordship and servitude (F 794); the wife is to be 'lady' (that is, sovereign (F 796)), but she has already promised to be a 'humble trewe wyf' (F 758). The Franklin's ideal marriage

therefore draws on elements of the apparently conflicting traditions of Christian marriage and courtly love; which is to say that as
well as criticizing the earlier tales he draws on them, except the
Merchant's. He cannot do without the 'pacience' which he finds
in *The Clerk's Tale*, but his emphasis on 'gentilesse' commits him
also to *fyn amour*. Moreover the doctrine is not complete with
this strange pair of bedfellows. The Franklin introduces a third
important term, 'trouthe', near the beginning, where it is made to
follow representatives of the language of courtliness ('gentillesse')
and Christian marriage ('humble trewe wyf'). 'Trouthe' is the
bond with which Dorigen makes fast the contract.

> F 753
> She thanked hym   and with ful greet humblesse
> She seyde 'Sire   sith of youre gentillesse
> Ye profre me   to have so large a reyne
> Ne wolde nevere God   bitwixe us tweyne
> As in my gilt   were outher werre or stryf
> Sire I wol be   youre humble trewe wyf
> Have heer my trouthe   til that myn herte *breste*'   breaks

'Trouthe' is the cement that holds together elements which
without it might run the risk of contradicting each other.

Despite all I have said about 'benign uninvolvement' I find this
part of the tale attractive and in its way impressive. There is a
weight to it as of ripe experience, which goes well with the gentle-
ness of the tone. But these daring paradoxes somehow fail to
excite. It is as if Chaucer is doing his best here, making this
discussion as good as it can be – in order to show that *this* best
isn't good enough. The marriage of Dorigen and Arveragus, the
exemplum to illustrate the doctrine, has not yet been done well
enough to make us give much importance to the Franklin's discussion; indeed in the first part of the story the doctrinal discussion seems more real than the characters.

The problem the Franklin tackles so boldly is: how to make
love permanent and dependable, how to ensure that it has to do
with 'trouthe'.

> F 767
> Love is a thyng   as any spirit free

he says, but at the same time he is trying (as the human race *does*
try) to bind love. The paradox of the freedom of love which is yet a
bond is at several of the centres of Chaucer and the problem is not,
after all, the exclusive concern of the people of the Middle Ages

Anything the Franklin manages to say about it may still be interesting.

But what he says seems less deeply true than, for instance, what we find in Book III of *Troilus and Criseyde* where the paradox follows from the story and is inseparable from the power of the story. The Franklin seems to be trying to fix his story in advance. He is no fool; he knows that the problem is not easily to be settled; but he does seem to think that if the paradoxes are balanced finely enough and both parties keep to the agreement in 'trouthe', all is *sure* to be well. He seems to offer a *guarantee* of love – and the result is the metamorphosis of the God of Love into something more like the Angel in the House.[1] The Franklin's couplet about the effect of 'maistrye' upon that shy creature, the God of Love, is very good.

> F 765
> Whan maistrie comth   the God of Love anon
> Beteth his wynges   and farewel he is gon

– but he himself might be accused of trying to make sure the God of Love stays, by clipping his wings. For all the paradoxes, the Franklin's initial discussion either solves the problem too easily or solves the wrong problem. One can object that his paradoxicality is not so true-sounding as the comic earnestness of the other end of Chaucer's career. *This* is more a real recognition of the power of love:

> PF 4
>   Love   that my felynge
> Astonyeth   with his wonderful werkynge
> So sore iwis   that whan I on hym thynke
> Nat wot I well   wher that I flete or synke
>
> For al be   that I knowe nat Love in deed
> Ne wot how that   he quiteth folk hir hyre
> Yit happeth me ful ofte   in bokes reede
> Of his myrakles   and his crewel yre
> There rede I wel   he wol be lord and syre
> I dar nat seyn   his strokes been so sore
> But 'God save swich a lord'   I can na moore

The Franklin dares say a great deal more, but there is nothing at the beginning of his tale like Troilus's recognition that when he has

---

[1]   Strong passions mean weak will, and he
    Who truly knows the strength and bliss
Which are in love, will own with me
    No passion, but a virtue 'tis.
          Coventry Patmore, *The Angel in the House,*
                Book I, Canto III

done what he can all rests with the gods – that the 'grete worthynesse' of love is found 'bitwixen drede and sikernesse' (III, 1315–16),
and nothing like the torments of Palamon and Arcite before
Theseus achieves for them anything like a *modus vivendi* with the
God of Love.

The Franklin's theme is the same as D. H. Lawrence's in
Women in Love: how to make the relations of the sexes 'valid and
precious', how to civilize the passions and connect them with the
life of the imagination and intellect, and the personal life with the
life of society. These are the problems of Gudrun and Ursula and
Birkin and Gerald Crich as much as of Dorigen and Arveragus.
Setting aside the difference of scale, the immediately obvious
difference between the two works is that there is nothing at the
beginning of Chaucer's tale to correspond with the struggles
Lawrence's characters go through – the battles, the wrestling with
language and each other – before they achieve anything whatever.
The Franklin seems to be trying to get there without doing the
work. Unless Chaucer can give something like Lawrence's power –
and unless he can derive it from a comparable involvement in
life – why need we spend very long on his tale?

III

The best parts of the earlier sections of *The Franklin's Tale* are
those where no attempt is made to involve the reader very deeply
and where the rather stock figures come in for a light dusting of
irony. Dorigen is not exempt. Arveragus leaves her temporarily
and she is plunged in grief.

> F 817
> For his absence   wepeth she and siketh
> As doon thise noble wyves   whan hem liketh

This is the right state to be in and Dorigen is following the convention even with enjoyment. Her grief is stated flatly and
generally:

> F 819
> She moorneth   waketh   wayleth   fasteth   pleyneth
> Desir of his presence   hire so destreyneth
> That al this wyde world   she sette at noght

Dorigen sets the wide world at nought a little too easily – just as
Aurelius later in the tale is too ready to give it away (F 1228) – and

any sympathy she receives from the reader is of the most general kind and tempered by amusement.

Aurelius, a late member of Chaucer's series of love-lorn squires, is treated throughout with a detached amusement which could have been heartless in a less benign or more naturalistic context. He is seen as unsympathetically as the wretched Damyan of *The Merchant's Tale*, but more in humour than contempt. 'No thyng dorste he seye'

> F 944
> Save in his songes   somewhat woulde he wreye
> His wo...

> F 947
> Of swich matere   made he manye layes
> Songes   compleintes   roundels   virelayes
> How that he dorste nat   his sorwe telle

And after his formal declaration of love ('"Madame" quod he' etc. (F 967)) the Franklin lets him down in a single line. It is only then that

> F 979
> She gan to looke   upon Aurelius

Dorigen says she will love him if the rocks are away, and Aurelius takes his leave in style:

> F 1010
> Thanne moot I dye   of sodeyn deth horrible

But he is not so fortunate. Instead, he goes home and makes a prayer to Apollo (described a little unfairly as 'ravyng') to work the miracle of removing the rocks. Despite the extremity of his torment Aurelius has time to remind Apollo that his, Apollo's, sister Lucina is more powerful than Neptune. Aurelius is then taken desperately ill with 'the loveris maladye Of Hereos' (A 1373–4) and the Franklin comments

> F 1084
> Dispeyred in this torment   and this *thoght*   anxiety
> Lete I   this woful creature   lye
> Chese he for me   wheither he wol lyve or dye

After *two years* during which Aurelius is

> F 1101
> In langour   and in torment furyus

his brother bethinks himself of the Magician. The desperate illness is mocked by the Franklin's literal interpretation of the figure of the wound of love's arrows.[1] A sursanure was the wound made when the head of a spear or arrow snapped off and remained inside the body. The Franklin says,

F 1111
His brest was hool   withoute for to sene
But in his herte   ay was the arwe kene
And wel ye knowe   that of a sursanure
In surgerye   is perilous the cure
But men myghte touche the arwe   or come therby

But now, with the search for the Magician, the cure is ridiculously sudden:

F 1165
    What sholde I make   a lenger tale of this?
Unto his brotheres bed   he comen is
And swich *confort*   he yaf hym for to gon   encouragement
To Orliens   that he up stirte anon
And on his way   forthward thanne is he fare

This light irony goes well with a curious unreality that pervades the tale's earlier scenes. The May-morning scene makes a useful contrast with the April of the opening of *The General Prologue*:

F 906
And this was   on the sixte morwe of May
Which May hadde peynted   with his softe shoures
This gardyn   ful of leves   and of floures
And craft of mannes hand   so curiously
Arrayed had this gardyn   trewely
That nevere was ther   gardyn of swich prys
But if it were   the verray paradys
The odour of floures   and the fresshe sighte
Wolde han maked   any herte lighte
That evere was born   but if to greet siknesse
Or to greet sorwe   helde it in distresse
So ful it was of beautee   with plesaunce

This is dreamily conventional. The lack of impetus in the rhythm joins with the emphasis on 'paint' and 'craft' and with the literary reminiscences to create a sense of unreality. (Another way of bringing this out would be to put the passage beside those lines of Donne in 'Twickenham Garden' where he may be remembering

---

[1] Cf. the opening of *Le Roman de la Rose* and of Gower's *Confessio Amantis* (in the latter the damage is done by a lance).

it.) This feeling of unreality culminates in the illusions of the Magician.

The unreality of his magic is brought out with some care – by this point in the tale we ought to be beginning to realize that whatever the meaning of this dreaminess may be, it is certainly intentional. In the first meeting with the Magician we are shown that though he has power to read thought he has no control over death (F 1179ff.); and the Magician's illusion-display is inter-mixed with a repeated and carefully recorded interest in his supper which makes the illusions seem even more illusory.

IV

My argument is to be, of course, that these feelings about the unreality of the earlier parts of *The Franklin's Tale* are just what Chaucer wants. The course of the tale subjects the marriage of Dorigen and Arveragus to the very Chaucerian test of severe adversity, and that changes their idea of the contract they have made. The tale has to develop something more than the amuse-ment, the irony and the benignity of the first parts; but the first parts make a very suitable base for such development.

Dorigen experiences in the course of the tale a series of shocks into wakefulness which culminate in the test of her 'trouthe'. The first – and the first sign that the tale is to be much more than a benignly paradoxical theory set off by elderly irony – is her reaction to the black rocks, a part of the tale whose significance is well shown by Mr Speirs. Dorigen's fear of the rocks takes the form of philosophical doubt. Chaucer, instead of telling us that Dorigen was afraid of the rocks in the general way he has told us she was sad at the departure of Arveragus, makes Dorigen speculate about Providence. The seriousness of her doubt is quickly apparent.

F 865
    Eterne God   that thurgh thy purveiaunce
Ledest the world   by certein governaunce
In ydel as men seyn   ye no thyng make
But Lord thise grisly   feendly rokkes blake
That semen rather   a foul confusion
Of werk   than any fair creacion
Of swich a parfit wys God   and a stable
Why han ye wroght   this werk unresonable?

There is no room for the black rocks amongst Dorigen's cosily perfect arrangements. They are the intransigent real world, thrusting in like the gods into *The Knight's Tale*. Her fear of the rocks speaks the reality of her love – for she feels it threatened and we feel the reality of the threat – but also its insufficiency to cope with things as they really must be if we are not to live in a dream. Dorigen cannot take the rocks as part of the divine plan (I do not mean it would be easy to do so); but later, when the rocks seem to have gone, she realizes that she has been impious.

> F 1345
> It is agayns   the proces of nature

This is the strong admission that the rocks were *in* 'the process of nature' and that therefore the will to sink them into Hell was against nature. This admission is Dorigen's awakening into a more real world, a kind of attainment of self-knowledge. It begins the crisis of the poem;[1] for the upshot of Dorigen's awakening is that the marriage is brought into collision with real trouble. Now, when Aurelius claims his due, is the time for Dorigen to emerge from the dreamy beginning into something more real and serious.

But even now Dorigen cannot fully realize the situation. Even in the dilemma in which she must either break her 'trouthe' to Aurelius or commit adultery and so be false to Arveragus, she finds something proper to do, which saves her from the agony of having to organize her own experience for herself.

'The Pleynt of Dorigen' is the most difficult part of *The Franklin's Tale*, because it is easy to misunderstand. It is a very long (F 1355–456) formal lament in which Dorigen, in confirming her resolution to kill herself rather than submit to Aurelius, is made to remember a long succession of fictitious and/or historical characters who did kill themselves in similar plights. The passage was evidently much admired in the fifteenth century, because several of the manuscripts give it a title or special illuminated capitals. But we of the twentieth century tend to be embarrassed by rhetorical set pieces and not to know what to do with them. So perhaps we try to imagine ourselves as medieval minds and make a determined effort to enjoy the rhetoric as it was enjoyed in the

---

[1] The much-admired passage about winter, beginning 'Phebus wax old' (F 1245) seems to me good not as an isolated thing but as a register of an almost tragic change of mood. Winter is so much more real than May in the poem because it announces the beginning of the real part and the end of conventionality.

Middle Ages (however that may have been). This seems to me quite wrong, a form of condescension to Chaucer, of which one should always beware. Chaucer is, after all, an artist; and if he puts this large rhetorical set-piece into his poem he may well be doing so because in some way the poem needs it. At any rate, a criticism which shows what the 'Pleynt' is doing in the tale will be more convincing than the assertion that Chaucer was pandering to the tastes of his age.

The 'Pleynt' is just what is wanted at this moment of the tale because it is Chaucer's way of showing Dorigen as at once genuine in her outburst and hopelessly imprisoned in a convention that can't properly express her feelings. There is a tension between the impulse which makes Dorigen keep breaking out again and again after she seems to have finished (lines F 1365-9, 1386, 1395-9, 1419-26) and the stilted formulae (What shal I say of...(F 1437) Lo which a wyf was...(F 1442) The parfit wyfhod of...(F 1451) O Teuta Queene...(F 1453)) which are her only way of expressing it. Dorigen looks naturally enough for comparable cases, but it is not quite natural that she should do it like this. (One recalls the Franklin's own opinion of rhetoric: F 727 My spirit feeleth noght of swich mateere.) There is real feeling here, but channelled into the wrong expression and conclusion (which also means there is something wrong with the feeling, which can't be separable from the expression). Sometimes too there seems something deliberate and forced about the emotion:

F 1368
Whan thritty tirauntz   ful of cursednesse
Hadde slayn Phidon   in Atthenes atte feste
They comanded his doghtres   for tareste
And bryngen hem   biforn hem in despit
Al naked   to fulfille hir foul delit
And in hir fadres blood   they made hem daunce
Upon the pavement   God yeve hem meschaunce

'ful of cursednesse', 'in despit', 'foul' and the last curse are all superfluous. Spontaneous feeling satisfactorily expressed would not need this sort of whipping-up.

The result is that Dorigen is not perfectly sincere. I do not mean she is telling lies or hypocritical, but that she rests in an insufficient expression: in not finding the right way of saying what she feels, she shows that she doesn't really know what she feels. This is even true at a quite obvious level:

F 1457
    Thus pleyned Dorigen   a day or tweye
    Purposynge evere   that she wolde deye

But what is she waiting for? If she has sufficiently defined her purpose all she has to do is carry it out. Instead she satisfies herself with this unwhole account of herself which leaves her 'purposing evere' but not getting on with it. And this is the judgment made by the action of the tale upon the genial opening: this is where the guarantees of love have led, to this insufficiency and insincerity.

What Dorigen is waiting for is, of course, Arveragus. He returns and achieves sincerity at once (as well as, incidentally, taking command in a way that makes the earlier insistence on the wife's rights seem a little trivial). At that moment of Arveragus's return the tale suddenly wakes right out of its cosiness into a human situation as convincing as anything in *Women in Love*. Arveragus hears Dorigen's account of what has happened and says,

F 1469
'Is ther oght elles Dorigen   but this?'
    'Nay nay' quod she   'God helpe me so as *wys*   certainly
This is to muche   and it were Goddes wille'
    'Ye wyf' quod he   'lat slepen that is stille
It may be wel   paraunter yet today
Ye shul youre trouthe holden   by my fay
For God *so wisly*   have mercy upon me   as sure
I hadde wel levere   ystiked for to be
For verray love   which that I to yow have
But if ye sholde   your trouthe kepe and save
Trouthe is the hyeste thyng   that man may kepe'
But with that word   he brast anon to wepe
And seyde 'I yow forbede   *up* peyne of deeth   upon
That nevere   whil thee lasteth lyf ne breeth
To no wight telle thou   of this aventure
As I may best   I wol my wo endure'

Arveragus decides that even in this extremity Dorigen must keep her 'trouthe'; he has a frail hope that 'trouthe shal delivere' (*Trouthe*, refrain). The rest of the story shows 'trouthe' as the one thing needful of the marriage, which at once makes it real and saves it. By keeping 'trouthe' Dorigen and Arveragus survive the test before which their marriage has not been fully real. The virtue of 'trouthe' saves the couple then moves outward in a beautiful spreading circle to Aurelius and then to the Magician. In the quoted passage 'trouthe' gains its more than theoretical force from its place in the story, from the extreme pain of Arveragus, held in check until the realistic bursting into tears. This emotion is attached to 'trouthe', which becomes charged with feeling as well as thought.

There my doubts about the tale's adequacy vanish. With this explosion of feeling a new impetus of energy enters the tale; and when the three representative ideas – courtly love, marriage, 'trouthe' – are stated again in order (by Aurelius to the Magician) the Franklin has at last shown his right to use them, having creatively demonstrated them and connected them with something real:

F 1595
        Arveragus   of gentillesse
   Hadde levere dye   in sorwe and distresse
   Than that his wyf   were of hir trouthe fals

V

This development of *The Franklin's Tale* affects the doctrine of its opening lines.

Dorigen and Arveragus begin with that paradoxical list of bargains, and they try to seal love into the contract with the seal of 'trouthe'. But why should this 'trouthe' of the beginning be the same as the 'trouthe' of Dorigen's joking promise to Arveragus? It might be argued that Dorigen and Arveragus are the victims of a linguistic fallacy: Dorigen uses the same phrase, 'have here my trouthe', in two places, and thinks that she is therefore in both places talking about the same thing.[1] But if Dorigen *thinks* her trouthe is plighted to Aurelius, it *is*, and she cannot back out without destroying also her 'trouthe' to Arveragus. In any case it seems to me Dorigen is right and that she has plighted her troth in both cases. (Sir Gawain is similarly right when he feels his 'trawthe' engaged to the Green Knight.) Moreover, Dorigen's bargain with Aurelius is as much as what she wants as her bargain with Arveragus: her 'no' is very firm, but she *wants* to go back to the idea of getting rid of the rocks. She plights her troth to Aurelius with the force of her wish for the world to be less threatening.

The determination of Dorigen and Arveragus to keep 'trouthe' is their wish to be true to each other and to their love; this is the test of their sincerity and their sense of what is real. But this sincerity turns upside down the neat if paradoxical understandings

[1] Cf. D. W. Robertson's commentary, discussed below, p. 272.

reached at the beginning. Everything is open again. 'Trouthe', which was the guarantee of the safety of love, is now the very quality that puts everything at risk. By this daring loyalty Arveragus and Dorigen add the final element of adventurousness which they have tried to organize out of their marriage and without which their lives are unreal. For the final paradox is that this 'trouthe' rather than the earlier arrangements brings the God of Love into the marriage. The emotions of Dorigen and Arveragus that I have pointed to, and their effect on Aurelius and the Magician, are more like the beating of the wings of 'beningne love'[1] than anything we have seen earlier in the tale. This is where we find the coalescence of Love, 'trouthe' and 'gentilesse' which the Franklin began by seeking.

But only because it need not have been so. The Franklin's example shows that things can fall out like this, not that they must. The objection to the opening was that Dorigen and Arveragus seem to be seeking guarantees of the prosperity of their love: but in the event we see the 'grete worthynesse' of love in the tale only when they abandon all guarantees and opt instead for hope, or faith, in 'trouthe'. It so happens that Aurelius is influenced to do a 'gentil' deed, and the lines that tell us so are fully convincing. He behaves as any decent man would have felt and behaved – and so shows that he has understood more of the language of love than we have hitherto given him credit for. The naturalness of his response allows us to see this development of the story as the true and right one. Nevertheless, Aurelius needn't have responded like that.

F 1499

This squier   which that highte Aurelius
On Dorigen   that was so amorus
Of aventure   happed hire to meete
Amydde the toun   right in the *quykkest* strete   liveliest
As she was bown to goon   the wey forth right
Toward the gardyn   ther as she had *hight*   promised
And he was   to the gardyn-ward also
For wel he spyed   whan she wolde go
Out of hir hous   to any maner place
But thus they mette   of aventure or grace
And he saleweth hire   with glad entente
And asked of hire   whiderward she wente
And she answerde   half as she were mad
'Unto the gardyn   as myn housbonde bad
My trouthe for to holde   allas allas'

            [1] *Troilus and Criseyde* III, 1261.

> Aurelius   thogh he wondred on this cas
> And was astonied   at the *nycetee*   simplicity
> Of Dorigen   to telle hir pryvetee
> 'My deere lemman Dorigen'   he sayde
> 'No fors thereof   ye ben nat now a mayde
> Now is no tyme   for swich cursed prudence
> Lat be thyn olde   spiced conscience'
> And with that word   he caughte hir by the queynte
> And faste upon hire eyen   than he preynte
> And than anoon   took hir in armes tweye
> And lad hir forth   ther as him liste to pleye

– it *could* have gone like that (setting aside the verse). Or alternatively the tale could have turned tragic. In any of these cases the point would have been similar, though the tale wouldn't have been as good. Dorigen and Arveragus would in any event have been true to their love – but love is a thing as any spirit free, and he might not have favoured them. In the end their fate is as much on the knees of the gods as that of Troilus in Book III or the Tercels of *The Parliament of Fowls*. So it is that when the Franklin asks his closing *questio amoris* he is using the word 'free' (usually something more like 'noble' or 'civilized') partly in its modern sense:

F 1622
Which was the mooste fre   as thynketh yow?

Chaucer is a wily writer and it should not really be surprising that the tale which at first seems to lay down the rules for guaranteeing permanent success in love should later be seen to belong with his other Boethian works in saying, as far as it says anything extractable, 'Hold fast to the best you know and can believe in – not that that will allow you to make any very certain sense of the wonders of the world...' Chaucer says so with the strength of the story, whereas the earlier rules belong to the deliberate weakness of the earlier parts of the story.

Women in Love has a comparable development, which is the justification for offering the comparison. Birkin is determined to break out of what he feels to be constricting conventionality into something he needs a new language to describe. But the bits of his new language we see are not superior to the old ('interpolarity' and so on). Ursula, on the other hand, wants to rest securely within the old language of love. One development is that Birkin has to come round in part to Ursula's point of view and see that the only way he can express newness of life is within the existing language. It is surprising that Arveragus should countenance adultery: it is almost the same surprise (coming, so to speak, from the other direction) that Birkin should countenance good old marriage. Both have to abandon their wish for a new certainty (I have in mind Birkin's wistful recognition at the end that he cannot simply give up the idea of a relationship like the one with Gerald: on the other hand he can't hope to find it). In both works the surprising upsetting of the original morality – made convincing because embodied in the story – is the artist's achievement of sincerity. Both writers show the terrifying openness of the bond of love; at the beginning and at the end of our literature this subject is the central concern of the great writer of the age.

Part Three:
Perspectives

I 2

Chaucer's Contemporaries:
1, 'Piers Plowman'

So far I have been talking about Chaucer as if he were one of our poets. I have been discussing his poems and the development of his genius in the hope that assumptions about the nature of his poetic achievement will be 'swallowed down' with the criticisms of individual poems. It is now time for me to show openly what, in the state of contemporary criticism of medieval poetry (below, Chapter 16, 'Chaucer and criticism'), I must think of as the cloven hoof. Those who have sailed so many leagues with me must be prepared for the avowal that I really do think Chaucer is an English poet. By this I mean that for those of us brought up in a community whose first language is English, and especially for those whose first language is English English, Chaucer is the oldest of *our* poets, the first of those we read naturally, by right, and before (though not without) the interposition of either translations or editorial explications of the poet's different world. ('Before', I mean, in logic not time – whether in fact we read first Chaucer or Professor Coghill is a personal accident.) I read Chaucer as if he were an English poet, as if the term we apply to T. S. Eliot or Pope or Donne extends also to him: I consider Chaucer in ways like enough to the ways of considering our other poets not to need another term.

Each English poet belongs, as well as to English literature, to his own age of English literature. I want to continue the case about Chaucer's status as an English poet by asking whether 'the age of Chaucer' – a phrase occasionally used even by critics who believe there is no such thing – can mean anything.

Mr John Speirs makes well the connection between Chaucer and two contemporary writers which I believe to be central to this question, and which I would like to pursue a little further than Mr Speirs does himself.

The place of *Sir Gawain and the Green Knight* – and *because* it is a great poem it is a central place – is in the English tradition. It belongs to the first great creative moment of (I shall dare to say) *modern* English literature – the moment of the *Canterbury Tales* and of *Piers Plowman*. These three English poems, though robustly independent from each other, are not accidentally contemporary.[1]

Chaucer was not alone. There is no evidence that he had read *Piers Plowman*, and it seems rather improbable that he had ever heard of *Sir Gawain and the Green Knight* or could have read it without a glossary; but these two very different poems belong with Chaucer. How they belong is our present subject: a preliminary formulation could be to say that like Chaucer both Langland and the *Gawain* poet are struggling, from the variously constricting conditions of what I shall call a 'pre-literary' situation, into something *we* can recognize as literary art. In this way Langland is more significantly Chaucer's contemporary than Gower, though the latter is in obvious ways closer to Chaucer, simply because Gower is not a great English poet.

If there are likenesses between the poetry of Chaucer and Langland, they are certainly not at the level of temperamental affinity or agreement about what poetry ought to do. If we can make anything of the proposition that they are significantly contemporary it can only be after conceding that in many important ways it would be hard to imagine poets with less in common.

Chaucer's vast range is common knowledge, but there is a group of subjects, interests or traditions missing in Chaucer, which are the very centre, or so it at first seems, of *Piers Plowman* – a group which presents the main alternative offered by English history to Chaucer's own range of interests. It would not be quite true to say that ecstatic or ascetic religion is absent from Chaucer's work, or even that he never has any ambition to exhort the reader to virtue (there are respectively the tales of the Clerk and the Parson). But it is certainly true that Chaucer is out of sympathy with ecstasy and the more abandoned kinds of pulpit oratory, and that these appear in *The Canterbury Tales* only when held in check by an irony that views them severely from the outside. But Langland sometimes sounds in his own person rather like the Pardoner in full spate of mad rhetoric. Again, Chaucer makes no direct pronouncements on the politics of church or state, except in terms so general that no

---

[1] John Speirs, 'Sir Gawain and the Green Knight', *Scrutiny* XVI (1949), 275; reprinted in *Medieval English Literature, The Non-Chaucerian Tradition*, (1957).

cap could be proved to fit any individual – a prudent course in a poet of high enough rank in the state to have lost his head, if things had gone a little worse, in the troubles of the nineties. Langland on the contrary is always passionately opinionated (like a wild provincial Dante) about the right ways for kings, popes and lords to behave. Chaucer seems to know nothing of the peasantry; his world is the civilized one of the courts, from which he can peer down no further than the lesser burgesses. Langland, in the very title of his poem and the development of his story, finds hope only in the peasantry.

Chaucer's own Plowman is the one thoroughly lifeless character in *The General Prologue* and, being a dead man, tells no tale. (Or perhaps he really is supposed to tell the spurious *Beryn* some of the manuscripts given him – Chaucer may have realized that the only hope of a Plowman's Tale was to get a text from somewhere else.) The trouble with Chaucer's Plowman is that he is seen so vaguely and sentimentally, quite unlike anyone else in the Prologue.

A 529
With hym ther was a Plowman was his brother	
That hadde ylad of dong ful many a fother	
A trewe *swynkere* and a good was he	worker
Lyvynge in pees and parfit charitee	
God loved he best with al his hoole herte	
At alle tymes thogh him gamed or smerte	
And thanne his neighebor right as hymselve	
He wolde thresshe and therto dyke and delve	
For Cristes sake for every povre wight	
Withouten hire if it lay in his myght	
His tithes payde he ful faire and wel	
Bothe of his propre swynk and his *catel*	goods
In a *tabard* he rood upon a mere	sleeveless coat

What is it that the establishment eternally demands of the populace? That it should work industriously and not strike, that it should refrain from riot and be religious in so far as the religion is of a kind to promote the bearing of crosses and the prompt payment of taxes. This is exactly what Chaucer, with some unction, likes in the Plowman. The earthy touches are an attempt to bluff us into believing that Chaucer is as well acquainted with the Plowman as with his brother the Parson. Chaucer can know and love the Parson because the Parson is literate and can write a sermon, but the Plowman can only plow. The alternative to this account is to see Chaucer's Plowman as a retort to Langland. Piers Plowman becomes a figure of Christ: Chaucer is perhaps just showing in a few lines what he thinks of the idea of our salvation by the lower orders.

Chaucer tells stories; Langland exhorts, often enough in a hectoring manner. Langland has something in common with Wyclif, and shows many of the traits of puritanism 200 years before they are supposed to have developed. One need not subscribe to the view of Chaucer as a merry old soul to see that he is out of sympathy with Langland's style of full and simple commitment to moral and religious positions. It fits that at a more personal level Chaucer notoriously makes jokes about his fatness, while Langland calls himself 'Long Will' and makes jokes about his thinness – a thinness that is a sign of an obsessive devotion to teaching and exhortation like, though less philosophical and more polemical than, that of Chaucer's Clerk.

Langland's interconnection of love, self-denial and practical politics has a very seventeenth-century smack to it. His anti-clericalism would have been at home in an Elizabethan conventicle, and he actually calls for the disendowment of the church over a hundred years before Henry VIII made his own the opinion that the common good would be better served if the lands of the monasteries were administered by the aristocracy. Langland then represents a very important and long-lasting thread of English life made of strands not found in Chaucer. Born in the seventeenth century it is impossible to imagine Langland a royalist (would he have been Bunyan?); in the eighteenth century his wild but conservative zeal would have found a home in the Wesleyan movement; in the nineteenth century he could have been a Christian socialist and later in great sympathy with William Morris; a few years ago I am sure he would have been found disapproving of Bertrand Russell from within the ranks of the Campaign for Nuclear Disarmament. Langland *is* (in Mr Speirs's phrase) the non-Chaucerian tradition. But is he a poet?

If Langland is just a preacher or a scholar he is incomparable with Chaucer, since Chaucer is a fully self-conscious literary artist – a phrase I can't much like, and which had it been possible in the English of his day I am sure Langland would have indignantly repudiated as a description of himself.

Sometimes it looks as though Langland's instincts are all against poetry. He will keep breaking away into denunciations or preaching. For instance, at the beginning of the 'Dowel' section Langland has to introduce the very important word 'inwitte'.

BI X 52
  Inwit and alle †wittes†   closed ben therinne
For loue of the lady *Anima*   that lyf is ‡ynempned‡
Ouer al in a mannes body   §he§ walketh and wandreth
Ac in the herte is hir home   and hir moste reste
Ac Inwitte is in the hed   and to the herte he loketh
What *Anima* is lief or loth   he lat hir at his wille
For after the grace of God   the grettest is Inwitte[1]

  * consciousness, conscience   † perceptions   ‡ named   § she

So far so good. But the poet then immediately succumbs to the temptation to preach a little sermon that has nothing to do with his definition of 'inwitte'.

59   Moche wo *worth* that man   that mys reuleth his Inwitte
And that be glotouns globbares   her god is her wombe
†For† thei seruen Sathan   her soule shal he haue
‡That‡ liueth synful lyf here   her soule is liche the deuel
And alle that lyuen good lyf   aren like god almi3ti

     * is to   † because   ‡ they that

Certain sins belong so strongly together in the fourteenth century that it is almost part of Langland's grammar for him to continue, once he has got started on gluttony, to a denunciation also of drunkenness: there is a sort of chain-reaction that leads him further and further from his subject into the more pleasant (to him) paths of moral thunder:

64   Allas that drynke shal fordo   that god dere bou3te
And *doth* god forsaken hem   that he shope to his liknesse

     * makes

Only now, when we have forgotten about it, does he return to 'inwitte'.

Here, of course, Langland is the opposite of Chaucer. The tag 'her wombe is her god' is used twice by Chaucer, in the tales of the Parson and the Pardoner. The latter makes an instructive contrast with *Piers Plowman*: instead of being led astray into sermonizing Chaucer shows mercilessly how meaningless that rhetoric is in the mouth of the Pardoner.

C 529
  The apostel wepyng   seith ful pitously
'Ther walken manye   of whiche yow toold have I
I seye it now wepyng   with pitous voys

[1] *Piers Plowman* is quoted from the great edition of W. W. Skeat (2 vols., Oxford, 1886).

That they been enemys   of Cristes croys
Of whiche the ende is deeth   wombe is hir god
O wombe   O bely   O stynkyng cod
Fulfilled of dong   and of corrupcioun
At either ende of thee   foul is the soun

This expert progression from the tearful by way of the portentous to the vulgarly humorous is done with great vigour and complete detachment: this is a speech that could well be learned by rote, and Chaucer cannot be suspected of sympathy with the Pardoner. Both these passages of Langland and Chaucer are close to real medieval sermons.[1] But Chaucer's is the artist's terribly clear picture of the thing as in itself it really is. Langland on the contrary slips into being a preacher, instead of showing or exploring the preaching. Here one might say that Chaucer is the poet, and that Langland's work, however well it does the preaching, is on a lower plane.

Nevertheless, my contention is that Langland's poem is itself the laborious working-out into real poetry, and that this makes *Piers Plowman* comparable with Chaucer's career.

Although Langland frequently lapses into the sub-poetic he can also be found doing the other thing, struggling for a vision of life truer than his pre-existing moral beliefs. Right at the beginning, Langland himself disapproves of Meed, but his poetry makes her comparatively sympathetic, and Conscience, the official morality of the episode, hard and priggish.

Perhaps the best-known passus, VI of the B-text, is about the proper ordering of the ranks of society. It begins with just the modification of medieval commonplace that one might expect of Langland the moralist. The ordinary classification into those who work (Piers the Plowman), those who fight (the Knight) and those who pray is made more interesting by Langland's inversion of the usual order of precedence to make Piers the Plowman dominant. The opening lines are also interesting, as is often the case with those passages where one can accuse Langland of preaching, because of the passionate decency which in real-life politics might be the opposite of enlightening. But there is nothing new in the essential division of responsibility between Piers and the Knight, the agreement that Piers shall work for both in return for the Knight's protection; and nothing seems to be gained by stating this allegorically.

[1] Cf. G. R. Owst's *Literature and Pulpit in Medieval England* (Cambridge, 1933).

B VI 25

'Bi seynt Poule' quod Perkyn   'ȝe profre ȝow so faire
That I shal swynke and swete   and sowe for vs bothe
And other laboures do for thi loue   al my lyf tyme
In couenaunt that thow kepe   holikirke and my selue
Fro wastoures and fro wykked men   that this worlde struyeth'

So far so ordinary. But Langland doesn't leave things at that.

By line 107 the policy is in operation and seems to be working well.

Now is Perkyn and his pilgrymes   to the plowe faren
To *erie* his halue acre   holpyn hym manye   plow
Dikeres and delueres   digged vp the balkes
There with was Perkyn apayed   and preysed hem faste

But then

117   seten somme   and songen *atte nale*   at ale
And hulpen erie his half acre   with 'how trollilolli'

and it is soon time for Piers to call in the Knight to do his duty in accordance with the contract. Here for the first time the passus begins to be more than neat schematization, and to admit the difficulties and passions politicians are likely to encounter.

156   A Brytonere a braggere   a bosted Pieres als
And bad hym go pissen with his plow   forpyned schrewe
'Wiltow or neltow   we wil haue owre wille
Of thi flowre and of thi flessche   fecche whan vs liketh
And make vs murie thermyde   maugré thi chekes'
    Thanne Pieres the plowman   pleyned hym to the knyȝte
To kepe hym as couenaunte was   fram cursed shrewes
And fro this wastoures wolueskynnes   that maketh the worlde dere
'For tho waste and wynnen nouȝte   and that *ilke* while
Worth neuere plente amonge the poeple   ther while my plow
    liggeth'
    Curteisly the knyȝte thanne   as his †kynde wolde†
Warned Wastoure   and wissed hym bettere
'Or thow shalt abugge by the lawe   by the ordre that I bere'
            * same   † nature demanded

Waster retorts with a direct challenge to the scheme of things. He simply says, with the utmost explicitness,

169   'I was nouȝt wont to worche' quod Wastour   'and now wil I
        nouȝt bigynne'

Thereupon the social structure collapses. The Knight is powerless to uphold the covenant.

Langland's honesty here is that of a 'clerk' not confined to his commonplaces, able to look beyond his study windows and see that the ruling classes *were* powerless to curb the demands of the depleted peasantry. Or, to put it differently, Langland's capacity to get free of medieval cliché is that no sooner does he begin to tell a story about his favourite clichés than the story runs away with him into a truth quite different from the cliché he started with or, perhaps, from anything he consciously wants. In this passus the story is necessary to what Langland is doing: it is by telling this story about his commonplace that Langland understands and alters it.

When the Knight lets him down Piers calls for Hunger to make the wasters work.

175 'Awreke me of thise wastoures' quod he 'that this worlde
         schendeth'   shame, destroy

Piers at this moment wants people to be driven to work, at any cost; and the observation is the obvious one that if people do no work hunger *will* come. But Piers takes the responsibility of 'houping after' him; Piers *wants* hunger. And Hunger does do what the 'curteys' Knight cannot.

176 Hunger in haste tho   *hent* Wastour bi the mawe   seized
     And wronge hym so bi the *wombe*   that bothe his eyen   belly
         wattered
     He buffeted the Britoner   aboute the chekes
     That he loked like a lanterne   al his lyf after
     He bette hem so bothe   he barste nere here guttes

And sure enough

186 Faitores for fere her of   flowen in to bernes
     And flapten on with flayles   fram morwe til euen
     That Hunger was nou3t so hardy   on hem for to loke

But before this, in face of the severity of Hunger powerfully created in Langland's verse, Piers is already changing his position.

181 Ne hadde Pieres with a pese lof   preyed Hunger to cesse
     They hadde ben *doluen* bothe   ne deme thow non other
     'Suffre hem lyue' he seyde   'and lete hem ete with hogges
     Or elles benes and bren   ybaken togideres
     Or elles melke and mene ale'   thus preyed Pieres for hem
                              * done for

This change is Langland's rising above the medieval common-place. Let hunger drive people to work – an idea attractive enough

208

to the armchair economist; and hunger does drive these wasters to
work. But Langland is able to see that if hunger is to make people
work it will be *like this*, a way of getting the work done which is
hardly pleasant to contemplate, and as far from a neat solution as
the original social contract turned out to be. So within ten lines of
having called in Hunger, Piers has to turn his attention to the
mitigation of Hunger's effects. And once Langland's inspiration
takes control he can go much further. As the passus continues the
rashness of the original call to Hunger becomes increasingly
apparent. Hunger, after the manner of political saviours, is easier
to call in than to get rid of. Yet Hunger is an ally, and Piers asks
his advice about the problem of wasters (even though *after* he has

202   preyed Hunger to wende
    Home into his owne *erde*   and holden hym there).   country

But the spirit of the question is utterly different from that of
Hunger's reply:

205 'Ac I preye the ar thow passe' quod Pieres to Hunger
    'Of beggeres and of bidderes what best be to done?
    For I wote wel be thow went thei wil worche ful ille
    For myschief it maketh thei beth so meke nouthe
    And for defaute of her fode this folke is at my wille
    They are my blody bretheren' quod Pieres 'for god bou3te vs alle
    Treuthe tau3te me ones to louye hem vchone
    And to helpen hem of alle thinge ay as hem nedeth
    And now wolde I witen of the what were the best
    And how I mi3te amaistrien hem and make hem to worche'
      'Here now' quod Hunger 'and holde it for a wisdome
    Bolde beggeres and bigge that *mowe* her bred †biswynke†
    With houndes bred and hors bred holde vp her hertis
    Abate hem with benes ‡for‡ bollyng of her wombe
    And 3if the gomes grucche bidde hem go swynke'

      * may   † work for   ‡ against

Part of Hunger's difference from Piers is that the savagery of
Hunger is seen to have its comic side. It continues to do so in a
passage where the comedy becomes quite inseparable from the
savagery. Piers asks Hunger for a remedy against starvation, and
Hunger, being hunger, can only prescribe himself.

255   '3et I prey 3ow' quod Pieres '*par charite* and 3e kunne
    Eny leef of lechecraft lere it me my dere
    For somme of my seruauntz and my self bothe
    Of al a wyke worche nou3t so owre wombe aketh'
      'I wote wel' quod Hunger 'what sykenesse 3ow eyleth
    3e han maunged ouer moche and that maketh 3ow grone'

Part of Langland's irony is directed against himself. Langland is certainly prone to admire the simple kind of social remedy that Piers's call for Hunger typifies. Langland certainly also has himself a quirky dislike and fear of doctors. But the attack on doctors to which Hunger continues – quite inappropriate here – makes the speaker more ridiculous than the doctors. Hunger misfires with one of the oldest European jokes, doctors who kill the patients, because *he* is killing the labourers.

270   'And ȝif thow diete the thus   I dar legge myn eres
      That Phisik shal his furred hodes   for his fode selle
      And his cloke of Calabre   with alle the knappes of golde
      And be fayne bi my feith   his phisik to lete
      And lerne to laboure with londe   for lyflode is swete
      For morthereres aren mony leches   lorde hem amende
      Thei do men deye thorw here drynkes   ar destiné it wolde'

We have now come all the way in the passus from simple social models and remedies with a family likeness to Bringing Back the Cat to a very effectively poetic criticism of such simplicities. This continues, getting further and further from any simple preaching as it becomes more freely poetic. When Piers says this in reply to Hunger's diatribe,

277   'By seynt Poule' quod Pieres   'thise aren profitable wordis
      Wende now Hunger when thow wolt   that wel be thow euere
      For this is a louely lessoun   lorde it the forȝelde'

his gingerly politeness is insincere. Hunger is now a disastrous all-powerful guest on an unwelcome visit of indefinite duration, who has to be cajoled away.[1] The ironies continue, with varying degrees of comedy and horror. Hunger's reply to Piers's politely-wrapped-up request for him to leave is in his own and only style:

280   '*Byhote* god' quod Hunger   'hennes ne wil I wende   promise
      Til I haue dyned bi this day   and ydronke bothe'

The passus then returns to real starvation. The author's point of view has now shifted completely since the opening: Hunger, called in by Piers, is now the monstrous enemy. Langland's poem is better even than a simple discovery would have been, registered in an ordinary change of mind – better than the 'return upon himself'[2] Arnold so much admired in Burke. Langland's showing

---

[1] I make this point differently and for a different purpose in Chapter 2 of my *Chaucer's Prosody* (Cambridge, 1971).
[2] 'The Function of Criticism at the Present Time', *Essays in Criticism*, first series.

himself the truth involves a deeper understanding of the whole problem: it is not simply a change of mind because, for instance, he does not condone the wasters. The passus continues,

> 301 By that it neighed nere heruest   newe corn came to *chepynge*
> Thanne was folke fayne   and fedde Hunger with the best
> With good ale as Glotoun tauȝte   and gerte Hunger go slepe
> * market

As soon as harvest comes there is an immediate return to the *status quo ante*. The difference is that we now see the problem differently, and can have no dependence on the wish for draconian remedies that made Piers first whoop for Hunger. The reader learns something by experiencing this story (though to say *what* ought to be to point back to the text).

This achievement is as poetic as Chaucer's and, in an obvious way, beyond Chaucer. One wouldn't know from *The Canterbury Tales* – splendid picture of England as that work is – that there had been any such events as the Black Death and the Peasants' Revolt: for the engagement – and the *poetic* engagement – with those parts of life, one goes to Langland.

When Langland tries to round off the Hunger passus with a bit of the good advice that is so central to his ambition one feels that the story he has told is better than he knows, and that it makes the advice perfunctory and thin:

> 322 Ac I warne ȝow werkemen   *wynneth* while ȝe mowe   gain
> For Hunger hiderward   hasteth hym faste
> He shal awake with water   wateoures to chaste

It is also fitting that when Langland leaves the story for a preaching end he goes a little crazy. The story has been a way of discovering a truth. But what are we to make of this? –

> 328 Whan ȝe se the sonne amys   and two monkes hedes
> And a mayde haue the maistrie   and multiplie bi eight
> Thanne shal Deth withdrawe   and Derthe be iustice
> And Dawe the dyker   deye for hunger
> But if god of his goodnesse   graunt vs a trewe

Two monks' (or monk's?) heads *what*? Multiply *what* by eight? And how shall death withdraw if Daw is going to die? Editors like to suppose this is a gnomic passage with a hidden meaning: if so, the most apparent thing about it is the style of the hiding. It is just raving, and, in the end, raving is the alternative in *Piers Plowman* to poetry.

Langland does, for all his preaching and raving, achieve art more often than one might have thought probable. If it were worth the space one could offer a commentary similar to the above on the Seven Deadly Sins passus (B-text V); I will make the point briefly from one sin. At first it seems that this passus is only an excuse for the denunciations of vice Langland's soul loved. But:

'So long as a religion is fully alive, men do not talk about it or make allegories about it.' To which we may reply that if Dante, Milton and Bunyan did not believe their religion it would be difficult to find anybody who did believe. It does not disprove the reality of Bunyan's temptation that he represented it as a struggle with a fishy-scaled monster. The articles of his creed required a concrete expression. Religion is dead when the imagination deserts it. When it is alive abstractions become visible and walk about on the roads.[1]

Langland's sins do come to life and walk about the roads; one result is that one can never be quite sure what they will do next – what the story will make Langland realize about them. Again we move out of simple moral exhortation into poetry, which explores further and realizes the sins more deeply. It is not that Langland ceases to care about the nature of the sins: Glotoun is more gluttony than Pernel Proudheart is pride *because* he is vividly individualized in that story about him. Glotoun is waylaid on his way to shrift, and the life of the passage is in making the reader feel imaginatively just how gluttony *would* succumb to this temptation:

> B V 304
>   Now bigynneth glotoun   for to go to schrifte
> And *kaires hym* to kirkeward   his †coupe† to schewe
>   Ac Beton the brewestere   bad hym good morwe
> And axed of hym with that   whiderward he wolde
>   'To holi cherche' quod he   'forto here masse
> And sithen I wil be shryuen   and synne namore'
>   'I haue gode ale gossib' quod she   'Glotown wiltow assaye?'
> 'Hastow au3te in thi purs   any hote spices?'
>   'I have peper and piones' quod she   'and a pounde of garlike
> A ferthyngworth of fenel seed   for fastyngdayes'
>   Thanne goth Glotoun in   and grete othes after
>   * runs   † guilt

I can still feel the temptation in 'wiltow assaye?'

For all the evident moral intent, the Glotoun passage really leaves the reader free to make his own conclusions. Gluttony is

---

[1] W. Hale White ('Mark Rutherford'), *John Bunyan* (1905), pp. 230–1; answering remarks by J. A. Froude.

shown in all its foulness (especially lines 36off.) but because Langland *is* showing us gluttony, and not merely telling us to eschew gluttony, he shows the demonic force that drives Glotoun into the tavern. One response, from those strongly enough inclined to gluttony to go against the grain of the poem's language, could well be, 'Well yes, I see what that life is – but it is the one I want: I see my desire strongly expressed there and I'm damned if my wife and mistress (line 364) are going to make *me* repent.' Langland's portrait of Glotoun is almost as free from overt moralizing as Chaucer's horrifying Summoner.

This is the difference between Langland and all the sermon literature with which Owst compares his poem. At Langland's best he rises into art which, so far as I know, even the liveliest sermons never do. In his various sources Langland finds the same elements that go into other devotional or prophetic writing – the rhetoric, the imagery, the *exempla*, the personifications. But in the sermons they subserve a simple moral purpose, whereas Langland can make art of them. He can do more here than Chaucer. *The Pardoner's Tale* is, of course, splendid: but that is *all* Chaucer can make of Langland's field. Langland's Glotoun is more an exploration, and less a perfectly observed thing, than the Pardoner's sermon on gluttony.

But if Langland climbs out of preaching into art it is not without a struggle. He himself was troubled in conscience by not knowing whether writing poetry was an activity of sufficient moral worth to devote himself to.[1] Would he not be better occupied in prayer? He raises the question in the interesting autobiographical passage in passus VI of the c-text. Reason rebukes Langland (clothed as a 'lollere') for not working. There is no social category of poets, and writing poetry does not count as work.

C VI 12
   'Canstow seruen' he seide 'other syngen in a churche
  Other coke for my cokers other to the cart picche...?'

---

[1] I am forced here to raise (if only in a footnote) the tedious question of how we know Langland is telling the truth about himself. (Cf. G. Kane, *The Autobiographical Fallacy in Chaucer and Langland Studies* (1965), and Jerome Mitchell, *Thomas Hoccleve* (Urbana, 1968), Chapter 1.) There is no independent evidence by which we can check what Langland says. But, firstly, he doesn't write as if he would lie casually, and, secondly, I am discussing not an hypothetical historical man called William Langland but the author of *Piers Plowman*. I know that the author of *Piers Plowman*, whether 'real' or a persona, has a worry about writing poetry which fits the character of the poem's narrator. I know that because it is in the poetry.

But Langland has just told us that he is

3   lytel ylete by   leyue me for sothe
           Among lollares of London   and lewede heremytes
           For ich made of tho men   as reson me tauhte

('Because I wrote poems about those men, as reason taught me.')

Reason is evidently divided on the question of whether poetry is work. Langland answers his protests, a little feebly and jokingly, by saying that he is too weak to work with sickle or scythe, and too tall to stoop to pick weeds (23–4). Reason is not satisfied and returns to the charge. Langland makes the further excuse that he prays for people (like Chaucer's Clerk). But why not then pray professionally, as a monk? One reason is that Langland has already mentioned his wife Kit, but the other, which he doesn't put to Reason, is that he wants to be a poet, in a society which has no place for the kind of poet he wants to be – which being the case, he cannot even state the case clearly. The nearest he comes is his claim (56) that intellectuals are excused from labour because they are distinguished by natural intelligence, which in Langland's case can only be evidenced by the poetry he writes. But he then escapes the issue by a characteristic, long digression about the folly of admitting illegitimate children to the priesthood. He seems again on the point of defending himself *as a poet* when he says,

83   For in my conscience ich knowe   what Crist wolde that ich wrouhte

– but he tries to explain this 'what' next line as 'preyers'.

Conscience, however, will not let him off so easily, and takes up the questioning:

89   Quath Conscience 'by Crist   ich can nat see this lyeth
     Ac it semeth nouht parfytnesse   in cytees for to begge
     Bote he be obediencer   to pryour other to *mynstre*'   monastery

Langland replies ambiguously with a reference to the parable of the hid treasure,[1] and he goes on

99   So hope ich to haue   of hym that is almyghty
     A gobet of hus grace   and bygynne a tyme
     That alle tymes of my tyme   to profit shal turne

But whether Langland is to 'redeem the time'[2] by prayer or, like T. S. Eliot, by creating poetry, does not appear.

Langland found it so hard to recognize and express his poetic

---

[1] Matthew xiii. 44. Conscience will not understand this coy reference.
[2] *Ash Wednesday* IV.

ambition for the same reason that Chaucer found it so hard to break out into *The Parliament of Fowls*. Both became conscious in pre-literary situations where ways of writing permitted dependent comment but not the criticism of life both in their different ways were pushing towards. The sermon tradition with which Langland was so much at home gave him the chance to denounce vice and to castigate the rich and proud of the earth. The mystical tradition with which his affinities are less simple gave him his language of love as 'triacle of hevene'. The groundswell of religious and social revolt allowed him to make Piers Plowman become almost the same as Christ. But there were no precedents for his flowering into irony and poetry, into a work where finally everything depends upon everything else. That required a creative originality comparable with Chaucer's.

Langland's success is less certain and more equivocal than Chaucer's: he often rests in the traditions from which his living impulse is to emerge: that is to recognize that there is a great deal of dull stuff in *Piers Plowman*. Langland rarely resists any opening, however slight, for yet another onslaught on the traditional enemies of Christianity or his own pet dislikes, the hermits, the lollards and the doctors. But the dullness is a condition for the moments of escape into real poetry.

The final sign that Langland did move in the direction of 'art speech' is the way he ends his poem in the B- and C-texts, and by the way that affects everything that goes before.

The 'Vision of Piers' and the long involved 'Dowel' section generally answer to the above account: they are full of everything from sternly orthodox morality to self-criticism and vulgar humour, and the poem redeems its dullness by the passages where Langland sets his imagination free. But with 'Dobet', the Christian life, Langland may seem to be abandoning his attempt at a criticism of life in favour of a more straightforward celebration of Christianity. This is to oversimplify; but at least with passus XVIII of the B-text (which Skeat, rightly in a way, calls the finest in the poem) it does begin to look as if Langland thinks he has solved his problems – which, whatever it may lead to by way of eloquence or religious fervour, is not a poetic thing to do. The passus is certainly, in parts, splendid. Langland is magnificently unafraid of using words like 'glory'; and he tells the Crucifixion with the whole weight of his Christian feeling. (Though even in this passus there are dull passages.) The passus is the culmination of the

religious fervour of the whole poem and ends fittingly with Langland's carrying his fervour back into real life as he wakes on Easter
morning and calls to Kit and Calotte

> B XVIII 427
> Ariseth and reuerenceth goddes resurrexioun
> And crepeth to the crosse on knees and kisseth it for a Iuwel
> For goddes blissed body it bar for owre bote
> And it afereth the fende for suche is the my3te
> May no grysly gost glyde *ther* it shadweth   where

But this is 'Dobet', and 'Dobest' is still to come. And 'Dobest',
better even than this perfervid joy, turns out to be a return to the
exploration of confusion with which the poem opens. At first
'Dobest' seems to be following 'Dobet' by telling the story of the
development of the church. Sometimes it seems too good to be
true; Langland seems not to realize that there is a certain inappropriateness in his figure of the church as a well-run farm in which
the evangelists are oxen and the fathers carthorses:

> B XIX 257
>   Grace gaue Piers a teme foure gret oxen
>   That on was Luke a large beest and a lowe chered
>   And Marke and Mathew the thrydde myghty bestes bothe
>   And Ioigned to hem one Iohan most gentil of alle
>   The prys nete of Piers plow

By the middle of B XIX Unity Holychurch is built and everything is
(as with Piers's social arrangements before the outburst of the
Waster) neat, perfect, and dull. But then Langland shows – to my
mind quite finally – that he is a poet before he is an apologist for
Christianity. He doesn't leave things perfect. Not only is Holychurch under attack at the end of the poem; the attack is successful.
There comes an authentic Waster-like note, which has the effect of
letting some life back into the poem, when Conscience's advice
that we should repent before going to mass is thus received:

> B XIX 394
> '3e bawe' quod a brewere 'I wil nou3t be reuled
> Bi Iesu for al 3owre Ianglynge with *spiritus iusticie*'

The poem ends with the defection from Holychurch of Kynde
(earlier, as Nature, equated with the creating God) and Lyf. The
general theme is given a peculiar force by its mixture with a
personal attack by age upon the narrator which is as shocking as
Hunger's onslaught on the wasters (B XX, 185ff.) and which helps

obscurely with the undermining of the earlier certainties. Finally a Friar Flatterer penetrates and spoils Holychurch, where Conscience, the hero of this part of the poem and as close in meaning to our 'consciousness' as 'conscience', has retreated for defence; whereupon Conscience abandons the church. The poem ends, perhaps with deliberate flatness,

B XX 378
'Bi Cryste' quod Conscience tho   'I wil bicome a pilgryme
And walken as wyde   as al the worlde lasteth
And seke Piers the Plowman   that Pryde may destruye
And that freres hadde a fyndyng   that for nede flateren
And contrepleteth me Conscience   now Kynde me auenge
And sende me happe and hele   til I haue Piers the Plowman'
And sithe he *gradde* after grace   til I gan awake   cried out

This makes the poem as much a pilgrimage as *The Canterbury Tales*, and in the same way. The end leads straight back to the beginning, where Langland is also walking

B Prol. 4
        wyde in this world   wondres to here

Dobest is the hard search for truth in poetry, however confused the search and the poetry sometimes are. Dobest too is the sign that all the parts of the poem are to evaluate each other dramatically, like the different kinds of love in *The Parliament of Fowls*; for it is only in this confused seeking, and in relation to much that is not splendid, that the splendour of the Resurrection passus can have its place: which, too, makes that passus itself better than it would otherwise be. Without what comes before and after it would be impressive, but it would not be the kind of criticism of life one finds in great poetry.

Piers Plowman as much as *Ulysses* is a work justifying its own existence; and its triumph is to establish itself as poetry rather than Christian apologetics. In it Langland succeeds in seeing what it is that he began by wanting to do. The poem is great enough to allow me to apply to the way its end leads back to the beginning those great lines of Eliot:

We shall not cease from exploration
And the end of all our exploring
Will be to arrive where we started
And know the place for the first time.[1]

            [1] *Little Gidding* v.

This is what Langland does in *Piers Plowman*. It can follow that one's reason for preferring his poetry to his moralizing is that it is a superior mode of knowledge. This is a development, from a pre-literary situation, comparable with Chaucer's; there is therefore some potential point in seeing Langland as contemporary with Chaucer.

13

Chaucer's Contemporaries: 2, 'Sir Gawain and the Green Knight'

Sir Gawain and the Green Knight shares with *The Canterbury Tales* the power of surviving academic treatment – even more strikingly because, unlike the latter, it is a poem only available to academics. It is, paradoxically, an English poem that we need to translate; and I have no wish to underestimate the difficulties of the poet's diction. But the main problems of reading this difficult poem are just what they always were.

Sir Gawain is, almost, a poet's poem, full of subtleties which may cause a stumble. But like all good difficult poems it gives itself to the reader who reads well enough; and in that way it is no more difficult for us than for its original audience, if it had one.

By calling it difficult I do not mean to suggest that the poem is obscure. The difficulties stem from the places where the poem is most clearly itself. In one sense it would be absurd to say that the character of the Green Knight is a difficulty: what could be more startlingly plain? Yet it is right that critics should have spent much effort (though not perhaps quite all the extant miles of text) on the problems raised by the Green Knight, and it is not surprising that so many critics are fooled by the Green Knight. After all, Gawain is a bit fooled himself. So if I discuss what I think are the difficulties in *Sir Gawain and the Green Knight* it is in the hope of making clearer the poem's success. And (in view of the very substantial body of published work which elucidates the poem in ways that seem to me to leave the difficulies intact) I had better say that I don't mean *Sir Gawain* is a kind of cryptogram with an answer or, on the other hand, that we could get anywhere by discussing anything that could be called the poet's 'technique'. Anything wonderful in the poem comes from following the poem and allowing it to *be* a poem.

We have to work out from what we can understand. If we begin with what is *not* difficult that may then be a base for exploring what *is*. Once we have got some confidence that we are reading a poem, the work is less hard.

We see quite soon, I think, the ordinary powers of the alliterative poet; these have been well remarked by Mr Speirs and Mr Spearing, the latter of whom writes of the passage describing the beheading of the Green Knight.

The sound and movement of the lines give the event an extraordinarily physical presence: in particular one notices the crunching sound as the blade shatters the bone ('the scharp of the schalk schyndered the bones'), and the gradual increase in speed from the labouring movement of 'Gavan gripped to his ax and gederes hit on hyght' to the monosyllabic and internally echoing plunge of 'the bit of the broun stel bot on the grounde'.[1]

But even here the *Gawain* poet is unusual, for he seems to have a rare grasp of the styles and subjects of the alliterative tradition so that the success is never *only* a matter of the 'sound and movement' of the lines. There is plenty of consonantal richness elsewhere in Middle English, but hardly anywhere else outside *The Canterbury Tales* poetry as concentrated and ordered as one finds, for instance, in the progression of the seasons at the beginning of the second fitt of *Sir Gawain:*

516   After þe sesoun of somer   wyth þe soft wynde3
        Quen 3eferus syfle3 hymself   on sede3 & erbe3
        Wela wynne is þe wort   þat waxes þeroute
        When þe donkande dewe   drope3 of þe leue3
        To bide a blysful blusch   of þe bry3t sunne
        Bot þen hy3es heruest   & hardenes hym sone
        Warne3 hym for þe wynter   to wax ful rype
        He dryue3 wyth dro3t   þe dust for to ryse
        Fro þe face of þe folde   to fly3e ful hy3e
        Wroþe wynde of þe welkyn   wrastele3 with þe sunne
        Þe leue3 laucen fro þe lynde   & ly3ten on þe grounde
        & al grayes þe gres   þat grene wat3 ere
        Þenne al rype3 & rotes   þat ros vpon fyrst
        & þus 3irne3 þe 3ere   in 3isterdaye3 mony
        & wynter wynde3 a3ayn   as þe worlde aske3
                   no fage[2]

[1] A. C. Spearing, *Criticism and Medieval Poetry* (1964), p. 27. This is not Mr Spearing's main point. His essay is worth attention.

[2] *Sir Gawain and the Green Knight*, ed. Sir Israel Gollancz (EETS, Oxford, 1940). I translate:

This is as much the concentration, for a purpose, of a traditional way of feeling and observing, as the comparable first section of *East Coker*. The poet is creating the movement of the seasons for its significance in Gawain's story – the sense of the lapse of time, and concomitant changes in the way the world appears to a man – and one can see that he is making art out of what elsewhere is only a possible element of art.

Another and quite different power of the *Gawain* poet comes out in the exchanges between Gawain and the Lady in Fitt 3. One of the many things Chaucer is supposed to have fore-run is the English novel; but I know of nothing in Chaucer so like a novel as the story in this fitt. Here the *Gawain* poet is using a novelist's eye for relevant detail, character and, above all, realistic dialogue, all made to subserve his interest in what is significant in Gawain's style of life. The last is perhaps not immediately apparent, but at any rate the way that the conflict of wills and desires is created in this verse is evidence that we have to do with the work of a talented literary artist.[1] And that is enough to establish some confidence that if we follow the clue through the labyrinth it is likely to be the one left by the poet. 'I give you the end of a golden string...' But what, if we may ask a question that will be thought crude, is *Sir Gawain and the Green Knight*'s subject?

The device of asking a question about situation or character, particularly a problem about love, was a favourite of the medieval poets, presumably as a way of involving an audience in consideration of their poems. *Sir Gawain* doesn't ask such questions, but I

> Afterwards, the season of summer   with the soft winds,
> When the West wind warbles   on weeds and seedlings.
> Grace is great for the plant   that grows outside,
> When the damping dew   drops from the leaves,
> To await a glad glance   from the bright sun.
> But then bustles in harvest   and grows bold soon,
> Warns it in face of winter   to wax quite ripe.
> With drought he drives   the dust to arise,
> From the face of the earth   to fly most high.
> Wroth wind from the heavens   wrestles with the sun;
> Leaves loosen from the lime   and alight on the ground,
> And the grass goes all gray   that green was before.
> Then all ripens and rots   that rose up at first,
> And so runs the year   in yesterdays many
> And winter winds round again   as the world needs,
>   No lie.

---

[1] For a detailed analysis of these scenes see D. Mills, 'An Analysis of the Temptation Scenes in *Gawain and the Green Knight*', *The Journal of English and Germanic Philology* LXVII (1968).

believe that each of the four fitts implies one or more questions
of this kind.[1] But one of the poem's subtleties is that these questions mask rather than directly state the chief preoccupations of the
poem. I will consider only two instances.

Who or what is the Green Knight? Is he human or faery? These are
the questions presented by the first fitt – presented so insistently that
the reader may be led to suspect that they are covering rather than
expressing the poet's real interest. He thrusts on us the question of
whether the Green Knight is a man, and gives evidence on both sides.
Green is the right colour for some sort of vegetation deity, and it
certainly isn't human to pick up one's head after decapitation. His
behaviour is 'runisch' ('mysterious'). Yet if the Green Knight is a
fairy he is a very solid one and

141   mon most I *algate*   †mynn† hym to bene   always   judge

This mixture of natures belongs with the poet's mixture of styles.
Green men, nature gods, fairies, belong to one kind of narrative,
realistic scenes to another. The folk ballads bring in the otherworld in an appropriate style, with a feeling of otherworldly
significance.[2] So, too, when Yvor Winters (whose best poems are all
distilled literary criticism) wants to recreate the feeling of our poem,
he writes something mysterious, 'runisch':

> Reptilian green the wrinkled throat,
> Green as a bough of yew the beard;
> He bent his head, and so I smote;
> Then for a thought my vision cleared.
>
> The head dropped clean; he rose and walked;
> He fixed his fingers in the hair;
> The head was unabashed and talked;
> I understood what I must dare...[3]

But the *Gawain* poet's introduction of the Green Knight is quite
unlike this. Far from making a hushed suggestion about the Knight's
most mysterious feature, his colour, the poet throws the colour
hard at us by reserving it for the last word of one stanza and then,
perhaps while we are still in a state of shock, repeating it throughout the next. The effect is not mysterious but startling.

143   For of bak & of brest   al were his bodi sturne
      Both his wombe & his wast   were worthily smale
      & alle his fetures folȝande   in forme þat he hade
            ful clene

---

[1] I owe the germ of this idea to a conversation some years ago with Mrs H. M.
Shire.   [2] Cf. 'Thomas Rymer', quoted above p. 154.
[3] 'Sir Gawaine and the Green Knight', *Collected Poems* (Denver, 1960), p. 113.

> For wonder of his hwe men hade
> Set in his semblaunt sene
> He ferde as freke were fade
> & oueral enker grene
>
> Ande al graythed in grene þis gome & his wedes...[1]

Even his horse is green. The last thing a poet should do if he is trying to insinuate the otherworld under cover of vague suspense is to tell us that it is surprising; but the Green Knight's sudden irruption is as surprising as if a fairy were to appear suddenly on television. It is wrong in the same way that it is wrong to try to prove the existence of ghosts by taking photographs of them: if there are ghosts they don't belong to the same world as cameras, and if there are creatures like the Green Knight they should not arrive in this way in Arthur's court.

But I don't mean the scene is 'wrong' in the poem. The Green Knight's entry is an obviously successful narrative *coup*: the story goes with such pace and naturalness that when reading we don't stop to make the above remarks. But talking about the fitt afterwards these are matters that are bound to be raised – and so I think the poet is doing it on purpose.

Again, one would not expect mysterious figures from the otherworld to be remarkable for quirkiness of character – even poltergeists or leprechauns retain their mysteriousness – but the Green Knight is the only out and out human personality in the first section of the poem. The aggressive inappropriateness of his rush into the hall and the poem belongs with his masterfulness in everything he does, his domineering rudeness and overweening air of command. The lines (301ff.) in which he enjoys the astonishment of the court and uses it to insult the assembled knights are amongst those which remind one of the powers of a novelist. The poet is making the tension between man and fairy as tense as

---

[1] I translate: 'For although his body was strongly-built as to back and chest, both his belly and his waist were properly slim, and all his parts accordingly, in the shape that he had – very pure. Great wonder people had of his colour, set visibly in his appearance: he went on like a hostile warrior, and all over inked GREEN. And all rigged out in green this warrior and his clothes...'

All the editors seem to me to make an unnecessary difficulty over 'enker'. It is, as they recognize, the French *encré*, 'inked' or 'dark'. But for reasons best known to themselves they want to say the Knight is bright green and so gloss the word (in the most recent case, the edition of R. A. Waldron, 1970) 'pure, intense'. But 'dark' makes excellent sense if one thinks of the colours which can be dark and gleaming at the same time that one finds in the medieval illuminated manuscripts. I think the Knight is the same colour as the leaves of his midwinter 'holyn bobbe' (206) – a dark, gleaming green.

possible. (And this is certainly not because he can't help it: in Fitt 2 he gives a very convincing example of the contrary, a realistic situation which gradually and subtly turns mysterious. The castle Gawain finds at the end of his wanderings (763ff.) is real enough, but manages to suggest itself at the same time as a fairy castle, which appears at the right moment, and which he approaches, as it shimmers through the trees, with mysterious suddenness; similarly though Gawain's main opponents on his journey through mid-Wales have been (naturally) the weather, and loneliness, he has also had to contend with foes ranging from animal to supernatural, and they are made to belong naturally together as they might in a folk tale.)

But the concentration on the Green Knight masks the poet's real interest in Gawain, and the questions about the Green Knight's nature mask the real question, the nature of the challenge he presents to Arthur's court. It is a characteristic subtlety that the character who is the real centre of the poem should appear at first as only a sort of impersonal politeness.[1]

The nature of the Green Knight's challenge may come clearer if we ask what he has in common with his other avatar, the Lord of the Castle. Both are domineering, but their most obvious common characteristic is sheer simple vivacity. Both of them are always full of beans, in and out of season. If one had to say what they stand for it would be hard to get much further than saying they are just 'life' – instinctive, irrational life. This is commonly recognized. 'He [the Lord of the Castle] has the profuseness and reckless vigour and the amorality of life on its purely natural level.'[2] Mr Berry then falls into a post-D. H. Lawrence linguistic fallacy. If the Green Knight is 'life' he *must* be the hero or, at least, to be admired and approved of: 'But in all his different roles, aspects, and appearances, there is a common amplitude and an amoral enjoyment of life that transcend [*sic*] limited human capacities.'[3] And 'Gawain...encounters something other than, and larger than, himself.'[4] One trouble here is that the 'life' Mr Berry suggests to me is a vegetable one, perhaps as befitting the Green Man. I have difficulty in restraining the brambles in my garden; they have an

---

[1] Mr J. Burrow shows in *A Reading of Sir Gawain and the Green Knight* (1966), how carefully the poet makes the contrast between the brashness of the Green Knight and the courteous self-effacement of Sir Gawain.

[2] Francis Berry, 'Sir Gawayne and the Grene Knight', *The Pelican Guide to English Literature*, Vol. 1 (1954), p. 156.

[3] *Ibid.*, p. 157. [4] *Ibid.*

amplitude that transcends my limited human capacities. Further, I do not deny that there is something splendid and wonderful about brambles, as about all life – only I wish they would grow else-where, and I'm certainly not going to admit that their amoral enjoyment of life is in any sense other than the physical 'larger than' myself. 'Life', that very important word, has to have a range even wider than 'love'. At one extreme it does no more than exclude the dead and the inanimate: and though to be lively is better than to be deadly, to say that something is alive is not necessarily much of a compliment. The life of the Green Knight does not seem to me a very admirable kind of life. In so far as it is amoral it is subhuman. It reminds me of Johnson on Fielding:

Fielding being mentioned, Johnson exclaimed, 'he was a blockhead'; and upon my expressing my astonishment at so strange an assertion, he said, 'What I mean by his being a blockhead is, that he was a barren rascal.' BOSWELL. 'Will you not allow, Sir, that he draws very natural pictures of human life?' JOHNSON. 'Why, Sir, it is of very low life...Sir, there is more knowledge of the heart in one letter of Richardson's than in all "Tom Jones."'[1]

The Green Knight is wonderful (since all life is wonderful) but hopelessly insufficient, pre-human.

His wife tries hard to be amoral, too. 'She has the morals of an alley cat.' But cats do not have morals, they have instincts and habits; and this seems to be the state the Lady aspires to. But she does want

1513   þe lel layk of luf   þe lettrure of armes

as well – 'the real game of love, the literacy of knighthood'. She makes no connection, however, between her flirtatious talking and what is to happen in bed. The first is fashion: Gawain has come down with the latest court turns of phrase[2] and she wants this grace before meat. The test she offers is the one we have mentioned many times before, the wish to make love an amusement. Her insistence on animality does not disqualify her for that game. To insist on one's animality is (as Mr David Sims said to me) a very human thing to do: animals do not insist on their animality, but human beings treating life as a game well may.[3]

[1] Boswell, 6 April 1772.
[2] Perhaps also with turns of another sort, such as Horner denies possession of. 'I have nothing that you came for. I have brought over not so much as a bawdy picture, no new postures, nor the second part of the *Ecole des Filles*; nor –' *The Country Wife*, I, i.
[3] Cf. Desmond Morris, *The Naked Ape* (1967).

The test the Lady offers is the old one Marie de Champagne gave to the troubadours: how to maintain human seriousness amidst the frivolities of court. But this is not so far from the Green Knight's own test as it may look. Perhaps he is just 'life', in the sense of energy before it is shaped and expressed in human consciousness. But that is again a way of saying that he is pre-human: for apart from human consciousness there is no *other* place where we can be aware of life. The Green Knight has to be observed externally because he has no human consciousness. To see the Green Knight as better than Gawain is a primitivism rather like seeing the Lady as better than Gawain: the test he offers is in a different way like the test she offers: both are challenging Gawain to find the sense of 'life' within human life. What to do with 'life'? – to separate it from talking, like the lady, or from humanity altogether like the Green Knight? The challenge is for Gawain to see how and why civilization, the human life of Camelot, is better than the proffered alternatives.

So if we ask what it is in Arthur's court that the Green Knight challenges, my simple answer would be, 'humanity'. The challenge is to whatever chances civilization gives us of making something humanly serious of life – which is all we *can* make of life. Can civilization survive the challenge of pre-human life or the challenge of life-as-amusement? If that is the question it is at least not a dead one.

This is equally the question in Fitt 3, masked (as preoccupation with the Knight in Fitt 1 masks questions about the court) by the reader's surprise at the Lady's goings-on. 'What ought Gawain to do?' is the question here, working at a level more profound than – though suggested by – our fascination with her antics. Here the disposition itself is a subtlety: we are not expecting the decisive test of Gawain yet and it is not until we have followed the story through that we realize the great test has already taken place.

To put this question differently: why does Gawain resist the Lady? For many critics this is a question that does not need to be raised. Gawain is dedicated to Mary and chastity and therefore must not go to bed with women, however pressingly invited. But what *sense* does his dedication make? Why can't he change his mind and achieve a less old-fashioned-looking morality for himself?

Gawain likes the Lady – which is hard to explain if one sees him as a courtly Joseph Andrews – because he is susceptible to women.

His dress and manners are sometimes reminiscent of Chaucer's Squire's; and flirtation is his ordinary relationship with a beautiful lady. He discriminates between the two ladies in the castle:

972 Þe alder he *haylses* †heldande† ful lowe
   ‡Þe loueloker he lappeȝ‡ a lyttel in armeȝ

          * salutes   † bowing   ‡ lovelier he folds

When at length the Lady asks him if there is anyone else Gawain does not mention chastity and only says he will have no lover 'the while' (1791). His own motive at the psychological moment is certainly in part a wish to keep chaste, but is also a fear of forgetting his mission and of betraying his host (1773–5); his chastity, that is, exists in connection with his effort to make some sense of his mission and be true to his knighthood in so doing.

   The Lady's test is certainly thorough. She tests at once all the knightly qualities and virtues, all the things whose connection makes Gawain a knight. This is what the story does with the strength of the temptation one feels in it. 'Any man who is not disturbed by the physical presence of Gawain's temptress should return to James Hadley Chase without further waste of time.'[1] How easy it would have been for Gawain to give it all up and 'play the loon'[2] for a while. Were it not better done as others use? He is closer to it, I think, than the editions admit. They all emend the decisive line with the minimum of fuss. From line 1766 the unique manuscript reads

> Þay lauced wordes gode
> Much wele þen watȝ þer inne
> Gret perile bi twene hem stod
> Nif Mare of hir knyȝt mynne

> For þat prynce of pris de presed hym so þikke
> Nurned hym so neȝe þe þred þat nede hym bi houed
> Oþer lach þer hir luf oþer lodly re fuse

This is the moment when Gawain has to take her or leave her; the emphasis is squarely on Gawain. But all the editions alter line 1770 to

> For þat prynces of pris   depresed hym so þikke[3]

---

[1] R. T. Jones, in the introduction to his edition *Sir Gawain and the Grene Gome* [*sic*] (Natal, 2nd impression, 1965), p. 2.
[2] 'She with a bishop played the loon' – old song.
[3] Mr R. A. Waldron's new edition – which will be found on the whole very useful – thinks this emendation so obvious that we are not even informed it has been made.

which is supposed to be translatable as something like 'For that princess of worth was pressing him so fiercely, was urging him so near the mark, that he needs must either take there her love or refuse it rudely.' I think on the contrary the manuscript makes the better sense. Gawain *is* in peril; 'Wiȝt wallande joye' has 'warmed his hert' (1762); with their 'smoþe smylyng & smolt' they have, paradoxically, 'smeten into merþe' (1763) so that it is a matter of course that

1768 Gret perile bitwene hem stod

and now 'that prince of worth was freeing himself so completely, was offering himself so near the point of no return, that he must either take there her love or refuse it rudely'.[1]

Chastity is important for Sir Gawain, but its importance is not something given: it is a sense he has to work out, with difficulty, in his encounters with the Lady. What he has to work out is the belief that his faith in his civilization is better than her alternative. He has in that sense to create the idea of chastity for himself. This may also help to explain why Gawain consistently treats the Lady with a courtesy she is quite unable to appreciate. For her, courtesy is a fashionable going through certain linguistic hoops; it is what a lady should say to a man before she lets him in (the nearest things in Chaucer are the love of Nicholas for Alisoun and Damyan for May). But 'curteysye' is Gawain's way of life, the virtues and values of fine life, as well as its airs and graces. By treating her courteously he is standing by the best he knows – whatever *she* makes of it.

This is not to say that Gawain fully understands the nature of his trial either before or after his fault has been pointed out to him. Perhaps his 'standing by the best he knows' is as little an explanation of the world as Duke Theseus's similar doctrine. Nevertheless, Gawain knows enough to take his lapse with due seriousness. He has failed at the very centre of the cluster of knightly virtues; when he accepts the girdle he shows he is unwilling to face death. Soldiers of any description have a right and a duty to preserve their life if they can, but the defining characteristic of any soldier is that if need be he has to be ready to die at the demand of his profession. Gawain's acceptance of the girdle is the hankering after a world in which this is not the case. The fault is not the whole truth about Gawain: it is more characteristic of

[1] I append a note on this interpretation after this chapter.

him that after it is committed he can manage, in a whole series of verses, to say 'Nevertheless, not as I will, but as thou wilt.'[1]

2158 To Godde3 wylle I am ful bayn
    & to hym I haf me tone

2208 Let God worche we loo
    Hit helppe3 me not a mote
    My lif þa3 I forgoo
    Drede dot3 me no lote[2]

He has committed the fault nevertheless. But Gawain's fault is one which the Green Knight, in his capacity as Life Force, can easily forgive:

2368 Bot for 3e lufed your lyf þe lasse I yow blame

For the Green Knight death is just the ultimate evil. He is like Jean de Meun's amoral Nature[3] whose concern is not with any significance there might be in life, but simply in keeping life going. Gawain's failure is to maintain his own values against the Green Knight's archaic belief that self-preservation is a great virtue. I do feel the Green Knight as primitively pre-Christian here: he couldn't possibly attain to a morality that says, 'Greater love hath no man than this, that a man lay down his life for his friends.'[4] So Gawain is right to take his fault seriously – but Arthur's court is also right to think Gawain heroic and the tale worthy of commemoration: whereas the Green Knight is simply and typically stupid when, after the terror of what Gawain thinks is to be the second beheading scene, he expects Gawain to return to the castle and continue the revelling as if nothing had happened. With this hindsight his earlier cruelty with the grindstone and the feints looks more like sheer insensitivity.

    The end of *Sir Gawain and the Green Knight* brings it very close to *The Knight's Tale*. Both poems use the figure of a knight, paradoxically enough, as an example of patience. A knight's business in the world is fighting, and virtually all that Chaucer tells us of his Knight in *The General Prologue* is that he fights properly. But the characters in *The Knight's Tale* have to suffer patiently the inflictions of the gods, and Gawain has to lie passive

---

[1] Matthew xxvi. 39.
[2] 'To God's will I am completely obedient, and to Him I have taken myself.' 'Leave it to God' [proverbial expression, literally, 'Let God work'] 'so, so... it helps me not a mote: though I lose my life, dread [or doubt] makes me [utter] no noise.'
[3] *Le Roman de la Rose*, lines 15902ff.
[4] John xv. 13.

before the attack first of the Lady then of her husband. It is only by being true to the best one knows that Gawain or Palamon can come through. But the stories are not this cliché; the stories create the idea with their own life. The unforgettable thing that makes Sir Gawain's patience not a cliché is the story's climax in the surely final image of patience, when Gawain has to look over his shoulder, see an axe descending on his naked neck, and

E 1151
Receyven al in gree   that God us sent

This incident, in its place in the story, tells us exactly what the poet means by 'trouthe'. So I agree with Mr Burrow that, for all its subtleties and convolutions, *Sir Gawain*'s theme is that of *The Clerk's Tale* and *The Knight's Tale*: the question of what loyalty to one's beliefs may entail, and what kind of sense it might make. These poets are contemporary in their creative use of the great words, like 'trouthe'.

Part of the point of these remarks has been to put something against Mr Speirs's essay where, I think, he allows his interest in pre-Christian ritual to confuse the meaning of the poem, by making the Green Knight more admirable than he really is. This being so I would also like to make the obvious remark that Mr Speirs established the reputation of *Sir Gawain* more surely than he could have done if he had written it himself. He was the first to see the poem as a poem and say so, and he has given anybody interested in poetry the chance of discussing the poem as such. Mr Speirs has also, of course, given me the centrally perceptive quotation at the beginning of the last chapter, which we must now consider.

II

What is it to be contemporary? Just to be alive at the same time? But 'the same time' is no longer an easy notion even in physics, let alone history. If contemporaneity is just being alive at the same time is then John Dryden contemporary with the Emperor Akbar? What would that tell us? Dryden is contemporary with India only to the extent that he makes contact with it – however oddly – in *Aurengzebe*, and elsewhere.

To be contemporary is somehow to belong together. Chaucer and Langland and the Gawain poet belong together whether or not they knew each other. They are of very different traditions;

Chaucer begins with Frenchified courtly poetry, Langland with sermons, the *Gawain* poet with alliterative romance; yet they are comparable in ways in which the writers, or even the literary traditions, in England before Chaucer are not comparable. There is no connection worth making between the *Ormulum, King Horn* and *The Owl and the Nightingale*: each belongs to a quite separate world; and the fact that *The Owl and the Nightingale* can't be seen in an age of English literature is one of the difficulties in judging it. The *Ormulum* and the *Ancrene Riwle* are more contemporary with the Anglo-Saxon homilies than with the early troubadour lyrics which were already being written in England at the same time as the former.

The comparability of our three poets – and to a lesser degree a small band of others like the authors of *Patience* and some of the extant lyrics – is that they all in their different ways make the decisive step forward into literary art. The *Gawain* poet is as far from the romances hypothetically his forerunners as Chaucer is from the material he turned into *The Pardoner's Tale. Sir Gawain and the Green Knight* is as much a criticism of life as *The Knight's Tale*. The former is a sport. (Though the other poems in the same ms. are ample evidence that *Sir Gawain* was not alone.) It has survived by a lucky chance; it had no influence on subsequent history; and it comes from an area of the country, the language and the literature which is far from Chaucer's territory. Yet it complements Chaucer. These poems all give us comparisons: they find their place in our literature by means of the comparisons, and the comparisons form our idea of the Age of Chaucer.

But if *The Canterbury Tales* and *Piers Plowman* and *Sir Gawain and the Green Knight* belong together it is only because they belong to us, as well as to the fourteenth century. My last chapter will return to and explore this proposition, but first I wish to suggest two further perspectives.

Note on line 1770 of Sir Gawain and the Green Knight

The editorial sense of the emended line (see p. 228) will not do for the following reasons: (1) the Lady is best and most often described as a 'wale burd' or something similar ('a choice girl') rather than a 'princess of price' – though perhaps the poet is being sarcastic. Gawain, however, is grouped with 'prynces of prys' at line 2398, and 'prys' is one of the words most frequently used of him; (2) 'depresed' is found in the poem in two senses but not the one demanded here;

(3) 'nurned', from a verb which seems (I write before the *Middle English Dictionary* has reached 'N') only to be found in the poems of the *Gawain* ms. and in *St Erkenwald* is, however, used often enough to give some idea of its meaning, which again is not the meaning demanded here; (4) the emended reading gives no apparent reason why Gawain's refusal must be unmannerly: he has been refusing politely throughout such earlier encounters as when she says

1224 I schal happe yow here   þat oþer half als

and one can supply a stage direction, *She leans over the bed to embrace him.* Why is it now more difficult if all the rousing is still on her side?

'Depresed' could mean either 'subdued' (as in line 6 where Gollancz derives the word from Old French *depresser*) or 'freed' (as line 1219, from Old French *despresser* or *despriser*).

'Nurn' seems to mean something like 'offer' or 'proffer', in so far as one can suggest a single modern English equivalent.

1822 'I will no gifteȝ for Gode   my gay at þis tyme
     I haf none yow to norne   ne noȝt wyl I take'

2443 'How norne ȝe yowre ryȝt nome   & þenne no more?'
('How do you offer your true name...?')

1661 Bot he nolde not for his nurture   nurne hir aȝayneȝ
('But he would not, because of his upbringing, offer [anything] in response to her.')

1668 Ande þer þay dronken & dalten   & demed eft nwe
     To norne on þe same note   on nweȝereȝ euen

('And there they drank and discoursed (?), and agreed afterwards again to try out [offer] the same business on New Year's Eve.')

Similarly *Cleanness*

65   An oþer nayed also   & nurned þis cawse[1]

(from the parable of the Great Supper: 'Another refused also and offered this reason.')

669 'Now innoghe hit is not so'   þenne nurned þe dryȝtyn
(where 'nurne' is just 'to say'.)

802   I schal fette yow a fatte   your fette forto wasche
       I norne yow bot for on nyȝt   neȝe me to lenge

('I shall fetch you a vat to wash your feet: I offer you/provide for you but for one night to stay near me.')

[1] *Early English Alliterative Poems*, ed. R. Morris (1869).

Also *St Erkenwald*:

195 Þe name þat þou nevenyd has & nournet me after
('The name you have named and offered to me.')

So, taking 'hym' as reflexive, the normal form, one arrives at the translation I offered. It does also answer my fourth objection to the editors: Gawain has to take her or be unmannerly because he is already somewhat far gone.

14

Scotland

Langland, the *Gawain* poet, and to a lesser extent the lesser writers, make an immediate context for Chaucer. There are also as many wider contexts as we choose to define; but before coming to the most important, the one we live in, I want to mention two further perspectives which come so naturally to any discussion of Chaucer as to be almost necessary.

I

I can best relate the Scottish poets of the late Middle Ages to the question of the place of Chaucer in our literature by showing that there might be some sense in the term by which they are often known, 'Scottish Chaucerians'. At first sight this might seem hard to maintain, for 'Scottish' may seem so much truer than 'Chaucerian', since *The Kingis Quair* and the poems of Henryson, Dunbar and Gavin Douglas, are all very Scottish but unlike Chaucer.

The great difference between England and Scotland at the end of the Middle Ages is summed up, on the Scottish side, in the poetry of William Dunbar. Anybody inclined to think of medieval Scotland as English should meditate on the difference of national culture expressed in the literary tradition of which he is the *a per se*.

Dunbar (like Lydgate in England) turned his hand to anything, with the major exception of the long stories which are central to Chaucer. Dunbar, like Lydgate, produced in large numbers songs, allegories, pious pieces and rhetorical *tours de force*, and additionally he flytes. He is obviously contemporary with Chaucer's later English disciples, but there is no mistaking the difference. Here is the beginning of a poem of Dunbar's that could not possibly have been written in fifteenth-century England.

Illuster Lodovick, of France most Cristin king,
  Thow may complain with sighis lamentable
The death of Bernard Stewart, nobill and *ding*,   (digne) noble
  In deid of armis most *anterous* and abill,   adventurous
  Most mychti, wyse, worthie, and confortable,
Thy men of weir to governe and to gy:
  For him, allace! now may thow weir the sabill,
Sen he is gone, the flour of chevelrie.[1]

(There are three more stanzas, variations on the last line occurring in the common manner.)

There is nothing here in the sentiment or even the phraseology that would have been strange in contemporary England. Many medieval elegists complain with lamentable sighs, 'to governe and to gy' is confined neither to Scotland nor to this period, and the very Scottish idiom of some of Dunbar's poems in lower style is, for obvious reasons, not to be found here. But if it is obvious that Dunbar is writing in the style befitting a public elegy that in itself may differentiate him from the English Chaucerians. Explicitly the poem is addressed to 'illuster Lodovick', but the striking thing about it, compared with the work of Lydgate or Hoccleve or Chaucer himself, is that Dunbar is obviously addressing a public in a public manner. It makes no difference that the 'public' may have been no larger than the Scottish court: the word 'public' is never needed when we are thinking of the work of the English Chaucerians. The audience addressed by Chaucer and his followers seems always to be either a small group – probably of ladies – or an individual: English courtly poetry always has a private air; the rose-garden in England and France is carefully enclosed. But with Dunbar's lines the formality of statement, the keeping his own personality well in the background, the rhetoric, all contribute to what we can recognize as public oratory, the opposite of the private and personal outpourings of Hoccleve or Skelton. English elegies could be full of ornate eloquence or could be genuinely felt, but the lack of an English elegiac style, the surprise one feels at the self-communing air, was the theme of my observations on *The Book of the Duchess*. Dunbar's public dignity and decorum is hardly paralleled in England until the lapidary style of Dryden and the eighteenth century.

And Dunbar's 'public' stance is not confined to the poems on naturally public subjects. It is as striking in the poems grouped by

---

[1] 'Elegy on the Death of Bernard Stewart, Lord of Aubigny', *The Poems of William Dunbar*, ed. W. Mackay Mackenzie (1932), p. 133.

Mackay Mackenzie under the heading 'personal'. The rightly famous 'Lament for the Makaris' begins with what might seem a purely personal emotion:

> I that in *heill* wes and gladnes,   health
> Am trublit now with gret seiknes,
> And feblit with infermite;
> *Timor mortis conturbat me.*

But even this is not so much the expression of a feeling as a seemingly disinterested description of the state. This is confirmed by the second stanza, which goes on immediately to appeal to generality, in which the writer is more strongly himself:

> Our plesance heir is all vane glory,
> This fals warld is bot transitory,
> The flesche is brukle, the Fend is sle;
> *Timor mortis conturbat me.*

Here the tone of public oratory is overt, and matches well enough the commonplace material. That the verse is not commonplace is a tribute to the way Dunbar manages to make the commonplace succinct and forceful, by making it the vehicle of the kind of feeling we like to think is personal, not public. The poem goes on for several stanzas to Dunbar's version of the *Danse Macabre*, before coming again to something particular and personal, a list of the Scottish poets death has killed.

> 77   He hes tane Roull of Aberdene,
> And gentill Roull of Corstorphin;
> Two bettir fallowis did no man se;
> *Timor mortis conturbat me.*
>
> In Dunfermlyne he hes *done roune*   whispered
> With Maister Robert Henrisoun;
> Schir Johne the Ros enbrast hes he;
> *Timor mortis conturbat me.*
>
> And he hes now tane, last of aw,
> Gud gentill Stobo and Quintyne Schaw,
> Of quham all wichtis hes pete:
> *Timor mortis conturbat me.*
>
> Gud Maister Walter Kennedy
> In poynt of dede lyis veraly,
> Gret reuth it wer that so suld be;
> *Timor mortis conturbat me.*

In several cases these lines are known to be personal, that is, about people Dunbar knew. But even here it is questionable whether there is much private feeling in the lines. They get their force from their place, following on from the

17   On to the ded gois all Estatis

section and from the lines about the English poets which are demonstrably a version of a common formula:

49   He hes done petously devour
      The noble Chaucer, of makaris flour,
      The Monk of Bery, and Gower, all thre;
         Timor mortis conturbat me.

Moreover the means of enforcing the feeling even in the case of Dunbar's acquaintances is the appeal to generality: 'all wichtis hes pete', 'gret reuth it were'. I don't feel the need to know anything about the personality of these people to understand Dunbar's poem: they are all just examples of general death, and the poem's strength is in its realization of this general commonplace. In this way it does not matter to the strength of the poem that the Scottish poets named are almost all mere names even to specialists in Scottish literature. The poem is good in so far as it is wholly limited by a poetic tradition and in so far as it is not at all the voice of the man William Dunbar.

   The same is even true of the little poem 'On his Heid-Ake'. What could be more private to a particular man than a headache? But Dunbar's reason for disliking the headache is that it stops him writing and joining in the social life which is his subject:

11   Full oft at morrow I upryse,
      Quhen that my curage sleipeing lyis,
         For mirth, for menstrallie and play,
         For din nor danceing nor deray
      It will nocht walkin me no wise.

But in the absence of the headache, presumably 'din, danceing and deray' do awaken him; and *then* the 'sentence' is not 'full evill till find' (8), because his meaning – his writing poetry – is his joining in this society.

   It is the same even with that very fine poem the 'Meditatioun in Wyntir': the 'I' of the poem is every courtier, and the feeling is as general as ever:

42   No gold in *kist*, nor wyne in cowp,   chest
      No ladeis bewtie, nor luiffis blys,
      May *lat* me to remember this,   prevent
      How glaid that ever I dyne or sowp.

Yit, quhone the nycht begynnis to schort,
It dois my spreit sum pairt confort,
   Off thocht oppressit with the schowris.
   Cum, lustie symmer! with thi flowris,
That I may leif in sum disport.

Perhaps lyric poetry generally is one man speaking for all, not for himself – but it isn't in fifteenth-century England. Thomas Hoccleve's poems are always about Thomas Hoccleve's feelings and how they are unlike other people's; a little further back, Chaucer's 'Compleynt to his Purs' is written about his own financial difficulties, not every man's.

Dunbar's generality is as much a creation of a court culture as the narratives of Chrestien de Troyes. Dunbar's strengths and limitations are both of this general kind: he can be at home only in what is generally acceptable, and that gives him the chance both to write some very good things and to show his language as that of a firmly established literature; but it also means that he is not a poet of the order of Chaucer.

Perhaps the most obvious general difference between the Chaucerians of England and Scotland is in their rhythmic traditions.[1] The iambic tetrameter of Dunbar is as characteristic of the Scots as the Lydgate line is of the English. The very assured tradition of metrical regularity in which Dunbar writes is at once more impressive and less potentially expressive than the balanced pentameters south of the border. One of the achievements of Chaucer's verse is to create an enormous range of the tones of speech within verse. Dunbar, at his best anyway, is not divorced from the life of the spoken language, but his speech-accents are those of the formal occasion in the great hall or even the open-air pulpit. This certainly implies a healthier tradition than was to be found in contemporary England, where the Chaucerians seem very in-bred and restricted to what can be said confidentially in a small room: at the same time it prevents an achievement of the magnitude of Chaucer's, or Dante's or even Langland's.

There are, of course, points of overlap between the English and Scottish poets. 'The Goldyn Targe' could be translated into literary English and mistaken for Hawes. But where the Scottish poets make the most effective use of Chaucer they are often farthest from him, as in Dunbar's *Tretis of the Tua Mariit Wemen and the Wedo* and Henryson's *Testament of Cresseid*.

---

[1] An aspect of this is that I think it appropriate to punctuate most of Dunbar's verse in the modern way.

The Tua Mariit Wemen and the Wedo is in its way, I think, a
great poem. It is also very characteristic both of Dunbar and of
Scotland. But still, in so far as these observations are true, the
poem is decisively inferior to the parts of Chaucer it is derived
from; and I hope if that can be shown it will take a stage further our
discussion of Chaucer as well as of Dunbar.

The Tua Mariit Wemen and the Wedo tells of the conversation
of the three characters of the title. Two of the three are unmistak-
ably based on Chaucer characters, though unlike them. The Wedo
is from the Wife of Bath, but without her exuberant love of love,
and one of the married women is based on May of *The Merchant's
Tale,* but is shown up by Dunbar much more relentlessly, in the
apparent effort to leave absolutely nothing concealed.

Dunbar begins, like the Merchant, by making ironical use of a
courtly setting.

1 Apon the Midsummer evin mirriest of nichtis
 I muvit furth allane neir as midnicht wes past
 Besyd ane gudlie grein garth full of gay flouris
 Hegeit of ane huge hicht with hawthorne treis...

Nothing could be more lulling to the experienced reader of medieval poetry than this beautiful and so conventional scene: it seems
as if we know exactly what is coming – some sort of dream vision
which will include love, handsome knights and beautiful ladies.
Sure enough the ladies arrive:

17 I saw thre gay ladeis sit in ane grene arbeir
 All *grathit* in to garlandis of fresche gudlie flouris dressed
 So glitterit as the gold wer thair glorius gilt tressis
 Quhill all the gressis did gleme of the glaid hewis
 Kemmit was thair cleir hair and curiouslie sched
 Attour thair schulderis doun schyre schyning full bricht

But when these three beauties are sitting comfortably

40 syne thai spak more spedelie and sparit no matiris

The last phrase is indeed a threat of what is to come, for the
principal subject of their conversation is the shortcomings of their
men. The first gives her account of bed with an old husband.
Chaucer draws a veil over the thoughts of May in a similar
situation:

E 1847
He was al coltissh ful of ragerye
And ful of jargon as a flekked pye

The slakke skyn   aboute his nekke shaketh
Whil that he sang   so chaunteth he and *craketh*
But God woot   what that May thoughte   in hir herte
Whan she hym saugh   up sittynge in his sherte
In his nyght cappe   and with his nekke lene
She preyseth nat his pleyyng   worth a bene

  * makes the noise of a high trumpet

After the economical picture of disgusting old January Chaucer leaves it all to the imagination, or God. Not so Dunbar: he tries hard to leave nothing to the imagination. Chaucer's refusal to go into detail has its own powerful effect, but for Dunbar there are no holds barred and no detail spared of any of them. He makes of the situation something very striking and successfully poetic, but something simpler and more self-committing than Chaucer's tale. I offer few glosses on this passage, leaving it to make its own way by the force of its native indecency.

89 I have ane wallidrag ane worme   ane auld wobat carle
  A waistit wolroun na worth   bot wourdis to clatter
  Ane bumbart ane dron bee   ane bag ful of flewme
  Ane skabbit skarth ane scorpioun   ane scutarde behind
  To see him scart his awin skyn   grit scunner I think
  Quhen kissis me that carybald   than kyndillis all my sorow
  As birs of ane brym bair   his berd is als stif
  Bot soft and soupill as the silk   is his sary *lume*   tool
  He may weill to the syn assent   bot sakles is his deidis
  With goreis his tua grym ene   ar gladderrit all about
  And gorgeit lyk twa gutaris   that war with glar stoppit
  Bot quhen that glowrand gaist   grippis me about
  Than think I hiddowus Mahowne   hes me in armes
  Thair may na sanyne me save   fra that auld Sathane
  For thocht I croce me all cleine   fra the croun doun
  He wil my corse all beclip   and clap me to his breist
  Quhen schaiffyne is that ald schalk   with a scharp rasour
  He schowis one me his schevill mouth   and schedis my lippis
  And with his hard hurcheone skyn   sa heklis he my chekis
  That as a glemand gleyd   glowis my chaftis
  I schrenk for the scharp stound   bot schout dar I nought
  For schore of that auld schrew   schame him betide
  The luf blenkis of that bogill   fra his blerde ene
  As Belzebub had on me blent   abasit my spreit
  And quhen the smy one me smyrkis   with his smake smolet
  He fepillis like a †farcy avert†   that flyrit one a ‡gillot‡

    † ailing carthorse ‡ mare

240

The poem continues in the same way which is at once very funny, quite relentless, and without any reticence. It ends with a final twist of the knife by asking a question, of insidious intent:

527   Ye auditoris most honorable   that eris has gevin
       Oneto this uncouth aventur   quhilk airly me happinnit
       Of thir thre wantoun wiffis   that I haif writtin heir
       Quhilk wald ye waill to your wif   gif ye suld wed one?

Dunbar wants to disgust the reader at the same time as amusing him: the answer to the question is something like, 'Ugh! What a thought!' But perhaps this in itself is similar to our response to *The Merchant's Tale*. The difference is that the 'ugh!' is half-way to disposing of Dunbar's poem. We may enjoy its vigorous language (it is a good sign here that the diction is so difficult) and its unrestrained humorous assault on women, but it is so unremitting, so completely regardless of any other possible styles of the feminine, that afterwards we may go our way feeling comparatively unscathed. The passage modelled on the Wife of Bath is similarly magnificent in its hints on how to court dozens of men simultaneously: but compared with Chaucer it is simple knockabout stuff, with none of the layer upon layer of malice I find in *The Merchant's Tale*:

476   Bot yit me think the best bourd   quhen baronis and knychtis
      And other bachilleris blith   blumyng in youth
      And all my luffaris lele   my lugeing persewis
      And fyllis me wyne wantonly   with weilfair and joy
      Sum *rownis* and sum ralyeis   and sum redis ballatis   whisper
      Sum *raiffis furght rudly*   with riatus speche   rave about rudely
      Sum plenis and sum prayis   sum prasis mi bewte
      Sum kissis me sum clappis me   sum kyndnes me proferis
      Sum kerffis to me curtasli   sum me the cop giffis
      Sum stalwardly steppis ben   with a stout curage
      And a stif standand thing   staiffis in my *neiff*   fist
      And mony blenkis ben our   that but full fer sittis
      That mai for the thik thrang   nought thrif as thai wald
      Bot with my fair calling   I comfort thaim all
      For he that sittis me nixt   I nip on his finger
      I serf him on the tothir syde   on the samin fasson
      And he that behind me sittis   I hard on him lene
      And him befor with my fut   fast on his I stramp
      And to the bernis far   *but* sueit blenkis I cast   just
      To every man in speciall   speke I sum wordis
      So wisly and so womanly   quhill warmys ther hertis

This throws in the reader's face an example of what it is to be 'wise and womanly'. But if we take the challenge seriously it is easy enough to resist: one thinks of other examples. Chaucer's tale is more sinister precisely because it is not the whole of Chaucer. Chaucer knows there are other things in the world – but that makes his creation of *this* thing much harder to shrug off. Dunbar's language, his use of the terms of love, is complete in, and completely exhausted by, this attack on love: he is comparatively simple-minded and single-minded; and the mind is that of Scottish literature. Dunbar leaves himself, and his tradition allows him, no room for the kind of development I find in *The Canterbury Tales* or in *Piers Plowman*. I do not intend this as an adverse judgment on either Dunbar or Scotland, but as the limitation that goes with their strength.

II

It is similar with Henryson's *Testament of Cresseid*, his continuation of the story of *Troilus and Criseyde*. I do not want to spend longer on the *Testament* (whose merit receives at least lip-service from academic histories of literature) than I need to show how firmly Henryson is bounded by the Scottish tradition.

The first difference from Chaucer is that *The Testament of Cresseid* is not really a story even to the extent that *Troilus and Criseyde* is. It begins with the poet's very well-written account of sitting down in winter to write, his inability to worship Venus, his thoughts about Chaucer's poem. This takes ten stanzas: the eleventh gives us most of the essential story, after which Henryson goes back to a lot of padding about the gods. Henryson perhaps saw *Troilus and Criseyde*, rightly, as a sequence of lyric moments; to which he added his own, the vision of Troilus failing to recognize, and giving alms to, the leprous Cresseide. This is very well done (stanza 72) and Troilus's half-remembrance of Cresseid is most poignant.

But why is *this* what Henryson wanted to add to Chaucer? – what in this so appealed to his imagination? He seems to have wanted the story as an example of mortality. The mortality of love is certainly one of Chaucer's own themes – necessarily so since he was trying for the final and complete picture of love – but Henryson wanted it clearer, plainer, simpler and more befitting his Scottish imagination. (This applies also to his gods: they have something of the force of Chaucer's but it is a more primitive force: cf. especially

Saturn, stanzas 22–4.) This is shown above all in the way he progresses from one strongly-felt commonplace to another. At first,
as I have said, the commonplace he wants to bring out is human
mortality. This is apparent in the gods' sentences, but especially
in the 'Plaint of Cresseid': Here she is addressing the 'Ladyis fair
of Troy and Grece' – and Scotland:

> st. 65
> Nocht is your fairnes bot ane faiding flour,
> Nocht is your famous laud and hie honour
> Bot wind Inflat in uther mennis eiris.
> Your roising reid to rotting sall retour:
> Exempill mak of me in your Memour,
> Quhilk of sic thingis wofull witnes beiris,
> All Welth in Eird, away as Wind it weiris.
> Be war thairfoir, approchis neir the hour:
> Fortoun is fikkill, quhen scho beginnis & steiris.[1]

The strength, here, is just in the feeling for the commonplace. But
the whole drift of Henryson's feeling – and tradition – is moving
him also to another commonplace: moral denunciation.[2] He seems
at the beginning of the poem deliberately to avoid it in order to
concentrate on mortality; but morality will out.

76   'O fals Cresseid and trew Knicht Troylus.

> 'Thy lufe, thy lawtie, and they gentilnes,
> I countit small in my prosperitie,
> Sa elevait I was in wantones,
> And clam upon the fickill quheill sa hie:
> All Faith and Lufe I promissit to the,
> Was in the self fickill and frivolous:
> O fals Cresseid, and trew Knicht Troilus.'

---

[1] *The Poems and Fables of Robert Henryson*, ed. H. Harvey Wood (Edinburgh,
1958), p. 121.
[2] Cf. Henryson's version of *The Nun's Priest's Tale*, which adds a character
called Sprutok who talks (very like Dunbar's Wedo) of replacing Chantecleer.
Chantecleer
> st. 74
> wes angry and held us ay in aw,
> And woundit with the speir of Jelowsy.
> Off chalmerglew, Pertok, full weill ye knaw,
> Waistit he wes...

In Harvey Wood's text Sprutok easily converts Pertok (Pertelote) to her point
of view: to which Pertok adds some scraps of morality:
> st. 75
> In lust *but* lufe he set all his delyte...   without

And the whole poem ends with a kind of serious parody of the advice with which Chaucer ends the tales of *The Legend of Good Women*:

86   Now, worthie Wemen, in this Ballet schort,
       Made for your worschip and Instructioun,
       Of Cheritie, I monische and exhort,
       Ming not your lufe with fals deceptioun.
       Beir in your mynd this short conclusioun
       Of fair Cresseid, as I have said befoir.
       Sen scho is deid, I speik of hir no moir.

The Testament of Cresseid is the result of a cold Scottish imagination (yet more genial than Chaucer's) at work upon Chaucer. Is it Henryson's own comment, or Scotland's? The question may show that the distinction would be unreal. Perhaps if we had much more of and knew more about the 'Scottish Chaucerians' they would not seem to belong so closely together: as it is, we see in both Henryson and Dunbar a tradition of creativity too strong for any great creative individuality. In *The Testament of Cresseid* we see Henryson beginning in one traditional feeling and moving into another, with perfect sincerity. One wouldn't want it otherwise.[1] But in the nature of this case he couldn't make the further move into what I have been calling 'criticism of life'.

This seems to me equally true of Henryson's fables – those very lively and charming poems which one yet sometimes feels like calling *only* charming and lively. I think Henryson wrote the fables because they gave him the chance of doing a great many different things in poetry – of bringing in a great range of poetic language – without forcing upon him (comfortable old schoolmaster as he seems to have been, enjoying his grimness in his study) the agony of poetic seriousness.

III

The paradox of a genuinely poetic language without a great poet may come clearer in a brief consideration of the work of Gavin Douglas.

It would be easy to show that Gavin Douglas is not a very striking genius. There is no reason to suppose his native abilities were greater than Lydgate's; none of his works is a masterpiece of the

[1] Cf. Del Chessell, 'In the Dark Time: Henryson's *Testament of Cresseid*', *The Critical Review* (Melbourne, no. 12, 1969), for a longer treatment of these questions.

order of half a dozen of Chaucer's or even of the best poems of
Dunbar. *The Palice of Honour* is only just interesting enough to be
read without strain. It consists largely of lists and catalogues,
culminating in a complete potted history of the world as seen by
Douglas in Venus's mirror. All the stock situations are there – the
May morning, the dream, the Court of Venus, the Palace of Honour
(by *House of Fame* out of *Assembly of Gods*). *King Hart* is a less
aureate work, and more serious, but it is open to the same objections as many of the allegories of the period: the lists of personified
moral qualities are no more convincing here than in *Magnyfycence*
or *The Ship of Fools*. There are some good things in the poem – the
arrival of Age before the house of King Hart and Dame Pleasaunce,
for instance – and they are all very like Dunbar and Henryson in
their grim Scottish power and their commonplaceness; but they
are too few and too separate.

The weaknesses of Douglas's Virgil translation are, again,
obvious enough. Unusually for its period it is a close and scholarly
translation, and it rebukes Chaucer and Caxton for their inaccura-
cies. But Douglas seems to have little feeling for Virgil; the work is
not his own in the sense that a good translator makes an author's
sense his own: it is Gavin Douglas because it is *not* Virgil.

Having said all that, one can ask how many pieces of writing in
English maintain for such a long stretch so high a degree of expres-
siveness. This strength of the Virgil translation as, so to speak,
sheer language, comes strongly out of any comparison with
Surrey's contemporary version of Book II which is supposed to be
the first example of English blank verse.

> There stands in sight an isle, hight Tenedon,
> Rich, and of fame, while Priams kingdom stood,
> Now but a bay, and rode vnsure for ship.[1]

> Thair standis into the sycht of Troy ane ile
> Weil knawin by name, hecht Tenedos vmquhile
> Myghty of gudis quhil Priamus ryng sa stude;
> Now is it bot ane fyrth in the sey flude,
> A raid onsikkyr for schip or ballyngare.[2]

Surrey's rather thin dignity is arguably more appropriate, but
Douglas takes two lines longer and gives himself the chance to

---

[1] *The Poems of Henry Howard, Earl of Surrey*, ed. F. M. Padelford, 2nd edn
(Washington, 1928), p. 115, lines 29–31.
[2] Virgil's *Aeneid* translated into Scottish Verse by Gavin Douglas, ed. D. F. C.
Coldwell (Scottish Text Society, 1957–64), Vol. II, p. 66, lines 15–19.

allow in a lot more, in quantity and quality, of the idiom of his language. When Douglas describes the ill-founded joy of the Trojans he gets it into the movement of the verse in a way that Surrey's decorum does not allow:

Surrey 32
Hether them secretly the Grekes withdrew,
Shrouding themselues vnder the desert shore.
And wening we they had ben fled and gone,
And with that winde had fet the land of Grece,
Troye discharged her long continued dole

Douglas 20
In desert costis of this iland thar
The Grekis thame ful secretly withdrew,
We wenyng thame hame passit and adew
And, with gude wynd, of Myce the realm had socht.
Quharfor al thai of Troy, blyth as thai mocht,
Thair langsum duyl and murnyng dyd away,
Keist vp the portis and yschit furth to play.

Surrey's last line concentrates so much on maintaining its own dignity that it is inappropriately doleful. Notwithstanding the greater trouble his language gives, one returns to Douglas much more readily than to Surrey. (In one way Douglas is as unfailing a well as Chaucer, though we had better not call it a well of English undefiled.) His superiority to Surrey is, not surprisingly, even more marked in scenes of action:

Surrey 618
And he an axe before the formest raught,
Wherwith he gan the strong gates hew and break.
From whens he bat the staples out of brasse,
He brake the barres, and through the timber pearst
So large a hole, whereby they might discerne
The house, the court, the secret chambers eke
Of Priamus and auncient kings of Troy.

Douglas p. 89, line 70
Bot first of al, ane stalwart ax hynt he,
The stern Pyrrus, to hew and brek the ʒet,
And furth of har the stapillis has he bet,
And bandis all of brass yforgyt weill:
Be that in twa the maistir bar ilk deill
Is al tofruschit, syne the hard burdis he hakkis,
And throu the ʒet ane large wyndo makkis
By the quhilk slop the place within apperis
The wyde hallys wolx patent al infeiris
Of Priamus and ancyant kyngis of Troy.

If there is any direct influence it is of Douglas on Surrey, not *vice versa*, but Surrey's version is not an improvement, at least in poetic strength.

Douglas's success is a peculiarly Scottish one. In contemporary England quite real talents like Barclay and Skelton (Skelton is more obviously endowed with genius than Douglas) were frustrated by the Chaucerian tradition and its demands. Douglas, not a major poet, can yet produce a long work of consistent liveliness and perhaps of more value than anything of Skelton's.

The Scottish tradition in poetry did not cut off the court poets from the resources of a rich language, and fifteenth-century Scottish poetry is remarkably impressive especially in comparison with the English: yet in its way the Scottish tradition was as inhibiting as the English. In Scotland, as in England after Lydgate, individual talent could do no more than express the tradition it sympathized with: hence Dunbar, Henryson and Gavin Douglas are at their best when least personal, when expressing with full conviction the commonplaces of their tradition in the liveliness of their language. The Scottish tradition brought the minor poets to full development, the English crushed them.

But it is still true that in Scotland we find a language of poetry without a major poet. And the 'Scottish Chaucerians' would be very hard to judge without such a poet in the near background. As well as the poet who made the great difference to the status of poetry, so that there could *be* poets, Chaucer is the great *point de repère* in our Middle Ages. Even if the phrase 'Scottish Chaucerians' registers in the main their difference from Chaucer, the comparison still holds and is still necessary. If we could not see their difference from Chaucer it would be much harder to see them at all.

15

Italy

I tried to say, with as little offensiveness as possible, and emphasizing that both sides of the comparison are well worth attention,
that Chaucer makes the 'Scottish Chaucerians' look primitive.
The question I want to ask now is whether the Italians make
Chaucer primitive in his turn. In particular, Dante enjoys in the
world at large and even in England a reputation to which Chaucer
has never attained. My questioning the justice of their comparative
fame will be more tentative even than the rest of this work, for my
Italian will not permit anything else. I can read Dante in the Temple
Classics text,[1] making frequent use of the facing translation: and if
this is thought to be scanty qualification for pronouncing on one
of the major European poets, I can only agree. But critics have to
chance their arm sometimes. Sidney's 'I think, and think I think
truely' is odd because the second part is implicit in the first; and I
offer these remarks about Dante because I think them true and to
the point. But there are degrees of confidence and rashness: and it
is not unserious to say that I would be glad to come back to this
chapter in a few years and be exasperated by it. Nevertheless I do
feel as if I have read Dante and can relate him to Chaucer – mainly
because I do feel some security in Chaucer as a centre to work out
from. It must be a common experience for English readers of
Dante, even those whose Italian is no better than mine, to find that
some of the cantos and many of the lines stick as firmly as Shakespeare's; and it may be true that (as Eliot argued) Dante is more
accessible to the Englishman with a smattering of Italian than
Shakespeare to the Italian with a bit of English.[2] But let us begin
with Boccaccio, an easier nut to crack.

---

[1] The *Inferno, Purgatorio, Paradiso* and *Vita Nuova* of Dante Alighieri, ed.
H. Oelsner *et al.* (1899–1906).

[2] T. S. Eliot, 'Dante', reprinted in *Selected Essays,* 3rd ed. (1951).

I

In an obvious way Boccaccio does make Chaucer look provincial. Boccaccio is a professional man of letters, a scholar and a critic. His *Genealogy of the Gods*, for instance, orders and considers its material with thoroughness and intelligence. English writers can display learning, but, for example Gower's *Mirour de l'Omme* is encyclopaedic only in the large number of facts it contains: the ordering of them is simply rhetorical. Boccaccio seems much more modern: one wonders how many of our modern works of scholarship will look so competent six hundred years hence. Boccaccio makes the English writers look amateurish.

He is very conscious, too, of the existence of criticism, which also helps to make him seem modern.[1] He is willing that his work should be criticized by competent judges, but fears the judgment of those who, without learning or taste, pretend to both. His main attack is on lawyers, who criticize poetry according to their professional standards, in particular by observing that you can't earn much money by being a poet. Boccaccio's defence is *not* that poetry is quite unlike litigation: he does see it as a profession like any other, but takes the line that money is not everything. His other defence is that his poetry, unlike their judgments, is immortal – a notion not much at home in England before the Elizabethan age.

This set of attitudes belongs to a tradition which feels itself secure, and has a serene dependence on its continuity quite unlike anything in the English fourteenth century. In a famous stanza of *Troilus and Criseyde* (II, 22–8), Chaucer indeed expresses a wistful consciousness of the changefulness of language, and in another (V, 1793–8), of the particular unsettlement of English, so that whether he is understood or not has to be left to God. Dante, of course, set out quite consciously to define a standard literary Italian (cf. *de Vulgari Eloquentia, passim*) and both Dante's confidence and Chaucer's uncertainty have been justified by the history of their respective languages.

Even *The Decameron* is a work of scholarship, comparable with Scott's *Minstrelsy of the Scottish Border* or Cecil Sharp's collecting of folk songs: Boccaccio seems to have drawn his collection from a vast experience of the taverns of Italy and to have put the bawdy tales,

---

[1] The relevant passages of *The Genealogy of the Gods* are translated from the Latin prose by Charles G. Osgood, *Boccaccio on Poetry* (Princeton, 1930); my summary is based on this translation.

as the most natural thing in the world, into that impeccable and lucid prose that anyone with any Italian at all can read without difficulty.

But the crucial comparison between Boccaccio and Chaucer is obviously the *Filostrato* and what Chaucer made of it in *Troilus and Criseyde*. If I re-tread this well-beaten path[1] it will be in the hope of getting more quickly to our destination, the question of Chaucer's provinciality.

Boccaccio's poem has none of the incoherence I pointed to in Chaucer's. C. S. Lewis's well-known case was that Chaucer medievalizes the *Filostrato*: often enough this 'medievalizing' amounts to confusing it; for most of the confusions and tensions can be traced back to an alteration of Boccaccio's plot or emphasis. In fact everything in *Il Filostrato* is explicable and straightforward.

There is no mystery about the kinship of Pandaro and Criseida: it is put forward as Troiolo's reason for not being forthright with Pandaro, and then becomes a tactical advantage since Pandaro has access to Criseida. There is no mystery either about what Pandaro is to get out of it. One young blood helps another in the expectation of some future *quid pro quo*; and if love is the great hunt it is natural for the huntsmen to stick together. Troiolo, who suffers from neither the bashfulness nor the scruples of Troilus, simply offers Pandaro his sister, or Helen, as a token of gratitude for services rendered.

> E perché tu conosca quanto piena
> benivolenza da me t'è portata,
> io ho la mia sorella Polissena
> piú di bellezza che altra pregiata,
> ed ancor c'è con esso lei Elena
> bellissima, la quale è mia cognata:
> apri il cor tuo se te ne piace alcuna,
> poi me lascia operar con qual sia l'una.[2]

There is no difficulty, either, about how to persuade Criseida. She has a reputation for virtue, but Pandaro believes – and nothing in the poem contradicts his belief – that

---

[1] Cf. especially C. S. Lewis, 'What Chaucer really did to *Il Filostrato*', *Essays and Studies* XVII (1931), and Ian C. Walker, 'Chaucer and *Il Filostrato*', *English Studies* XLIX (1968).

[2] *Il Filostrato* III, st. 18; Giovanni Boccaccio, *Opere*, ed. Cesare Segre (Milan, 1966), p. 831. The stanza is translated like this by R. K. Gordon in *The Story of Troilus* (New York reprint, 1964), p. 60: 'And that thou mayest know what great good will I bear thee I have my sister Polyxena, prized above others for her beauty, and also there is with her that fairest Helen, who is my kinswoman – open thy heart if either is pleasing unto thee – then leave it to me to work with whichever it be.'

II 27

>ogni donna in voglia
>vive amorosa, e null' altro l'affrena
>che tema di vergogna; e s'a tal doglia
>onestamente medicina piena
>si può donar, folle è chi non la spoglia
>e poco parmi le cuoca la pena.
>La mia cugina è vedova e disia,
>e se 'l negasse non gliel crederia.[1]

So Pandaro's plan is simply to offer Criseida a man (II, 37). Criseida, whose desires are as explicit as Pandaro calculates (II, 117 etc.) and who moreover thinks that unless she satisfies them her complexion will suffer (II, 116), almost, as Professor Muscatine said of May, 'just succumbs' (II, 139–40).

Troiolo and Criseida find exactly what they are looking for, and they know in advance what it is. The poem is much more sexually forthright than Chaucer's, and at this level fully successful.

III 32

>E la camiscia sua gittata via,
>nelle sua bracca si ricolse avaccio;
>e strignendo l'un l'altro con fervore,
>d'amor sentiron l'ultimo valore.[2]

Their 'ultimo valore' is very unlike Chaucer's 'grete worthynesse'. A few stanzas later Boccaccio praises love:

III 38

>Deh, pensin qui li dolorosi avari,
>che biasiman chi è innamorato
>e chi, come fan essi, a far denari,
>in alcun modo, non s'è tutto dato,
>e guardin se, tenendoli ben cari,
>tanto piacer fu mai da lor prestato,
>quanto ne presta amore in un sol punto,
>a cui egli è con ventura congiunto.

>Ei diranno di sí ma mentiranno,
>e questo amor, dolorosa pazzia

---

[1] Gordon translates this (*ibid.* p. 42): 'every lady leads an amorous life in her wishes, and...naught but fear of shame holds her back; and, if full contentment can be given to such desire without loss of honour, he who takes her not is a fool, and not overmuch, I think, does the penalty grieve her. My cousin is a widow and desirous; and if she were to deny it, I should not believe her.'

[2] Gordon, p. 62: 'and, casting off her shift, she quickly threw herself into his arms. And each with fervour held the other close, and they did feel the utmost sweetness of love.'

con risa e con ischerni chiameranno,
sanza veder che solo una ora fia
nella qual sé e' denar perderanno,
sanza aver gioia saputo che sia
nella lor vita; Iddio gli faccia tristi,
ed agli amanti doni i loro acquisti.[1]

All for *what* or the world well lost? Boccaccio's characters act as if
the best thing in life were a disconnected moment of sexual ecstasy.
There may be something to be said for that point of view; nor do I
wish to suggest that there is no poetic conviction in *Il Filostrato*.
But it misses Chaucer's splendour because its poetry is serving
something outside itself: it creates values by pointing elsewhere
and saying, 'Look, that's what matters.' Whereas Chaucer is a love-
poet (the term can be rigidly exclusive on occasion) and creates love
within his language. 'For I repeat, it [the language of love] is not
saying that anything has happened, and it is not describing anything. Nor is it the expression of a sensation or feeling. It is the
expression of love.'[2]

Boccaccio's poem has its own incoherence, of a much more
radical kind than Chaucer's, to the extent that it does try to be a
love-poem. It hangs together in the way I have been describing –
like the *Decameron*, where the same game is played, all the men chase
all the women (as well as the boys), and where the deducible rules
are as strict as what is supposed to be found in Andreas Capellanus. But Boccaccio gives *Il Filostrato* a frame which makes one
judge it by serious standards. The narrator is himself hopelessly in
love with a lady who has gone away: the poem is an offering to this
love. But he can't have it both ways: if love is just the *'ultima valore'*,
the languishing of the Troiolo of the later cantos, and of the narrator,
is just an unmanly weakness which ought to be settled in the style
of Pandaro by transferring the passion to another girl. Perhaps
this is what Boccaccio is trying to show himself in the poem; perhaps it is his Cure for Love. But if so the poem is a decisively

---

1 Gordon, pp. 62–3: 'Ah, let the wretched misers think of this, who blame him
who is in love and who has not wholly given himself, as they do, to gaining
wealth in some way; and let them consider whither, holding it very dearly as
they do, it ever offered such delight as is offered in a single moment to him
who has been happy in his love. They will say yes, but they will lie; and with
laughter and gibes they will call this love a painful madness; and they see not
that in a single hour they will lose themselves and their wealth without having
known in their lives what joy is. God make them unhappy and give their
possessions to lovers.'
2 Rush Rhees, 'Religion and Language', *Without Answers*, p. 123.

lesser thing than Chaucer's. Boccaccio, trying to reduce love to splendid sex, is cauterizing it: in the end he leads us back to the great game of love, so much less dangerous than the Venus-worship of Book III of *Troilus and Criseyde*. What Boccaccio excludes is exactly what Chaucer alone has the courage and the poetic power to make the centre of his poem.

At a surface level it is true that Chaucer looks gauche and provincial by Boccaccio's side, at least in *Troilus and Criseyde*. Chaucer is struggling into literature in a backward land and in a language which had none of the prestige and continuity of the literary language of Italy. Nevertheless, if poetry is about what is deep in life, about what matters, and about making sense of the gods, it is Chaucer who is the great poet and Boccaccio merely the consummate man of letters.

It is one thing, however, to measure Chaucer against Boccaccio – or against Petrarch or the other lesser Italians. The real question is whether Chaucer can hold a candle to Dante, and, if not, whether we Chaucer critics, blinded by our xenophobia and insularity, are not spending too much time on the lesser poet who, perhaps, is properly seen only in the penumbra of the greater.

III

There is a certain contradiction between two parts of the idea of Dante current in England and, it may be, between two ambitions realized in his poetry. On the one hand he is the Dante of the '*dolce stil nuovo*'[1], admired by Arnold for the high seriousness of

In la sua volontade è nostra pace[2]

by T. S. Eliot for the *universality* of his language,[3] and by himself, in *de Vulgari Eloquentia* for having established a standard Italian. This is Dante the great impersonal poet, the magisterial successor of Virgil. And this part of the idea of Dante fits well the deliberate unity of the career which leads him on a complete journey from love through Hell and Purgatory to the sight of God. Everything seems in place in Dante, the poet of the serene high Middle Ages.

On the other hand Dante is a poet of particularity and particular

---

[1] *Purgatorio* XXIV, 57.

[2] *Paradiso* III, 85; the Temple Classics text has the better-looking 'e' for 'In'. This is the line which Arnold says is 'altogether beyond Chaucer's reach' ('The Study of Poetry').

[3] *Selected Essays*, p. 239.

passions, who comes out well in quotation, in places like the few lines about the awful gluttonousness of Cerberus:

> E il duca mio distese le sue spanne,
>   prese la terra, e con piene le pugna
>   la gittò dentro alle bramose canne.

> Qual è quel cane che abbaiando agugna,
>   e si racqueta poi che il pasto morde,
>   chè solo a divorarlo intende e pugna...[1]

Or the avaricious and the prodigal, the former of whom 'shall arise from their graves with closed fists; and these with hair shorn off':

> questi risurgeranno del sepulcro
>   col pugno chiuso, e questi co' crin mozzi.[2]

One of Dante's bests is when he is magisterial and passionate at the same time, as in the superb denunciation of Florence (*Purgatorio* VI).

But the difficult central case, and the one that allows me to distinguish these two sides of Dante (which as I have described them *need* not be distinct) is what Dante makes of love, and the journey it leads him on. At the beginning of the *Vita Nuova* the superb confidence of the style is the perfect expression of the feeling. Nothing could be in sharper contrast with Chaucer's early fumblings than the effortless rightness with which Dante expresses the voice of his heart:

In quel punto dico veracement che lo spirito della vita, lo quale dimora nella segretissima camera del cuore, cominciò a tremare sì fortemente, che apparia ne' menomi polsi orribilmente; e tremando disse queste parole: *Ecce Deus fortior me, qui veniens dominabitur mihi.*[3]

By going into Latin – by going even further than his Italian style from the merely personal – Dante achieves a personal sincerity. Dante equally hits the right nail with great force when later in the *Vita Nuova* he realizes what his love for Beatrice has to do with his poetry. He makes what is surely the classical definition of the

---

[1] *Inferno* VI, 25–30. 'My Guide, spreading his palms, took up earth; and, with full fists, cast it into his ravening gullets. As the dog, that barking craves, and grows quiet when he bites his food, for he strains and battles only to devour it...'

[2] *Inferno* VII, 56–7.

[3] *Vita Nuova* II. 'At that point I verily declare that the vital spirit which dwelleth in the most secret chamber of the heart began to tremble so mightily that it was horribly apparent in the least of my pulses, and trembling, it said these words: "Behold God stronger than me, who coming will dominate me."'

finality of love, 'Io ho tenuti i piedi in quella parte della vita, di là dalla quale non si può ire più per intendimento di ritornare'[1], and this leads, with the logic of poetry, to Dante's seeing his words about this love as that which cannot fail him:

Madonne, lo fine del mio amore fu già il saluto di questa donna, di cui voi forse intendete; ed in quello dimorava la mia beatitudine, chè era fine di tutti i miei desiderii. Ma piochè le piacque di negarlo a me, lo mio signore Amore, la sua mercede, ha posta tutta la mia beatitudine in quello, che non mi puote venir meno.[2]

This does strike one as a poetic leap into truth – much more so than the manoeuvres Dante reports earlier, where his solemn tone goes badly with the courtly twists he is describing, and one sometimes wonders whether he is imposing on himself.

Though this moment of the *Vita Nuova* is so good in itself, it betrays Dante into placing a mistaken reliance on his inspiration, his feeling for Beatrice. He has here achieved

> The final certitude of speech
> Which Hell itself cannot unlock.[3]

But Dante can never realize that such certitude is transient: he will hang on to it like grim death. Troilus is also certain of his love, but *he* finds it 'betwene drede and sikernesse'. Dante's magisterial certainty is quite different – and, I would suggest, really less secure. Poetry cannot fail, Dante feels: it is as certain as love and language. But he is without the complementary sense that poetry is also as frail as love and as language.

Dante *uses* Beatrice: he makes his love subserve his other ends, which are in control. This is not a way of making love more certain, on the contrary it is, in the course of the *Divine Comedy*, a way of losing its life. Dante will not submit himself humbly enough to his own inspiration; he will force it to do what he, the strong-willed Florentine, thinks it should do.

Even setting aside the *Convito*, where he has allegorized the poor girl almost out of existence, Dante's confidence that the praise of

---

[1] *Vita Nuova* XIV. 'I have set my feet in that region of life beyond which one cannot go with intent to return.'

[2] *Vita Nuova* XVIII. 'Ladies mine, the end of my love was once this lady's salutation of whom I ween ye are thinking; and therein dwelt my beatitude, for it was the end of all my desires. But since it hath pleased her to deny it to me, Love, my lord, by his grace, hath placed all my beatitude in that which cannot fail me.'

[3] Yvor Winters, 'For the Opening of the William Dinsmore Briggs Room, Stanford University, May 7, 1942', *Collected Poems* (Denver, 1960), p. 131.

Beatrice guarantees his poetry and that what she says cannot err is not borne out by his text. It is not true that he is most sure or convincing when writing of her or at her dictation: and the more certain he becomes, the less is his certainty justified by the poetry. Turned into pure light in the *Paradiso*, Beatrice is much less interesting than when she was merely a woman in the *Vita Nuova*. But that is something Dante cannot and will not recognize, for his certainty is disconnected from his inspiration.

Take the famous case of Paolo and Francesca. Dante creates the moment of their love with as much immediacy as Cerberus's gluttony.

> Per più fiate gli occhi ci sospinse
>   quella lettura, e scolorocci il viso;
>   ma solo un punto fu quel che ci vinse.
>
> Quando leggemmo il disiato riso
>   esser baciato da cotanto amante,
>   questi, che mai da me non fia diviso,
>
> la bocca mi baciò tutto tremante...[1]

This, one might say, is heavenly. That would not quite be just: but we might certainly ask what 'paradiso' means if the love that informs it is never of this kind. And Dante's sympathy with Paolo and Francesca is fully conscious, as well as transparently there in the poetry. He says

116   Francesca, i tuoi martiri
     a lagrimar mi fanno tristo e pio.

('Francesca, thy torments make me weep with grief and pity.')

And the episode ends when Dante faints out of compassion. Nevertheless, there they are in Hell, amongst the carnal sinners. They are in Hell because, outside his poem, Dante's belief is that they have sinned. But the belief doesn't enter the poetry – except in the line which immediately follows the passage I quoted:

137   Galeotto fu il libro, e chi lo scrisse

('The book, and he who wrote it, was a Galeotto [Pandar].')

Milton, having allowed himself a similar flight of poetry, rebukes it with a similar direct intervention:

[1] *Inferno* v, 130–5: 'Several times that reading urged our eyes to meet, and changed the colour of our faces; but one moment alone it was that overcame us. When we read how the fond smile was kissed by such a lover, he, who shall never be divided from me, kissed my mouth all trembling...'

from Morn
To Noon he fell, from Noon to dewy Eve,
A Summers day; and with the setting Sun
Dropt from the Zenith like a falling Star,
On *Lemnos* th' *Ægæan* Ile: thus they relate,
Erring...[1]

Dante's moral intent is here in conflict with his inspiration. It is the same with the tale of the fate of Ulysses, a passage rightly singled out by T. S. Eliot for special praise. Yet here, too, Dante is forcing a moral onto the poetry, not discovering or creating one in the poetry. Ulysses and his companions set out on a voyage of discovery which one sympathizes with with the force of half a millennium of European history:

'O frati,' dissi, 'che per cento milia
    perigli siete giunti all' occidente,
    a questa tanto picciola vigilia

de' vostri sensi, ch' è del rimanente,
    non vogliate negar l' esperienza,
    di retro al sol, del mondo senza gente.

Considerate la vostra semenza:
    fatti non foste a viver come bruti,
    ma per seguir virtute e conoscenza.'[2]

This again speaks from the heart of Dante's inspiration; and again the morality seems dictatorially imposed.[3] They achieve the sight of Purgatory (the moment of terror and achievement has something of Conrad's phrase 'We sighted the southern ice' in the tale *Falk*) and then – God intervenes. But I am left admiring Ulysses and thinking that perhaps his adventure was worth death. I think at worst he ought to be in Purgatory:

[1] *Paradise Lost* I, 742–7.
[2] *Inferno* XXVI, 112–20: 'O brothers!' I said, 'who through a hundred thousand dangers have reached the West, deny not, to this the brief vigil of your senses that remains, experience of the unpeopled world behind the Sun. Consider your origin: ye were not formed to live like brutes, but to follow virtue and knowledge.'
[3] Croce almost says so: 'Ma Ulisse, che, ardente sempre della volontà di conoscere il mondo e gli uomini, non ritenuto né da dolcezza di figlio né da pietà verso il vecchio padre né da amor di moglie, con canuti compagni a lui fidi, si mette ancora pel mare alla scoperta della parte non conosciuta della sfera terrestre; Ulisse, che infiamma i suoi compagni con le alte parole: "Fatti non foste a viver come bruti, Ma per seguir virtude e conoscenza"; è una parte di Dante stesso, cioè delle profonde aspirazioni che la riverenza religiosa e l' umiltà cristiana potevano in lui contenere, ma non già distruggere.' Benedetto Croce, *La Poesia di Dante* (Bari, 1921), p. 98.

133   n'apparve una montagna bruna
per la distanza, e parvemi alta tanto
quanto veduta non n' aveva alcuna.

Noi ci allegrammo, e tosto tornò in pianto:
chè dalla nuova terra un turbo nacque,
e percosse del legno il primo canto.

('There appeared to us a Mountain, dim with distance; and to me it seemed the highest I had ever seen. We joyed, and soon our joy was turned to grief: for a tempest rose from the new land, and struck the forepart of our ship.')

It is not that Dante is rebuking a presumptuous venture beyond the limits of humanity: he is here against the search for significance itself, which is, nevertheless, the life of this poetry. At the beginning of the second Canto of the *Paradiso* Dante uses an image of his own journey that puts one in mind of Ulysses:

7   L' acqua ch' io prendo giammai non si corse
('The water which I take was never coursed before.')

– the difference is that Dante feels his voyage guaranteed:

8   Minerva spira, e conducemi Apollo.
('Minerva bloweth, Apollo guideth me . . .')

Despite the title of *La Vita Nuova*, the vision Dante wills is not of a new heaven and a new earth, but of an order that is quite immutable and independent of human vision. It is true that the *Comedy* is a voyage of discovery out of the 'selva oscura' of the first Canto – that Dante finds what can be shown him by Virgil or Beatrice – but the discovery is of something pre-existent. Whereas there is more pure creation of what is discovered in Shakespeare or Chaucer.

One result of Dante's domineering over his inspiration is that this magisterial judge of human values can be petty and dull. It is notorious that Dante's enemies find themselves in Hell; he does not always even wait for them to die before pronouncing the last judgment. This taking upon himself the role of God could succeed only if his judgments were as just and calm as he believes them to be. But Dante is sometimes mean, vengeful and spiteful. Virgil approves of Dante's curse of Filippo Argenti with a speech that savours a good deal of the deadly sin of 'envye', the delight in doing people down:

Quanti si tengon or lassù gran regi,
   che qui staranno come porci in brago,
   di sè lasciando orribili dispregi![1]

This is as bad as the opposite view, of Chaucer's Monk, that there
is necessarily something tragic in coming down in the world. Dante
goes on to suggest to Virgil that before they leave they should have
Filippo dipped in the mud (53), to which Virgil agrees with
peculiarly grave unction:

56   tu sarai sazio;
   di tal disio converrà che tu goda.

('Thou shalt be satisfied; it is fitting that thou shouldst be gratified in
such a wish.')

Similarly the insult to Florence at the beginning of *Inferno* XXVI,
which begins superbly, turns spiteful and petty within a few lines.

Put beside this the unrealization of much of Dante's Hell and
Heaven. Dante is certainly able to strike some of the different
terrors of Hell into the reader. But there is a lot that does not come
across; many of the pains are not painful, because the reader is not
called on to imagine them. In Canto XXI of the *Inferno* a new load of
Barrators arrive in Hell and are thrown into boiling pitch. But
there is something domestic and pleasant, rather than painful or
terrifying, about the whole episode. The pitch is (lines 7ff.) like
that boiled in Venice in winter to caulk damaged ships; the sinner
is kept under like this:

55   Non altrimenti i cuochi ai lor vassalli
     fanno attuffare in mezzo la caldaia
     la carne con gli uncin, perchè non galli.

('Not otherwise do the cooks make their vassals dip the flesh into the
middle of the boiler with their hooks, to hinder it from floating.')

This is the canto, too, where we are introduced to some of the
demons – but their pettiness, dirt and farting would make them
more at home in a morality play than a great epic poem. Poets can,
of course, make something terrible of the pettiness of evil (how
ordinary much of the nastiness of Shakespeare's witches is!) but
that doesn't seem to be Dante's point here.

Another sign of the unwholeness of Dante's greatness is that his
conjunction of the Christian and classical worlds is as insecure – as

---

[1] *Inferno* VIII, 49–52. 'How many up there now think themselves great kings,
that shall lie here like swine in mire, leaving behind them horrible reproaches!'

much a product of will and tradition and as little of inspiration – as Milton's. In Dante Iddio and Giove are interchangeable, and the geography of Hell is Virgil's: but of course Virgil, though Dante's God-appointed guide, is himself condemned to Hell. The classical elements *can't* coexist with the Christian (though there is not hing quite so absurd as Milton's War in Heaven): but Dante (and Milton) *will* have it so.[1] Their masterful determination – in b oth cases at the heart of the work, so that one could not will it otherwise – is sometimes the enemy of poetry.

There are long similes in *Troilus and Criseyde*, but not de-liberately epic ones of the kind Dante and Milton insert, because they are proper to epic poetry, though as far as I can see they are never expressive and (in Dante's case) sometimes let down the intensity of a passage.

I offer as a good example of Dante's failings Canto XVI of the *Purgatorio*. At the end of the preceding canto Dante and Virgil have been overtaken by a cloud of smoke; in Canto XVI they are in it, and the image is so well done that when (lines 13–15) Dante gives us a glimpse of himself trying hard not to lose Virgil we can take it as emblematic of his journey as a whole:

> m'andava io per l' aere amaro e sozzo,
> ascoltando il mio duca che diceva
> pur: 'Guarda che da me tu non sie mozzo.'

('So went I through the bitter and foul air, listening to my Leader who was saying ever: "Look that thou be not cut off from me."')

But Dante insists on explaining this image of the fog. Meaning is forced into explicitness: and with the explanation the image loses its interest.[2] The spirits in the smoke

24   d' iracondia van solvendo il nodo
('They are untying the knot of anger.')

Further, it is notorious that Dante's Hell is more interesting than his Heaven; and this involves a judgment on the poem that is at once literary–critical, moral and theological. The *Paradiso* is Dante's attainment of the state in which

---

[1] Cf. the ludicrously inappropriate prayer to Apollo. *Paradiso* I, 13.

[2] Cf. '"And I saw heaven opened, and behold a white horse; and he that sat upon it was called" – there my memory suddenly stops, deliberately blotting out the next words: "Faithful and True". I hated, even as a child, allegory: people having the names of mere qualities, like this somebody on a white horse, called "Faithful and True"...A man is more than mere Faithfulness and Truth, and when people are merely personifications of qualities they cease to be people for me.' D. H. Lawrence, *Apocalypse*, Chapter I.

già volgeva il mio disiro e il *velle*,
  sì come rota ch' egualmente è mossa,
 l' amor che move il sole e l' altre stelle.[1]

Dante's rebelliousness is now at an end as his whole nature con-
forms to the promptings of Love. At last, he thinks, will and inspiration are one. Perhaps; but that may be because will has finally
vanquished inspiration; and this must be the end of both, since
Dante's poetry has always proceeded from the tension between his
feeling and what he wants to do with it. The rest must be silence.

Dante's perfection at the end of the *Paradiso* is perfect pride; the
Paradiso can be seen as the record of his damnation at least as
naturally as of his salvation. Self-justification and self-pity (Cantos
XVI–XVII) lead to this final bare assertion, which is Dante's final
farewell to his poetry. This follows naturally from Virgil's last
words to Dante, which would have appealed to Nietzsche in his
madder mood:

Libero, dritto e sano è tuo arbitrio,
 e fallo fora non fare a suo senno:
per ch'io te sopra te corono e mitrio.[2]

But the sanity of Dante's will can only show itself in our being
convinced by the judgments the poetry makes – which as the
poem progresses I increasingly fail to be.

This is not merely the objection that Dante is without proper
English modesty. The objection is that the development in the
Paradiso is not done into the poetry, and so there is no reason for
the reader to believe in Dante's progress in virtue and wisdom.
There is so much asserted in the *Paradiso* and so little shown: and
even more frequent is the assertion that Dante has done or seen
something too great for words. But experience that cannot be
expressed in words is not a poet's salvation: it is his nemesis. When
Dante tells us (XXXIII, 49ff.) that he has looked on God, the supreme
light, I don't believe him, because there is no supreme light in the
poetry at this moment. On the contrary this vision follows from the
granting of his prayer to Mary to

[1] *Paradiso* XXXIII, 143–5. 'already my desire and will were rolled – even as a
wheel that moveth equally – by the love that moves the sun and the other
stars.'

[2] *Purgatorio* XXVII, 140–2. 'Free, upright, and whole, is thy will, and 'twere a
fault not to act according to its prompting; wherefore I do crown and mitre
thee over thyself.'

Vinca tua guardia i movimenti umani.[1]

I am more interested in Chaucer's and Shakespeare's genius for seeing God within 'i movimenti umani'.

Dante is determined to separate out Heaven so that it has nothing in common with earth and only communicates with Hell on extraordinary occasions. In Canto XII a group of spirits

25   insieme a punto ed a voler quetarsi,
         pur come gli occhi ch' al piacer che i move
         conviene insieme chiudere e levarsi...[2]

This is characteristic of Dante's metaphysical poetry at its best: yet the image here links us to earth against his will, for the power of moving one's eyes only belongs to people who have had to learn it and can lose it again. More generally one can make to Dante's heaven the objections Johnson made to Milton's hell. The 'want of human interest' is felt here too; the characters are less substantial than those of the *Inferno*. Having committed himself to portraying them all as light, Dante denies himself any creation of the quasi-novelistic kind that is often so impressive earlier. The ludicrous case is when St Peter expresses his rage (XXVII, 10ff.) by glowing red.

The strength of the earlier books is above all their very convincing observation of human passions, but the *Paradiso* works not by observation so much as a kind of linguistic magic which before I read Dante I innocently thought had been invented by Professor J. R. R. Tolkien. In *The Lord of the Rings* there is a scale of values dependent entirely upon linguistic manipulation and not at all upon observation of life. Hobbits are more or less all right but are infinitely inferior to Gandalf the Grey: he, moreover, is later transfigured into the even better White River. Orcs are bad creatures but they are nothing to the Black Riders of Mordor. Worse still, however, is the balrog. A word *a* is coined then *b, c* ... are developed from *a* by comparatives, whether explicitly or by being made adjacent in the same work. This is just what Dante does with the beauty of Beatrice in the *Paradiso*. Each time they go up into the next heaven she is more beautiful and more purely light. But this linguistic magic is almost the opposite of poetic creation: certainly it is the opposite of realization. Dante's frequent boasts that what

---

[1] XXXIII, 37: 'Let thy protection vanquish human ferments.'
[2] 'accordant at a point of time and act of will, had stilled them, like to the eyes which at the pleasure that moveth them must needs be closed and lifted in accord...'

he has seen is inexpressible are assertions of his superiority to language: but his language does not bear out his claim.

In the end Dante's determination that Beatrice cannot err[1] is hubris: when he links it with her instructions to him to write, it becomes simple bluff.[2] It is a kind of confidence trick when Dante uses the heavenly spokesmen to answer the outstanding questions of history or philosophy (such as what language was spoken in Eden). Only poetic realization could bring off what Dante tries to do in the *Paradiso;* but realization has increasingly given way to self-assertion of a peculiarly self-righteous kind.

I conclude that Dante is really a genius of fits and starts who never achieved the final sincerity of knowing it. Dante does need his feeling for Beatrice and his other less beautiful passions: he does also need his great will to unity and formality. But the great poetry comes from these things separately or in uneasy and temporary balance: it is a hit-and-miss kind of poetry which creates no sense of the wholeness of sanity of the poet's soul. If *The Divine Comedy is* a whole it is because of a triumph of the poet's will which is far from sane and which is the enemy of the great poetry in Dante. Chaucer looks, and is, much more tentative than Dante, but I think Chaucer's the surer genius of the two. In a sense Dante's poetry is a means of *not* knowing himself. (These are hard words to use of a poet whose greatness I do not deny: but I think they are true, and it is also certainly true that Dante's reputation is unlikely to be touched by any words of mine.)

The difference I see between Chaucer and Dante will be plain enough to the reader of earlier chapters. Chaucer is, at the beginning of his career, a man searching in chaos whose great poetic triumphs are all variations on the theme that *nothing*, with no exceptions, can be depended on or guaranteed. Chaucer's *oeuvre* makes a natural criticism of Dante's certainties.[3] Chaucer's genius belongs here with Shakespeare's – exploratory, adventurous, and not afraid of indecorum. Chaucer's is a higher kind of poetry than Dante's.

My justification for saying so is that the difference between the

---

[1]   Secondo mio infallibile avviso...
Paradiso VII, 19: 'According to my thought that cannot err...'
[2] *Purgatorio* XXXII, 103ff.
[3] Chaucer's criticism is conscious, too – but that is of comparatively little importance. Chaucer's fear of stellification and distrust of Fame (in *The House of Fame*) is a retort to those numerous passages of *The Divine Comedy* – for example, *Inferno* IV, *Purgatorio* XXVI – where other poets take Dante at his own valuation.

poets is essentially the difference between the literatures of Italy and England; and it will be almost my final task in the present discussion to show why that is not a nationalistic *non sequitur*.

Beatrice announces herself to Dante at a wonderful moment of the *Purgatorio*:

> Guardami ben: ben son, ben son Beatrice.[1]

She is, she is indeed Beatrice – and the wonder is Dante's belief. This is a moment when his certainty is fully expressed in the emotion of the poetry. It is just as much the centre of Shakespeare that when King Lear, his pride battered out of him on the heath with his very personality, comes to himself, *his* achievement of truth is the poignant uncertainty, quite out of his earlier character, with which he says

IV vi
>   Pray do not mocke me:
> I am a very foolish fond old man,
> Fourescore and upward,
> Not an houre more, nor lesse:
> And to deale plainely,
> I feare I am not in my perfect mind.
> Me thinkes I should know you, and know this man,
> Yet I am doubtfull: For I am mainely ignorant
> What place this is: and all the skill I have
> Remembers not these garments: nor I know not
> Where I did lodge last night. Do not laugh at me,
> For (as I am a man) I thinke this Lady
> To be my childe *Cordelia*.
> COR. And so I am: I am.

Lear learns what love is as effectively as Dante: Lear is at last able to recognize that the love of father for daughter and daughter for father is not a fact of nature but a gift of grace. But the realization is so fragile, so hard to come by – so easily swept away by those terrible closing scenes.

I sometimes think the central line of Chaucer is

F 1473
It may be wel   paraunter yet to day

– which would, again, take us straight back to the Shakespeare of the last plays, where the survival of life against the odds of a savage world is shown as miraculous.

Dante's sincerity is like Tattycoram's in *Little Dorrit*. She has to

---

[1] *Purgatorio* XXX, 73.

count up to twenty to allow her passions to subside. When she gets to twenty she is able to return quite sincerely to the framework of feeling approved by Mr Meagles, Mrs Meagles and Pet. But Chaucer, and Shakespeare, are always trying to find out what they mean: their great and final achievements are the process of discovery – and not the discovery of something pre-existent. I would say that Chaucer creates the idea of patience in English by writing *The Clerk's Tale*. (This does not imply he could have done so without the aid of other people and the language.) And that is a higher creativity than Dante's.

But I think it would be a bad thing if I could find a cultured Italian to agree with me. These things are bound to look different from different viewpoints: which is not to say that there is no truth in literary criticism. Each national literature is a centre from which to view the rest: I feel at home with Chaucer as I cannot with Dante. If English is one's first language, one naturally takes the greatest kind of poetry to be Shakespeare's – and Dickens's, and D. H. Lawrence's, and Chaucer's. Otherwise one goes against the grain of one's own language, and can be at home nowhere. I do not see how a great English poet could think Dante greater than Chaucer, except in despair of English. And I do say that T. S. Eliot's debts to Dante, so obviously a strength in *The Waste Land* and *Little Gidding*, are in this other way a weakness, and one that it is relevant to think of when considering the peculiarly limited and equivocal nature of Eliot's greatness. If Eliot's endeavour to extend English poetry into our century could have been as daring and English as Chaucer's, if Eliot could have gone back to Chaucer as well as to Dante, English poetry might have survived his death. Eliot's hankering after the Dantesque kind of impersonality and certainty is, at least sometimes, the disguise of an unconfidence in the creative habit of his own language. (Not that one wishes to sound ungrateful for what Eliot, or Dante, did give us, or that in the end one could imagine them otherwise.)

'What *is* English literature?' asks Dr Leavis. 'It is a question to which an English school should be constantly working out the answer.'[1] Chaucer's difference from Dante is one reliable mark of our literature. It only remains for me to ask formally how our literature defines Chaucer and *vice versa*, why the questions might matter, and – first – what is wrong with the usual answers.

[1] F. R. Leavis, '"English" – Unrest and Continuity', *The Times Literary Supplement* (29 May 1969), p. 571.

16

Chaucer and Criticism

Poetry can only live, in the reader, in the present. This is a truism, but so central a truism that we may hope to move from it to something less obvious.[1] The comparison of Chaucer with other medieval poets is a natural way of defining his place; but it is not always realized that, even in the case of the most abstruse comparisons, the position we are trying to define is Chaucer's place in English literature. It is worth stating and exploring some of the implications of this obvious proposition if only because it is so far from obvious to many of the most influential Chaucer critics that our common ways of reading Chaucer may try to deny it. The context in which we read Chaucer is our language of modern Chaucer criticism, the set of presuppositions, expectations and standards without which there is no reading but which, if wrong, get in the way of reading. And it is fair to say that, on the whole, modern Chaucer criticism makes itself weak by trying to separate Chaucer from English literature.

Unless Chaucer is in some sense one of our poets he is not a poet at all; but Chaucer's work is medieval, and so it is also true that any good reading of Chaucer must be a concentrating of attention on a certain part of the past, and in that way belong to history. Chaucer can only speak here and now, but he must speak with a voice from the fourteenth century. These complementary truisms have turned for modern criticism into the horns of a dilemma. For both these true and necessary propositions – that Chaucer's poetry is still alive in English, and that to know Chaucer is to know something of the past – have, separately, got critics into conceptual tangles which obstruct appreciation of Chaucer and obscure the question which criticism, explicitly or not, is always asking: How and how much does this poetry matter to us?

The historical muddles are the more influential. Since the

---

[1] For an exposition where the idea becomes very much more than truism, see F. R. Leavis, *English Literature in Our Time and the University* (1969), p. 68.

demise of 'Chaucer the cheery dear old man'[1] there have been several different important attempts to emphasize Chaucer's pastness by substituting for present reading some more verifiable discipline of history. How do we know our impressions of Chaucer's poems are true? This question can lead to the trap of attempting some historical guarantee: Chaucer *must* mean so-and-so if we can anchor his poems to something in history that we can know certainly. The two most important historical attempts on Chaucer have been the works of the late Professor C. S. Lewis, and of Professor D. W. Robertson, Jr.

From the short Preface to Lewis's posthumous book, *The Discarded Image*, emerge three quite different ideas of what the book is to do. At first it seems we are to be given a key to all the notes: 'I cannot boast that it contains much which a reader could not have found out for himself if, at every hard place in the old books, he had turned to commentators, histories, encyclopaedias, and other such helps.'[2] There the promise is of a vast mass of 'background' knowledge, parts of which will rise temporarily into the foreground to illuminate particular texts. (This is tantamount to offering us a language: but languages are not learned in this way.) Next Lewis uses the image of a map: 'To be always looking at the map when there is a fine prospect before you shatters the "wise passiveness" in which landscape ought to be enjoyed. But to consult a map before we set out has no such ill effect.'[3] This image presents in a mild way what I believe to be the decisive fallacy. The map is of those things outside poetry that will give the poems their place. But the map that is essential for the reader of literature is the relation of poems to each other, and that cannot be given to anybody before he sets out. We make our own 'map' literally as we go along: seeing relations is a great part of the thinking that follows reading, perhaps even part of reading itself. Until we know poems by reading them (there is no other way of knowing them) they cannot be said to exist for us, much less to exist in relation to each

---

[1] So I began to write before remembering that this old soldier, though somewhat fading, is by no means dead. He is still going strong for instance in T.W. Craik's *Comic Tales of Chaucer*, which tells us on p. 153 that '*The Merchant's Tale* is dirty enough, like some of the other comic ones, in its way; but Chaucer's sureness of touch, as an artist and as a man, makes the dirt a pure kind of dirt, and the story one at which we can be glad.' Dr Craik is here using a phrase from Hardy: all the same, to have one's dirt and eat it so happily is a symptom of the old tradition. Another example is Helen Storm Corsa's *Chaucer, Poet of Mirth and Morality* (Notre Dame, Indiana, 1964).

[2] C. S. Lewis, *The Discarded Image* (Cambridge, 1964), p. ix.   [3] *Ibid.*

other and other things. Lewis's kind of 'map' is secondary, except in so far as he means the presuppositions about what is worth attention that are given to us by spoken and unspoken literary history. But, again, that notion of what there is to read is in a broad sense the function of the language, not of Lewis's kind of book. On the other hand there is, I hope, a place for the comparison of maps (which is called 'literary criticism'): but that is another way of objecting to the image, for our critical maps are of terrains which are only there to the extent that other map-makers agree. Really we have to do not with maps but travellers' tales, and part of our problem is to distinguish reliable travellers from the other kind. Lewis also says,

> there are travellers who carry their resolute Englishry with them all over the continent, mix only with other English tourists, enjoy all they see for its 'quaintness', and have no wish to realize what those ways of life, those churches, those vineyards, mean to the natives...I was writing for the other sort.[1]

But the alternatives Lewis offers are not the real ones. The 'other sort' could only be the travellers who like Lady Hester Stanhope 'go native'. To know what things mean to the natives one must in the end *be* a native. A travelled English friend points to a couple of ordinary-looking cushions partly obstructing the rear window of a car, says, 'The owners of that car must be Chinese, because those are devil-cushions', and goes on to explain that some expatriate Chinese provide this accommodation for the car's resident demons. This tells me something I didn't know, but doesn't and can't tell me what these cushions are to their Chinese owners.[2] To know that would be to be naturally at home with a 'world-picture' that we cannot enter without abandoning our own. Lewis, for all his intelligent sympathy with the ways life went in the Middle Ages, was never a native of the Middle Ages. 'Resolute Englishry' is obviously not the best attitude for our compatriots abroad – but it is equally and as importantly true that I can't stop being English just by stepping off a boat at Calais. On the contrary the Englishman is reminded more insistently of his Englishness by being in a foreign land.[3]

[1] *Ibid.*, p. x.
[2] Cf. Wittgenstein's discussion of the difficulty of understanding anyone else's 'world-picture' (by which he doesn't mean 'world-view') in *On Certainty* (Oxford, 1969).
Since writing this I find that it is paralleled by a discussion in Mr Michael Black's 'Reading a Play', *The Human World*, no. 1 (1970).

Lewis's ambition is to be *sure* he has understood a medieval poem, by seeing it as its original audience saw it; and that we can simply never do. The original audience is as much a construction of our modern imagination as the poem, but, unlike the poem, is not based firmly on a text in a language. We cannot know what people thought of literature in the Middle Ages except from what they say or imply, which isn't much. In any case this offers an infinite regression: to understand Chaucer as he was understood in the fourteenth century one needs to know (say) Boccaccio, Boethius, Augustine and *Le Roman de la Rose*. But what makes us think we have understood *them*, if we can't understand the poetry of our own language?

Many other scholars fall into Lewis's error of not fully recognizing the inevitable pastness of the past and simultaneously not seeing the necessity of present reading. Mr Bateson, in the passage discussed above (pp. 5–8), writes as if he believes he really was present at the first reading of *The Parliament of Fowls*. The basic attempt is always to construct a model of the Medieval Mind and insert it into the readers' minds so that they react to poems as people with medieval minds used to. Lewis writes about Medieval Man almost as if there were a separate species so called, like Neanderthal Man (or more, I suspect, like Piltdown Man).[1] Such attempts are in any case desperate (Cf. 'If a lion could talk, we could not understand him.'[2]). Moreover I have noticed they always make the Medieval Mind out to have been a very feeble sort of mind,[3] fascinated by astrology and far-fetched interpretations of the Bible, and making no difficulty over believing the incredible. To objections that the medieval poets do not suffer from this Medieval Mind its constructors always retort, in effect, 'Yes, but that is because the poets were eccentric. You can only understand them with reference to this real centre, the Medieval Mind.' Lewis says,

In every period the Model of the Universe which is accepted by the great thinkers [who in every period agree with each other?] helps to provide what we may call a backcloth for the arts. But this backcloth is highly selective. It takes over from the total Model only what is intelligible to a layman and only what makes some appeal to imagination and emotion.[4]

---

[1] See the first paragraph of *The Discarded Image*.
[2] Wittgenstein, *Philosophical Investigations*, p. 223e.
[3] Cf. its equally feeble child, the Renascence Mind: 'Two concepts dominated the mind of Renaissance England. One was the Ego, the other was Hap or Fortune', F. W. Bateson, 'Renaissance Literature', *Essays in Criticism* XIII (1963), 129.   [4] *The Discarded Image*, p. 14.

The 'great thinkers', that is, form the centre (they are also enlightened enough not to take their Model ' quite so seriously as the rest of us'[1]) and poetry is comparatively weak-minded and peripheral. The 'thinkers' are the priesthood in possession of the sacred mysteries without whose knowledge we cannot approach the poets. In that case the *study* of poetry is hard to justify; but my main objection concerns, again, what I think is Lewis's misunderstanding of the language of poetry. Is 'the model' so much a result of philosophical construction? Is it not more like the unimaginably complex web of significances we call a language, which poets work on as directly and profoundly as philosophers? We shall have to recur to this discussion.

Lewis's bent is to deny our first premise, that Chaucer only exists in present reading. He consistently argues that reading in the Middle Ages was not what it is for us. (This no doubt is true: and in so far as it is true we cannot know what reading in the Middle Ages was like.) But it does not follow, as Lewis wants to say, that it is impossible to accommodate Chaucer within our modern ways of reading – to make him one of the poets of our language. Lewis is most explicit in a trenchant early essay:

> Boccaccio, we may surmise, wrote for an audience who were beginning to look at poetry in our own way. For them *Il Filostrato* was mainly, though not entirely, 'a new poem by Boccaccio'. Chaucer wrote for an audience who still looked at poetry in the medieval fashion – a fashion for which the real literary units were 'matters', 'stories', and the like, rather than individual authors.[2]

I have been trying throughout to counter this view by seeing Chaucer as an individual author in an age of our literature: the main present point, however, is that even if Lewis is right about the attitude of Chaucer's audience it doesn't follow that we should try to imitate that audience. It would even be better to argue teleologically and see Chaucer groping towards a modern reading. Perhaps he is pointing forward to what we make of him and would have been delighted to be recognized as what we mean by a poet. (Did not Shakespeare have to wait over a hundred years for full recognition of his seriousness?) But whether or not – we have no alternative to reading Chaucer now, if at all, and to remaining ourselves as we read him.

I would follow Arnold and change one of Lewis's tenses. What

---

[1] *Ibid.*
[2] 'What Chaucer really did to *Il Filostrato*', *Essays and Studies* XIX (1932), 59.

we are trying to do is to see something as in itself it really is. We can later if we wish argue that the poetry *was* the same (or different) in the fourteenth century: but that is a secondary matter. The first fact must remain the present reading of Chaucer – to be sure, a present recreation of this part of the past.

Every 'historical approach' I have yet encountered rests on the belief that our recognizable centre of interest lies outside the poetry that we want to read; but as we approach the centre it always, in my experience, recedes like the end of the rainbow or more like an *ignis fatuus*. This will I hope come clear in the briefest possible consideration of the work of Professor D. W. Robertson, Jr.

Professor Robertson defines the 'historical criticism' he practises as 'that kind of literary analysis which seeks to reconstruct the intellectual attitudes and the cultural ideals of a period in order to reach a fuller understanding of its literature'.[1] This mild-looking formula is the basis of a massive endeavour to prove that we know what it is that the medieval poets are saying before we read them.

For Professor Robertson the centre from which we come to the poems is the moral teaching of the medieval church. Like Lewis, he is after a 'native's-eye view' of medieval poetry, but he 'goes native' by way, especially, of St Augustine: 'To establish the background for an hypothetical reconstruction of Chaucer's view of poetry, we must begin with Augustine's indispensable work.'[2] The ambition is worked out both in *Fruyt and Chaf* and in the vast *Preface to Chaucer* (beside which, appropriately, the mere collected works of Chaucer may look insignificant). To discover what Chaucer meant we must define the intellectual climate in which he wrote and the common ideas he knew, and that will permit us to define what Chaucer *must* have thought – which turns out to have been exactly what the church told him.

The *Roman* [*de la Rose*] is a humanistic and poetic expression of ideas which Chaucer could have his parson in the *Tales* state in a straight-forward way, but which he, as a court poet, could state most effectively in ways suggested by the *Roman* and by other poems like it.[3]

By this argument *The Parson's Tale* is more reliably an expression of the real Chaucer than his poems, and can additionally be used to explicate the French poems; and all Chaucer's poetry becomes a

[1] 'Historical Criticism', *English Institute Essays*, ed. Alan S. Downer (1950), pp. 3–31.
[2] Huppé and Robertson, *Fruyt and Chaf*, p. 6.
[3] D. W. Robertson, Jr, *A Preface to Chaucer* (Princeton, 1963), p. 104.

versified 'statement', or disguising, of ideas which are found in a pure form elsewhere. Similarly, arguing that *Troilus and Criseyde* is a Boethian poem and that therefore Chaucer disapproved, because it is concupiscent, of the love of Troilus and Criseyde, Professor Robertson writes, 'If Chaucer had shown any inclination to doubt the wisdom of his philosophical master, we might have reason to approach his poem with something like a romantic point of view. But such doubt would have been strange indeed in fourteenth-century English court circles.'[1] How is Chaucer to show his inclinations? Professor Robertson discounts everything except formal statement and for that he looks to Boethius not Chaucer. But it is precisely because Chaucer *was* strange in four-teenth-century England, because he would have stood out as strange in any imaginable human group, that he is still worth attention.

Professor Robertson makes this comment on a passage of *The Franklin's Tale* discussed above on pp. 193ff.

> When the time comes in the Franklin's story for Arveragus to assert his husbandly authority, all he can do is to advise his wife to go ahead and commit adultery. As a lover, he can have, as Andreas implied, no real objection to this action. He is, at the same time, only enough of a husband to threaten his lady to be quiet about what she does 'up peyne of deeth'. And that is not to be much of a husband.[2]

Arveragus orders Dorigen to 'keep her troth', which he knows may involve submission to the lust of Aurelius. For Robertson this is the same as advising her to go ahead and commit adultery. The difference is one of tone, which this critic ignores as effectively as the characters of *The Merchant's Tale*. Professor Robertson and the Franklin might, as it were, be describing the same event – but 'the same' only by the rules of a divorce court, not by the rules of Chaucer's language of poetry. Professor Robertson concentrates on the quasi-referential use of language: talking about adultery is his way of making sure no nonsense is talked about the poem. But to ignore Arveragus's and Dorigen's pain in their plight at that moment of the poem is to ignore the story and the way it is told – that is, whatever makes Chaucer's poem a poem.

In any case Robertson's (or any other) attempt to explain Chaucer's poetry according to the doctrines of St Augustine is certain to fail. If we pay Augustine the compliment of treating him as a thinker rather than the possessor of a medieval mind, we have

---

[1] *Ibid.*, pp. 472-3.   [2] *Ibid.*, p. 472.

to see that his notion of how language can have meaning is mistaken in such a way that poets demolish it, by implication, as they write poetry. Augustine, in Professor Robertson's perfectly accurate account of his position (which Robertson calls 'an aesthetic attitude which became typically medieval') says that obscurity is 'divinely ordained to overcome pride by work, and to prevent the mind from disdaining a thing too easily grasped. It stimulates a desire to learn, and at the same time excludes those who are unworthy from the mysteries of the faith. But it is also pleasant'.[1] The pleasure is the kind we get from solving riddles: if the meaning is hidden it is pleasant to have to discover it. The point about a riddle is that it has an answer: anyone who can understand the riddle can acknowledge the correctness of the answer. But Augustine wants to say that the answers to the riddle of the Old Testament are a special knowledge owned and guaranteed by the church.

'Thy teeth are as flocks of sheep, that are shorn, which come up from the washing, all with twins, and there is none barren among them.' St. Augustine assures us that for a reason he does not understand holy men are more pleasingly described for him as the teeth of the Church, which cut off men from their errors and soften them so that they may be taken into the body of the Church.[2]

But this answer to the riddle makes no sense within the language of the riddle. If I simply deny that these words are a description of the teeth of the church, Augustine has nothing to fall back on to convince me but authority, the naked assertion that they do mean what he says because he says so. It is hardly a parody of Augustine's position to say that anything can mean anything else, provided the church insists on it. This is not a defensible idea of language; in particular it is not a defensible idea of poetry. Any real poem means precisely what it says ('what it says' including any symbolical or allegorical significance it may have): the evidence is that we can know what poems mean.

Augustine was, of course, writing at a particular time, when faced with a particular problem (it is difficult to imagine a great philosopher being so irrational if that were not so). The problem was: what to do with those books of the Bible securely within the canon but whose meaning, as far as the naked eye can see, has nothing to do with Christianity. Augustine's way out was to assert that the Song of Songs is an allegory about the church as the Bride of Christ – not a convincing piece of literary criticism. This was

[1] *Ibid.*, p. 53.　　　[2] *Ibid.*

the origin of those fourfold interpretations designed to reassure the faithful that the Bible doesn't mean what it says. It is true also that some medieval poets seem to invite interpretation similarly disconnected from what they wrote. Dante had an occasional weakness for such 'tacning';[1] nonetheless the *Divine Comedy* is great not because of its invitations to scholiasts, but as a poem.

In so far as Chaucer is a poet – to the extent that his poems express his meaning – Professor Robertson's kind of commentary is out of place.[2] Its distinguishing mark is that it always ignores the poetry, the movement of verse and tone that tell us what is happening in a poem.

Chaucer can only show his 'inclinations' in the way he writes; but Mr Robertson's ambition is to ignore the way Chaucer writes so as to be sure (so runs the crazy logic) of knowing what he means. The result is that Mr Robertson on Chaucer (like Augustine on Solomon) is always trying hard to prove that the poet cannot possibly have meant what he says. The *Preface* tells us what the poet must have meant, which leaves what he actually wrote as a kind of optional extra, *quod est absurdum*. And there is the same procedure of establishing one unknown by another that I remarked in Lewis's work: for what is it that allows us to believe, if we can't read Chaucer, that we can read St Augustine – a Latin writer separated from us by a much greater gulf of history?

The only way Professor Robertson could make his case that Chaucer disapproves of Troilus, Criseyde, all the eagles in *The Parliament of Fowls*, Palamon, Arcite, Dorigen, Arveragus *et al.*, would be to show how Chaucer's tone tells us what he is doing; instead the poems are treated as prose paraphrases of themselves, made to fit a conviction of what they *must* be saying. Robertson's generalizations about the medieval poets can, also, be inapplicable to some writers: the central statement that 'medieval artists were not much concerned to express their private feelings' (p. 13) is

---

[1] This is the word used by the Owl boasting of her knowledge in a passage where it is not taken very solemnly; *The Owl and the Nightingale*, line 1213.
[2] Cf. Rodney Delsanta, 'Christian Affirmation in the *Book of the Duchess*', *PMLA* LXXXIV (1969). This essay says that the repetition of horn-blasts suggests the resurrectional trumpet of the New Testament. No doubt it does to Mr Delsanta: but the essence of the procedure is that he doesn't need to show why it should to anyone else. The meaning is not *in* the language: this is a game with no rules. Cf. also Koonce, *Chaucer and the Tradition of Fame*, p. 93: 'Venus's lechery is also symbolized by her doves, birds said to be especially disposed to "acts of Venus". When accompanying the true Venus, Bernard [Silvestris] affirms, they are indicative of chastity.'

contradicted by the work of the troubadours, who began it all, and by the best poetry of that very medieval writer Thomas Hoccleve. But the more serious objection is that 'private' is used here in a way that tends to deny the existence of literature. For if there is nothing between the fully, demonstrably public on one hand and the private-and-personal on the other, where does literature live?

Professor Robertson's *Preface* is a failure to read Chaucer that justifies itself by asserting that reading is impossible; to which I think the most proper retort is, Sour grapes! I can read Chaucer, though not so well as I want to; I have also met or read the works of others who can read Chaucer. If Professor Robertson can't, it is rash of him to publish so weighty a tome on the subject.

I come away from *A Preface to Chaucer* feeling no wiser than when I started; and similar feelings of frustration overcome me when I read all those backgrounds to medieval literature which, at a lower level, try to achieve ambitions similar to Lewis's or Robertson's, by providing a complete spectrum of medieval life. A much better than average member of this class is Mr D. S. Brewer's *Chaucer in his Time* (1963). I dip into this book and am fascinated – especially, as in the case of *A Preface to Chaucer*, by the pictures – without ever, somehow, coming away enlightened. Books like this never get further than giving the reader a heap of jarring atoms – facts – and leaving him to do all the work of creation himself. Mr Brewer seems so unsurprised by the past that he feels no need to try to understand it. He contents himself with a few assertions of the order of 'Englishmen were violent, unruly and unstable as children'[1] which he can then refer back to as sufficient explanation of the amazing facts the book is full of. Wyclif fulminated against absentee priests but 'drew most of his income for most of his life from parishes from which he was himself absent'[2]. Mr Brewer calmly sees in this 'the natural inconsistency of the age'. Again, 'Although astrology seems pure nonsense to us, it was the basis of much of the most advanced science in the fourteenth century, and Chaucer's Doctor is not a quack for believing it.'[3] Why not, though? How can astrology be the basis of a *science*, unless our words are to lose all meaning? Alternatively, would Mr Brewer be happy to have been treated by Chaucer's doctor and, if not, why not? He doesn't see that it is necessary to explain. The result is a kind of insulation from the past: in the olden days it seems that anything could happen – and

---

[1] *Chaucer in his Time*, p. 12.   [2] *Ibid.*, p. 232.   [3] *Ibid.*, p. 100.

so nothing can be surprising and, in the end, nothing in the past can have meaning in the present.

A related confusion is the belief (most commonly held by editors) that before we can understand Chaucer's language we must have a great deal of information about what his words mean – as if there could be a list of the objects they refer to. The *Introduction to Chaucer* by Mr Maurice Hussey and others – a volume many teachers of Chaucer must have found most useful – commits this error not in the crude form but in a way interesting enough to be worth discussing.

The greatest difficulty comes with the names of concepts connected with larger and less definable medieval systems of ideas – ideas of the nature of man and his position in the universe. In such cases, we still use the words... but as conceptions of man and the world have changed, the words have gradually shifted in meaning, until, in their modern form, they may be a positive barrier to our understanding. Here one may mention *nature*, *vertu*, *wit* and *corage*: all are extant in modern English, but for an understanding of how they are used by Chaucer, some knowledge of the medieval 'world-picture' is necessary...for their meaning such words [ethical terms] depend not on definite intellectual systems, but on vaguer assumptions about human life and conduct, assumptions which are sometimes indeed unformulated. Thus a little more needs to be said here about the social background to medieval ethical terms, since it is from this background that the words draw their strength.[1]

One could quibble at some words and phrases, but Mr Hussey is here identifying the main problem clearly. It is, however, just because the people of the Middle Ages had unformulated assumptions that aren't ours that we *can't* get far by saying a little about social background. If somebody told me that if you sail a ship far enough south you will come to the Mount of Purgatory, I would think he was mad, because if you sail far enough south you get (as we all take for granted although few of us have been) to Antarctica. Being told that in the Middle Ages they thought Purgatory was where we think the South Pole is, doesn't help at all: it merely suggests that in the Middle Ages everybody was mad. Yet this isn't one of the difficulties given me by that canto in which Ulysses and his companions set sail to Purgatory. I just take this mad geography, in the *Inferno*, in a way I couldn't if it were offered as a piece of information – if it were *not* assumed. So, too, with the moral terms, like those mentioned by Mr Hussey, or 'trouthe' or 'gentilesse'. I don't believe that any amount of discussion of medieval social fabric will tell anybody what these words mean.

[1] M. Hussey *et al.*, *An Introduction to Chaucer* (Cambridge, 1965), pp. 185–6.

But Mr Hussey is right to see this problem of the changed 'world-picture' as a linguistic problem. I want, however, to invert some of the things he says. How could we understand what language leaves unsaid? Precisely as we do with our own language: by using the language and being as sensitive as we can to its assumptions. I 'swallow down'[1] Dante's Mount of Purgatory without any trouble: so too I understand 'gentilesse' and the social order in which it lives when I read Chaucer well. It is true that words have their meaning in the lives of individuals in society and that in that way words draw their strength from a 'social background': but it is also true that language gives sense to the 'background' and a home to the unstated assumptions. Languages work *as if* the world were so-and-so: to know how the world appeared to Chaucer (in so far as that can be done) we read the poems and imagine the world as if it were what they demand to make sense. So I would also turn an earlier sentence of Mr Hussey's upside down: for any understanding of the medieval 'world-picture' a knowledge of how these words are used by Chaucer is necessary.

Our only hope of reading Chaucer is to stay inside his language: if we can do so that is itself evidence that the historical problems need not be insuperable and that we are keeping the poems alive by present reading in a language that belongs to our own language. So, too, when we are judging poems. A recent editor says of the harpies of Dunbar's *Tua Mariit Wemen and the Wedo*:

> Their attitude has to be considered against the economic background of medieval society, where the giving of dowries played an important role in the arrangement of marriages and the wife often found herself the sole executrix of her deceased husband's estate. Even poor girls sought to acquire a suitable dowry by receiving alms and imitating the practices of the better-endowed classes. For this reason, the impact of Dunbar's anti-feminist satire today is probably more savage and less comic in its effect than it was when he wrote it. Although for the modern reader the rose-garden maidens [*sic*] are gold-diggers (of a type presumably common in James's materialistic court), the coarseness of their sentiments and the lewdness of their conversation must be considered against its appropriate social setting and not judged in accordance with Renaissance poetic idealization of the married state.[2]

No, the appropriate setting for the poem isn't some hypothetical Scotland where we can never belong, but the language of the poem, which can still have its powerful effect, and *our* language – the kind of setting shown by using of the poem words like 'coarse' and

---

[1] Cf. Wittgenstein, *On Certainty*, p. 21e.
[2] *The Middle Scots Poets*, ed. A. M. Kinghorn (1970), introduction, pp. 17–18.

'lewd'. It is characteristic that this sort of well-meaning historical commentary should weaken the impact of the poem.

One of the weaknesses of the various historical approaches is that they are not properly historical. They suffer from old-fashioned fallacies about the objectivity of history. Real historians have a much greater respect for imagination and a much greater distrust of 'background' than these literary critics; Collingwood[1] has had more of an effect where history is a real discipline. Professor Christopher Brooke's *The Twelfth Century Renaissance* is, quite rightly, much closer in its method to literary criticism than any of the histories of literature I have consulted.[2]

We are all trying to understand Chaucer's language: but it is an open question, to say the least, whether Mr Hussey or Professor Robertson or C. S. Lewis can do as much as one interested reading of *The Canterbury Tales*.

Any investigation of Chaucer must be, I repeat, historical: we try to see a product of the life of the distant past as in itself it really is. But the historical approachers so rarely have a proper notion of the delicacy of their task, of the difficulty of understanding the language of six hundred years ago. In the end how much better Chaucer shows us his world, for those willing to go with him! The poet, by writing his tales, is forced to attend to what matters and to put it with due order and emphasis. Chaucer gives us ideas of what life was like and how people thought and felt which are bound to make the efforts of commentators seem crude and unfocused. Chaucer is the main source of evidence about himself; and so the common characteristic of the practitioners of the historical approaches is that they all prefer something other than the main evidence: which is a failure of, amongst other things,

---

[1] R. G. Collingwood, *The Idea of History* (Oxford, 1946), especially pp. 245ff.

[2] Historians *can* go wrong, of course. I think of such comments on the current fashion for quantification as these, in a review by the distinguished historian, Professor Geoffrey Barraclough: 'The essential point about the new quantitative history is that it offers a way out of the historian's predicament. Its essential purpose is to establish objective criteria enabling history to move...to a new level of scientific exactitude by the elimination – so far as is possible in any science – of subjective factors.' *The New Year Review of Books* (4 June 1970), p. 55.

This certainly is a way out of the historian's predicament: it saves him from being a historian. The 'subjective factors' include whatever makes history history. Otherwise there are only facts. A fact can only become a historical fact by being taken into history, an imaginative construction. Even where history depends on modern methods of processing facts, its depth is a depth of imaginative understanding – as in Peter Laslett's *The World we have Lost* (1965).

historical method. If one discounts the main source of evidence, the only one that can still communicate to us directly and with some precision, the task of reading Chaucer becomes hopeless.

This is not to say that criticism of Chaucer is easy: when criticism loses sight of the fact that Chaucer belongs to the past as well as to the present it becomes the other horn of the above-mentioned dilemma. Mr A. C. Spearing's *Criticism and Medieval Poetry* must be seen as a brave attempt to produce real criticism which begins by impaling itself on this critical horn. For it is as easy to be thwarted by inadequate notions of criticism as of history; and Mr Spearing's initial account of his critical concern places the centre of interest outside the poems as surely as Professor Robertson's historical approach. Mr Spearing, too, knows in advance what he is going to find.

Probably the greatest advance in method made by literary criticism in this century has been the development of techniques for the detailed analysis of literary texture. As a result of this development, which has taken place over the last forty years or so, we have now reached a position where the approach to literature most commonly taken up by British and American critics has become one that is variously called 'critical analysis', 'practical criticism' or simply 'close reading'. This approach involves a minute scrutiny of the verbal detail of works of literature, and the scrutiny is designed to bring out certain effects in particular... What is especially sought after in literature is 'concreteness' of texture – the evocation or re-creation in words of sensory perceptions and bodily movements.[1]

But what could be the point of such an interest in literature unless to serve as a reminder to those who have forgotten what sense-perceptions are like? It would be literature for the paralytic. The thing missing is any notion of significance. One of the greatest passages of English verse re-creates sensory impressions and bodily movements just to make them, at that moment, hopelessly insignificant:

> To morrow, and to morrow, and to morrow,
> Creepes in this petty pace from day to day,
> To the last Syllable of Recorded time:
> And all our yesterdayes, have lighted Fooles
> The way to dusty death. Out, out, breefe Candle,
> Life's but a walking Shadow, a poore Player,
> That struts and frets his houre upon the Stage,
> And then is heard no more. It is a Tale
> Told by an Ideot, full of sound and fury
> Signifying nothing.[2]

---

[1] A. C. Spearing, *Criticism and Medieval Poetry* (1964), p. 1.
[2] *Macbeth*, v, v. Cf. S. W. Dawson, *Drama and the Dramatic* (1970), pp. 3-4.

The 'strutting and fretting' and the 'sound and fury' are certainly created in these lines, mainly by their rhythmic patterns; but they are created to be continually let down into 'signifying nothing'. It is not the re-creation of sensory perceptions that counts, but what Macbeth does with them. Johnson gets the general point as clear as need be in his remarks (in the *Lives of the Poets*) on Pope's *Essay on Criticism*: 'Motion, however, may be in some sort exemplified; and yet it may be suspected that even in such resemblances the mind often governs the ear, and the sounds are estimated by their meaning.' Poems certainly do re-create sense-impressions, but for some purpose. *What* purpose it is the business of the poem to express; and we can't know it before reading the poem.

Mr Spearing's book is not rendered useless by his inadequate idea of criticism: it is a triumph of sense over theory. But it is true that his application of 'close reading' to the hapless poets sometimes spoils what he has to say. For instance of a passage of *The Legend of Good Women* which looks to me like two hereditary conceits muddled together[1] Mr Spearing says, 'Every line...yields an almost physically palpable texture'; and he later writes, 'When Chaucer wants to express violent physical action he normally does so directly through violence of sound.'[2] But – setting aside the question of whether we really know what sounds Chaucer intended – why should it matter even if we do find a palpable texture in these lines? It is (once again) Chaucer's sounds *in language* that make a poem – and our problem.

The two critics who have been quoted time and again in these pages, Messrs Speirs and Muscatine, seem to me in their very different way superior to the rest because they both frequently throw light on Chaucer as I believe he really is, a fourteenth-century poet being read now. Professor Muscatine has, of course, a declared historical theme; Mr Speirs, too, has a sense of the past, as well as of the present, more convincing than Professor Robertson's.[3]

---

[1]   *LGW* F 125
       Forgeten hadde the erthe   his pore estat
       Of wynter   that hym naked made and mat
       And with his swerd of cold   so sore greved
       Now hath th'atempre sonne   all that releved
       That naked was   and clad him new agayn
[2] *Criticism and Medieval Poetry*, pp. 16, 19.
[3] Another work of some distinction where a sense of the past is inseparable from an appreciation of Chaucer's poetry is Mr R. O. Payne's *Key of Remem-*

Since I have made so much use of these two critics I would like to pay my formal tribute to them. I remember thinking when *Chaucer and the French Tradition* came out, 'At last! a critic with a really first-rate mind, who is willing to treat Chaucer with the same kind of attention that Shakespeare gets' – and I am still grateful for Professor Muscatine's work, though I do now sometimes think that its resemblance to one of the cleverer schools of Shakespeare criticism is all too close. Mr Speirs is quite different in such a way that he complements the strengths as well as the weaknesses of Professor Muscatine. The latter is not free from a certain brilliant facileness, especially in his theoretical passages; but the quality that makes Mr Speirs the critic I am most grateful to is his great honesty, which is more than absence of guile, and which makes him focus on the things that really matter. Mr Speirs always tells just what he thinks of a poem, a rare virtue in our field; and no critic can do more than that, though some might do it better. Mr Speirs too is at least unique amongst the Chaucer critics in that one could have wished him to have written more.

brance (New Haven, 1963). Some of his remarks make necessary comments on the Robertson attitude to the past:

'It is far more respectable historical method to judge the fourteenth-century mind by the kind of appeals that were made to it than the other way around, because ultimately we can guess at what a fourteenth-century reader might have understood only by examining the texts he was evidently expected to understand. Any other method reverses usable procedure and leaves us working from inference back to evidence, with nothing from which to derive the inference' (p. 3).

'In short, there is no legitimate way in which to wish off onto the courtiers of Edward III and Richard II the job of understanding Chaucer's poetry for us' (p. 4).

17

Chaucer the Father

Chaucer is the father of our splendid English poetry; he is our 'well of English undefiled', because by the lovely charm of his diction, the lovely charm of his movement, he makes an epoch and founds a tradition.[1]

But corruption must utterly have destroyed the fabric of human society before poetry can ever cease...And let us not circumscribe the effects of the bucolic and erotic poetry within the limits of the sensibility of those to whom it was addressed. They may have perceived the beauty of those immortal compositions, simply as fragments and isolated portions: those who are more finely organized, or born in a happier age, may recognize them as episodes to that great poem, which all poets, like the co-operating thoughts of one great mind, have built up since the beginning of the world.[2]

I

Chaucer's composition of *The Canterbury Tales* is the creation of English literature.

The 'frame' of *The Canterbury Tales*, the pilgrimage, and the intercourse of the narrators, has rightly been much admired. We see a wide range of representative temperaments and traditions, intellectual, social, sexual; and because we see them in individuals talking and behaving, values define each other in the way social groups, as well as plays, do define values. The pilgrimage is Chaucer's final step into drama, his last exploration of his world, whose elements define each other and whose connections form a whole. If so *The Canterbury Tales* are more Chaucer's criticism of life than the Moral Ballades. In all senses *The Canterbury Tales* are a journey in Chaucer's company across fourteenth-century England.

The tales have the impersonality of great art, but the impersonality, while allowing Chaucer to make his imaginative exploration,

[1] Matthew Arnold, 'The Study of Poetry', *Essays in Criticism*, second series.
[2] Shelley, *A Defence of Poetry*.

does not excuse him from a responsibility and concern that can only be, in another sense, personal. He expresses *his* world, which means telling us what he really believed about it, though not in such a way as to render his opinions capable of extraction. *The Canterbury Tales* are the record of a 'questing after significance'[1] as serious as Shakespeare's or Tolstoy's.

The journey across that England is in a real sense the creation of that England. Go back 200 years before Chaucer and where is England? Wales is there, and Ireland, and even Scotland after a fashion; but in England there is an Anglo-Norman aristocracy living on estates scattered across England and France, speaking French and distinguishing England from France only according to whether the patois spoken by peasants and the lower orders of the priesthood was Germanic or Romance. French was spoken at court, Latin in church and law, English in the fields: with such a situation it is not easy to imagine just what the word 'England' might have referred to. 'Chaucer's world' is more than a figure of speech and it does not mean the complete list of objects or even of words that he knew. By seeing England whole, by seeing the connections between the parts, Chaucer created the whole he saw. The thing is not separate from the idea of it. Chaucer's tales, more than one would have thought possible to a single work, create an idea of England – which we share, in imagination, to the extent that we read Chaucer. Chaucer's commitment is not to particular opinions or even beliefs, but to the exploration and evaluation of the kinds of life made possible by English. If Chaucer does manage to make his poetry 'full of humanity'[2] it is because he manages to concentrate the life of the English language. That is the same as seeing England.

The extraordinary feat of genius I am pointing to, the seeing England whole in *The Canterbury Tales*, is the creation of a national literature, a place where a nation can begin to find and recognize itself. Chaucer was able to do this only because he found the English language – and, of course, the society whose sense it expressed – ready for him: English, whose range of styles in the fourteenth century was wider (including the styles of court, churchmen and peasantry) but also more closely interconnected than ours. But if that English is the rich record of a civilization it is only, as

---

[1] F. R. Leavis, '*Anna Karenina*: Thought and Significance in a Great Creative Work', '*Anna Karenina' and Other Essays* (1967), p. 12.

[2] Ford, *The March of Literature*, p. 639.

far as we are concerned, through Chaucer's power to make it so – and to do that now, in a language we recognize as our own. Chaucer recognized the different powers of English and brought them together. He did not, as used occasionally to be thought, himself compose the English language; but he did make it, with the help of his contemporaries and his readers, the language of a great literature. If English had no great literature it would not be the language we know, even with the same grammar and vocabulary.

The life of Chaucer's language is not mere vivacity: he is no Green Knight of literature. If Chaucer is 'full of humanity' it is by means of his literary achievements; for his connection of different people and styles is made by connecting hitherto separate literary traditions. His fulness comes from a great *critical* effort. In England before Chaucer there was no English literature, only a variety of different literary traditions, with no common centre. Pre-Chaucerian English literature was generally[1] functional in different ways. Different traditions met different demands. If a devotional poem were requested, the traditional sentiments came readily in the traditional diction. The demand for romances was met by a quite different set of writers with a different style. Other equally insulated traditions were, for example, the sermon in its various kinds, the Boethian moral discourse, the fabliau, and the folk-ballad.

In some departments of medieval literature the demand was so long-lasting and unchanging that formulae to satisfy it grew up which any literate person could use with minimal variation. By the fifteenth century the stock of phrases usable in English courtly lyrics was almost fixed: all the courtier had to do was put them together in some sort of order, or programme Lydgate – that medieval prophet of computer-poetry – to do it for him.

The varying functions of literature in English before Chaucer centred on two main facts, the church and the aristocratic courts. Literature was a variety of activities on the periphery of these centres.

One of the marks of a pre-literary situation is that writers are not independent enough to comment on what they are doing. The church generated a large and constant demand for the various kinds of moral, religious and devotional literature, but it is no disrespectful comment on one of the most impressive collective human achievements to say that the medieval church could never

---

[1] I make clear the way in which I except *The Owl and the Nightingale* from this generalization, above, pp. 36–41.

have given birth, unaided, to modern literature. It was impossible, for instance, for the composer of a saint's life to criticize his own activity: a writer who appraised the value of what he was doing is just unthinkable in the early Middle Ages. The church provoked plenty of blasphemy and coarse humour, but not criticism – not, that is, until the emergence of literature: I argued that *The Prioress's Tale* is a criticism and evaluation of a part of medieval Christianity. The church could and did produce comment on life that could be fierce and full of vivacity: but the comment was always (for instance in the popular sermons I know) dependent upon given values. The only place where poetry could develop into a criticism of life was the court: but I have also tried to show what a major achievement it was when the medieval poets managed to break out of their natural role as courtly entertainers into some seriousness we can call criticism of life.

The great bulk of *The Canterbury Tales* exemplifies the hitherto separate traditions of medieval literature. Chaucer does almost everything: his literary range is enormous, and that is the way he achieves his social range. But by being of more than one tradition and by making the different styles evaluate one another Chaucer rises into independent comment.

Chaucer's bringing together of these different traditions creates a common language of literature. By evaluating what really mattered in life to Chaucer it creates at once a world, a literature and a criticism of life. And Chaucer's creation of a literature can affect us by asking what really matters to *us*; for the need to satisfy more than one audience leads directly to Chaucer's power to address us without scholarly mediation. One of the ways in which he creates our literature is by addressing, for the first time, the common reader. And that, again, is to say that in *The Canterbury Tales* our literature becomes for the first time a criticism of life, a creator of values because a creator of language.

The works of a pre-literary culture, not being self-sufficient, need a context in their culture before they can be understood. The miracle cycles are very impressive, but not as plays. They can never be performed again, because they need the conditions of performance dictated by their place in the life of their times. To appreciate them now we have to try to picture them in their own time, to imagine what they must have meant to people: the plays do not carry their sense in their text.

But Chaucer, talking to such a variety of readers (even if always in small courtly groups), can talk also to us. His is the first English literature after *Beowulf* to carry its own world with it: and this I believe to contain the hint of a way out of our critical–historical dilemma. Chaucer carries the life of his times imaginatively into *The Canterbury Tales*: to read them well is the same as being acquainted with Chaucer's world. He defines words by using them in stories. What does Chaucer mean by 'trouthe'? He means what Arveragus says to Dorigen at the climax of *The Franklin's Tale*, and we understand the word in so far as we enjoy the story Chaucer wrote.

If Chaucer creates a literature, it is our literature he creates – with our co-operation. When we say 'English poet' we are using words which have their sense in the language in which we talk of our own literature. 'English poet' has a whole set of associations and limitations: for instance it could not just be taken as the name of an occupation. We can call Chaucer an English poet, and the author of *Sir Gawain and the Green Knight*. I would be made uneasy about calling Gower an English poet only because he isn't much of a poet. To call Langland an English poet would be to stretch the term, but only a little, and I am ready to do it. But we couldn't call Laȝamon or Orm English poets within the range of meaning of the phrase. We should also need different words for the authors of *Beowulf* or *The Wanderer*, mainly but not wholly because those works are not in English.

The 'grammar' of our phrase 'English poet' and the rest of the words we use to talk of our literature expresses a range of ideas about our literature as a whole, and gives us ways of thinking about it that are of at least comparable validity when used of any part. I naturally think of Chaucer as an English poet, but *Beowulf* belongs to another group of ideas and ways of thinking.

Reading Chaucer has something in common with living in an old house. It is possible to live in a fourteenth-century manor, and to know it as well as any other house; and only living people can do so. But life in the house would itself be contact with the past: part of knowing that it is a house is knowing that it is an *old* house, different in many ways from a modern house. If I live in an old house I don't necessarily know what its original inhabitants made of it; I do know that it is the house they lived in (even though 'house' might have had a very different role in their lives) surviving into our different times. This analogy shouldn't be pressed too far; but I do say that we read Chaucer in English as much as Pope or Wordsworth, and that part of the reading, as also in the cases of Pope and Wordsworth, is meeting a life different from and older than ours. Chaucer may or may not be definably relevant to our modern problems – so may an old house, and there may be good reasons for keeping old houses that are blatantly 'irrelevant' – but one reason for reading Chaucer is that his poetry is a great chance of not being alive *only* in the present. Literature (the extreme case of language) saves us from being merely personal: a sense of the past is one mark of humanity, and 'olde bookes' save the consciousness permitted by our language from being restricted within the view of a few generations. The poets of a literature give a culture the unique chance of sharing a sense of the past, which speaks in living voices and says what can no longer be said. Our willingness to listen is the preservation, 'alive and changing in the present', of at once our literature, the fullness of our language, and our consciousness of belonging to a national culture.

None of this need be so. English literature is not a natural object to which a name is attached like a label; it is within our power to treat Chaucer as something other than an English poet. The critics' consignment of Chaucer to history suggests the possibility.

I would like to 'conclude of this longe serye' by trying to suggest some of the reasons why Chaucer should remain an English poet; and I shall try to prevent that from making the discussion external to Chaucer's poetry, by vindicating at the same time the very odd-looking phrase 'Chaucer the father of English Poetry'.

II

Why used Chaucer to be called by that odd title, 'the Father of English Poetry'? 'Father' is conveniently vague, with an illusory air of biological precision.

When we are told that Mr. So-and-so is the father of the House of Commons, it never occurs to us to suppose that all the other members are his offspring; what we understand is that the fact that he has been there the longest is thought to give him a larger stake in the place, to make him in a sense [equally analogical] its owner.

The word 'father', or its equivalent in other languages, is most commonly used in the sense of the owner of children, but when we try to find out what it is that makes a man the owner of children we learn that the fact that he has or has not begotten them has little or nothing to do with it. He is their owner or father because he has performed a magical

287

rite which is believed, explicitly or implicitly, to have transferred to them a portion of what may be called his life-essence.[1]

So if we call Chaucer the father of English poetry we need not mean that he metaphorically begot the other poets, only perhaps that he is a kind of magical head of the family, transferring to the rest 'a portion of...life-essence'. But how much could that say? I want to show that if we recognize Chaucer as the father of English poetry we can get clearer the sense of how he belongs to the past and the present.

In the case of the English court poets of the fifteenth century the biological image would do: it would be impossible to imagine Hoccleve or Lydgate without the (so to speak) genetic influence of Chaucer – which is not to blame Chaucer for Lydgate: a father is not responsible if his adult children go to the bad. After the Chaucerians the direct links between Chaucer and the English poets are few and unimportant. The Chaucer tradition was decisively broken in the sixteenth century and after 1550 only eccentrics like Spenser thought of allowing Chaucer any direct influence on their work. From 1550 until he began to be starch to the Englit. courses, Chaucer's status as a living classic was somewhat precarious. So when Mr Speirs makes his gallant attempt to rescue the fathership of Chaucer I have to dissent, at least from this way of putting it: 'It needs to be recognized that not only the poets but the great English dramatists and their successors, the novelists, form one unbroken development – the *main* development – from Chaucer...'[2] He is more acceptable when he goes on '...they are masters of the language of which Chaucer is, before them, the great master'. But that would place the succession in the language, not in any conscious literary continuity – which is, I think, as it should be.

If Chaucer is the father of English poetry it cannot be in the way Homer was the father of Greek poetry or Shakespeare is the father of English drama. No cultured Greek could be unaware of Homer and his achievement; no modern English dramatist, except of the illiterate school, can ignore Shakespeare. But most English writers, like the great critics, can and do ignore Chaucer. Yet if he is not the English Homer he can't on the other hand be the English Ennius, since we do at least pay lip-service to the idea that Chaucer is a subtle literary artist.

Chaucer's development into 'art-speech' – and Langland's, and

---

[1] Lord Raglan, 'What is a Father?', *Jocasta's Crime* (1933), p. 180.
[2] *Chaucer the Maker*, p. 20.

the *Gawain* poet's – is, I argued, the creation of a literature. It also has to be the creation of the *idea* of a literature: a language in which literature can not only be written, but talked about. Chaucer changed the meanings of words like 'poet' and 'tale'; for after Chaucer a tale naturally means what he wrote, as well as things like *King Horn*. The usual notions of literary influence are here too narrowly literary. Chaucer need have no direct conscious influence on the other poets to be seen as their father. His influence is profounder: when he changed the idea of poetry in English he influenced all succeeding writers, including the ones who never read him, by giving them a language in which literature was already accomplished, by saving them from having to repeat his own prodigious work on the foundation of a literature.

This, I think, is part of what the English Chaucerians meant by their everlasting and unanimous praise of Chaucer for what seem to us all the wrong reasons. There is much I find hard to understand in their picture of Chaucer as the great rhetorical embellisher of the language, documented in the first hundred or so pages of Miss Spurgeon's collection.[1] Any understanding comes from an effort of historical imagination, the attempt to sympathize with the very odd ethos of fifteenth-century court poetry. But the Chaucerians do seem to be on to a train of thought somewhat like the above. Hoccleve says,

> O deth þou didest naght harme singuleer
> In slaghtere of him but al þis land it *smertith*[2]   woundeth

Why does he see the death of Chaucer as harming all this land? Not because his feeling is impersonal: the rest of the passage is a strikingly personal outburst. Compare his version of the usual compliments to Chaucer's rhetoric:

> O maister deere and fadir reuerent
>   Mi maister Chaucer flour of eloquence
> Mirour of fructuous entendement
>   O vniuersel fadir in science[3]

Lydgate, who says '...of your language / he was the lodesterre'[4] also calls Chaucer 'þe flower of poets in our English tung and the first that euer elumined our languaege with flowers of rethorick eloquence'[5] and writes

---

[1] *Five Hundred Years of Chaucer Criticism and Allusion*, ed. C. F. E. Spurgeon (Cambridge, 1925).   [2] *Ibid.*, Part I, p. 21.   [3] *Ibid.*   [4] *Ibid.*, p. 37.
[5] *Ibid.*, p. 14. (This is a text probably rewritten in the sixteenth century.)

My mayster Chaunceer / did his besynesse
And in his dayes / hath so wel hym born
Out of our tounge / tauoyden al Rudnesse
And to Reffourme it / with Colours of swetnesse
Wherfore let vs / yiue hym lawde and glorye
And putte his name / with Poetys in memorye[1]

If 'al þis land it smertith' at Chaucer's death and if we 'putte his name / with Poetys in memorye' he did alter our language. He established poetic styles and subjects in a way his disciples could imitate, but more generally he was the 'flour of eloquence' because he showed English to be a language capable of poetry. Chaucer *made* English capable of poetry. Putting his name with poets in memory is at once a tribute to the poetry in itself and an affirmation that he is the founder of poetry in our tongue. Caxton says, 'For to fore that he by his labour enbelysshyd / ornated and / made faire our englisshe / in this Royame was had rude speche & Incongrue.'[2] But now, it is implied, English is a language in which poetry can be written. The point is a good one even though we are unlikely to agree with the idea of poetry held by the English Chaucerians.

Add to this my observation that the fourteenth century is the first age of our literature. The fourteenth century is the 'Age of Chaucer' because Chaucer makes it so in expressing it. We can make something of the idea of Chaucer's fatherhood so long as English is a language of poetry and so long as we find the idea of English literature a useful conception and mean by it more or less what has been meant in recent centuries. Arnold is making an essentially similar judgment both when he says 'He [Chaucer] has gained the power to survey the world from a central, a truly human point of view' and when he says 'with him is born our real poetry'.[3] But this can only apply as long as we go on creating English literature in our reading.

To make our map of English literature we relate works of literature to each other and to other things – to life, one might say. Without the relating to each other the works themselves exist only incompletely: even these parts derive from a whole. When a poem is incomparable it is uniquely hard to judge. Most of the time I think I am right to value *The Owl and the Nightingale* highly, but I acknowledge the possibility that it may be merely a pale imitation of the great lost work of its century. I think highly of *The Owl and the Nightingale* because, in the first place, it seems to me a most

[1] *Ibid.*, p. 37.   [2] *Ibid.*, p. 62.   [3] 'The Study of Poetry.'

interesting poem; but to try to believe this opinion I relate the
poem, however tenuously, to French and early Chaucer or, better,
I relate it to my own language by translating it. Neither of these are
ideal relations, but they are the best available, and without them
one is at sea about the poem and can't know where it belongs. (Or:
imagine what it would be like to think of *Romeo and Juliet* without
Antony and Cleopatra as a comparison: one would be in the dark
about how seriously to take the former.) The general form of what
I am trying to illustrate is well stated by Mr Rush Rhees:

> Art is serious in its 'ideas'. A piece of music is written in musical phrases
> or in music, as a poem is written in language and in poetry. Wittgenstein
> said in conversation once that Schubert's *Wiegenlied* is clearly deeper than
> Brahms' *Wiegenlied*, but that it can be deeper only in the whole of our
> musical language...
>
> What is said in a sonnet (say Drayton's 'Since there's no help, come
> let us kiss and part') could not be said in another form. But it could not
> be said at all, unless there were other poems and other sonnets.
>
> It was possible for Drayton to write a great sonnet or a weak one because
> people were writing and had written poetry. It was possible because there
> were those differences – the differences between great poetry and weak –
> in which are rooted the reasons why men write poetry at all. And it was
> possible, finally, because poetry already had the relation to the rest of
> language which it did.[1]

Chaucer does not quite, in Eliot's phrase, 'change expression', he
founds expression: he makes poetry possible and in that sense
creates the language for other writers and for us. (Of course, if
Chaucer had not founded English literature somebody else would.
But then it would not have been the same literature.)

So Chaucer is the father of English literature not by begetting it
or influencing it but by creating its form. Once something has been
done like this, and recognized, other comparable though different
things can be done, given a supply of genius and the continuity of
reading and thought about the literature which are an important
part of a civilization.

But if a father is as Lord Raglan says an owner of children, we
have to bear in mind, too, that children are sometimes known to
disown their father. The 'unbroken development' Mr Speirs wants
to find from Chaucer to the present day is an achievement of our
reading and thinking. It is not like the unbroken development of
the city of London or the unbroken growth of an oak tree. We make
Chaucer the father of English literature when we find that he

---

[1] 'Art and Philosophy', *Without Answers*, pp. 136-7.

naturally belongs, in our thinking, in the whole of English literature. Chaucer's position as the magical head of the family of our literature certainly is natural, but separate from our reading and thinking there is no guarantee that our literature does not start with Shakespeare, with the nineteenth century (as some of the more relevant of our new English departments pretend) or (as their students wish) with the Beat poets.

The continuing delight we feel in the poetry of Chaucer is the sign that we should continue to think about him. So long as there is something wonderful about Chaucer's poetry, the English language will continue to be a language of great poetry of which Chaucer is the father.

Index

293